Mystical Magical You

Written and Illustrated by

Wilda B. Tanner

WILD
COMET
PUBLISHING
LLC

Columbus, OH

© 2004 by Wild Comet Publishing LLC
P.O. Box 26115, Columbus, OH 43226-0115
All rights reserved. Published 2004
Printed in the United States of America

Cover: "Angelic Invitation to the Light" by Emery Bear
Book design and layout: Robin Smith/Emuses
Book Production Coordinator: Brad Buck/Wild Comet Publishing LLC

Library of Congress Control Number 2003116106
ISBN 0-9747006-1-4

Dedication

This book is lovingly dedicated to Ken Landon Buck, my son and artist friend, who has always encouraged and believed in me, even when I didn't believe in myself. It was only with his unfailing support and encouragement this book was finally finished.

Thank you, Ken.

Wilda Tanner

Acknowledgments

This book was made possible by a number of people. The family played a large role, with our matriarch Wilda Tanner performing the leading role of research and the writing. My brother Ken and myself with others worked through the proofing and edits. My wife Rachael, newborn son Alec and our dog Pro gave me support and allowed me the time needed to maintain the flow of Wilda's best selling *The Mystical Magical Marvelous World of Dreams* while preparing this book for printing. Thanks must also go to my wonderful cousin and Washington D.C. lawyer Beverley Ramsey for all those non-billed hours of legal and other useful advice. There was much help from other people, especially Robin Smith, who was able to take on any task from laying out the text to graphic arts to sage business acumen. And thanks to Christina Wald for making my Wild Comet logo sketch presentable. And finally, thanks to the many others who had a hand in making this happen.

Brad Buck
Production Coordinator
Wild Comet Publishing LLC

Other books by the same author:

Follow Your Dreamzzz: A How-To Book on Dream Interpretation

The Mystical Magical Marvelous World of Dreams

Contents

Foreword xiii

Chapter One: Ye Are Gods 1
    Know Ye Not That Ye Are Gods? 2
    The Law of Love 3
    Creating 3
    Cosmic Clock 3

Chapter Two: The Truth About You 5
    Your Lightbody 6
    Your Body's Vehicle — The Real You 6
    You Are Greater Than You Think 7
    Learning to Recognize Auras 8
    How Your Aura Affects Others 9

Chapter Three: The Process of Creation 13
    How Thoughts Become Things 13
    Thought Form Construction 14
    Some Common Thought Forms 15
    Love and Affection 18
    Floating Thought Forms .20
    Directed Thought Forms .21
    Race Consciousness 23
    The Effect of Your Thoughts 25
    Thought Forms Collect in Your Aura 27
    Boomerangs 28
    In the Beginning 28
    Major Lessons 29

Chapter Four: The Laws of Creation 31
    Thoughts Are Things 32
    Problem Perpetuators 36
    Worry 36
    Breaking the Laws 37
    Fears 37

Chapter Five: The Prison of Limited Thought 39
- Poverty Teachings 40
- We Live in an Abundant Universe 41
- Poverty Is a Learned Condition .41

Chapter Six: Understanding Your Belief System 43
- Your Subconscious Mind 43
- Decisions Conform to Your Basic Belief System 45
- The Power of Your Beliefs 45
- Adelade, the Unpaid Maid 46
- Abuse 47
- Low Self-Esteem 48
- Fears 52
- Poverty 55
- Physical Abuse 56
- Seeing Victimhood for What It Is 59
- Some Interesting Facts About Criminals and Victims 60
- Anger 60
- The Damaging Effects of Anger 61
- Three Laws to Consider 64
- Blame Game 66
- Know Thyself 67
- Your Growing-Up Years 68
- The School of Life 70
- Summary 70

Chapter Seven: Changing Your Beliefs 73
- Story of Two Brothers 73
- Accepting Our Lessons 74
- Old Concepts vs. the New 74
- Burning Bridges 75
- Escape from Prison 75
- Good Self-Esteem Is Important 76
- Measuring Your Self-Worth 77
- Learning to Love Yourself 78
- I Don't Understand All That I Know 79
- Self-Forgiveness 79
- Cleaning Your Mental Closet .79
- Reviewing and Cleansing Old Stuff 81
- The People Pleasing Syndrome 83
- Common People-Pleasing Traits 83
- The High Cost of People Pleasing 84
- Understanding Your Dilemma .84

Sure Cure for People Pleasing 85
Challenging People Who Challenge You 85
The Final Touch 86
The Healing Power of Love 86
Self-Talk 88
Attaining a State of Well-Being 89
Problems Are Messages You Need to Heed 90

Chapter Eight: Your Journal: An Important Tool for Growing . . 93
Getting Started 94
Reward Yourself for Each Goal Reached 95
Summaries Are Important 96
Dreams As Guidance 96

Chapter Nine: Decisions, Decisions 99
Promises 100
The Burden of Things Undone 101
Beautiful Morning 102
Depression 102
Your Own Little World 103
Gaia 103
Marital Agreements 105
The Importance of Forgiveness in Cleaning Up the Past . .106
Dropping Your Burden Through Forgiveness 107
Cleaning Up Your Past 109
Dealing With Undecided Items 109
Promises, Promises 110
Things Wanted and Things Not Wanted 112
Success Is a Feeling 112
Failure Is a Fatal Attitude 113
Faith 113
Worry Is Negative Goal Setting 113
We Always Have Choices 114
Procrastination Is a Self-Defeating Habit 114
Procrastination Reality Check .115
Not to Decide Is a Decision to Do Nothing 115
Make Clear Decisions for Tomorrow Today 116
Knowing What Is Right for You 116
Intellect vs. Intuition 117
Prayer and the Holy Grail 117
Intention 117
The Only Way to Have Happiness Is to Choose It 118

Chapter Ten: Goal Setting ...121
  Never Judge the Present by the Past ...122
  Planning for Success ...122
  Goals Give Your Life Direction ...123
  Guidelines for Goal Setting ...123
  True and False Goals ...124
  Your Life Purpose ...125
  Laying Out the Guidelines ...126
  Setting Goals for the Year ...127
  Setting Your Daily Goals: The Things-To-Do List ...127
  The Importance of Preparing the Way ...129
  Get It All on One Page ...130
  A Goal Book ...131
  Making Changes ...132
  Some Helpful Hints ...133
  Let No One Rain on Your Parade ...133
  Plan Your Work and Work Your Plan ...133

Chapter Eleven: Creating Your Heart's Desires ...135
  Timing ...136
  Your Basic Stance ...137
  Changing Your Thoughts ...138
  The Man with the Hose ...138
  Choosing Your Creative Goals with Care ...139
  Health, Wealth, and Loving Relationships ...139
  Moving from Where You Are to Where You Want to Be ...140
  Going from How Bad It Was to How Sweet It Is ...140
  Building a New Consciousness ...141
  A Simple Outline ...153

Chapter Twelve: Nurturing Your Creations ...155
  Adelade, the Unpaid Maid—the Saga Continues ...155
  Keeping Your Word ...156
  Discipline ...157
  Start Your Day with Clear Intent ...157
  Maintaining a Joyful Stance ...159
  Join the Joy Team ...160
  Putting It All Together ...160
  Seeing Is Believing ...160

Chapter Thirteen: Rediscovering Your God-Self 163
- Guardian Angels 163
- Recognizing Your God-Self 164
- Understanding Ourselves 164
- The Soul Is Who We Really Are 165
- Which Side Are You On? 165
- You Are Unique 165
- Finding Your Soul Purpose 166
- Feeding the Soul 167
- Working with Your God-Self 167
- Answers from Your God-Self 167
- Guidance 168
- Practice Awareness 169
- Intellect Always Argues with Intuition 170
- Body Signals 170
- Your Soul Knows 171
- Impulses 171

Chapter Fourteen: Meditation: Getting in Touch with Your God-Self 173
- Prayer as a Prelude to Meditation 173
- Meditation Is Prayer Without Words 174
- The Call to Worship 174
- My God-Self Contact 175
- Comments on Meditation 176
- Making a God-Self Connection 176
- Preparation for Meditation 176
- Meditation 177
- Recording Meditations in a Journal 180
- Some Meditation Seed Thoughts 180
- Mini Meditations 181

Chapter Fifteen: Body Talk 183
- Coming in as a Soul 183
- Becoming Disenfranchised 184
- Development of the Personality Self 184
- Your Soul Speaks 185
- Soul Talk 185
- How Your Body Talks to You 186
- Body Talk 187
- How Illness Speaks to You 187
- Stress Is the Main Cause of Illness 189
- Love Is the Only Law We Need 192

    The Message of Tension 192
    Solar Plexus—Your Radar Screen 192
    Ignorance Is Not Always Bliss .193
    Who, What, When 194
    Once Illness Strikes 194
    A Little Touch of Healing 196
    Be Kind to Yourself 196

Chapter Sixteen: Mirror, Mirror on the Wall 199
    People as Our Mirrors 199
    Seasons and Cycles 200
    Parents 200
    Karmic Lessons and Family 201
    Inherited Family Beliefs and Misconceptions 202
    A Note to Parents—Present and Future 204
    Siblings 206
    Friends 206
    Authority Figures 207
    Mates and Partnerships 208
    Coworkers 209
    Problem People 210
    How It Works 210
    The Faults You See in Others Are Your Own 211
    The Saga of Broken Promises 212
    Reprogramming Ourselves 214
    Minimizing Problems and Avoiding Nasty Repeats 215
    Putting It All Together 215

Chapter Seventeen: Surroundings as Symbols 217
    Living Room 218
    Kitchen 218
    Bedroom 219
    Bathroom 219
    Basement 220
    Closets and Cover-ups 220
    Confrontation Is Cleansing 221
    Message of My "House from Hell": What It Taught Me . . .221
    Message of Your Home: What It Tells You About Yourself . .222
    Final Analysis of Your Home .223
    Workplace: Your Home Away from Home 224
    Procrastination Is the Name of the Game 224
    Disorder: Failure to Make Decisions 225
    Your Automobile: An Extension of Yourself 226

Your Neighborhood: Another Reflection of Your Thoughts . . 227
What You Think Is What You Get 227
Guidelines for Choosy Creators 228

Chapter Eighteen: Circumstances as Symbols 231
Discomfort Is Your First Signal for Change 232
Patterns of Change 232
Cycles 233
Repeated Signals 233
Dealing with Problems Constructively 234
Boundaries 235
New Decisions 238
Typical Problems We May Face 238
Changing Your Thinking: Finding a New Attitude 240
The Universe Is a Safe and Loving Place 240

Chapter Nineteen: When Things Go Wrong 241
Repeating Patterns and Problems 242
The Story of No Goals 242
Misery Is Not a Place to Live 243
Do a Review 244
Check Your Goals 244
A Day of Joy 245
Check Your Focus 246
Stress-O-Meter 247
Addressing Your Stress 248
Check Your Basic Belief System 248
Laying the Groundwork for Success 248
Positive Support for Your Beliefs 249
Supportive Self-Talk 249
Improving Your Skills 250
Understanding Your Mis-Creations 251
When Problems Occur 252
Problems Are Lessons in Disguise 253
Problems Stimulate Our Growth 253
Problem Situations Made Easier 254
Dealing with Disappointments 255
Problem Prevention 255
Greeting New Things with Loving Acceptance 256
Check Your Score 256
The Purpose of Our Lives 257
Ten Talents 258

Chapter Twenty: Your Life, Your World, Your Universe 261
Your Own Little World 261
Vibration 261
Vibrational Harmony 263
Living More Consciously 263
In Tune with the Universe 263
Joyful Creating 264
Follow Your Bliss 264
Staying in That Happy, Loving, Vibrational Place 264
Sharing Personal Upliftment 265
Helping One Another in Positive Changes 265
Improving Family Affairs 266
Neighborhood 266
Community 267
Weathering the Storm 267
Tornado Alert 268
The Ripple Effect of Being Connected to Your God-Self ..269
You Are Creating Your Future Now 269
Expanding Into Planetary Consciousness 269
Earth Changes 270
Gaia 270
People Changes 271
The Universe 272

Bibliography 273

Appendix I: Recommended Reading by Subject 279

Appendix II: Reincarnation Facts and Quotes 283

Appendix III: Ceremonies and Rituals 291

Index 297

Foreword

Having written the foreword to *The Mystical Magical Marvelous World of Dreams*, I was eager to read Wilda Tanner's newest manuscript, and I was not disappointed. She continues her fine and convincing teaching with each of us in mind.

Mystical Magical You follows in the style of Wilda's acclaimed (fourteen reprints!) *Mystical Magical Marvelous World of Dreams*. She opens the door gently and invites us to glimpse the path to a higher way of knowing ourselves.

Throughout the volume, the author speaks soft words—as a guide and a friend escorting us on the journey. Her style is to address a variety of topics in a direct, easy-to-understand manner. *Mystical Magical You* introduces an amazing number of spiritual and self-empowering concepts, adjusting our awareness each step of the way. "What, when, where and how" is the usual format of delivering information. The onion is peeled layer by layer, revealing data, answers, and encouragement. Wilda excelled at introducing an awakening one to new insights and showing the way. Here she continues to lead and teach—"as we dig fifty one-foot holes," a favorite expression of mine.

It is important to realize that the role of all religion—with its outer structure, doctrine, and dogma, whatever they might be—is to lead us toward our own personal spirituality. Often we have begun the journey before we sense the awakening of the "Presence Within" has assumed leadership and is walking us into the greater light.

Tools to assist the process abound in this exciting volume. They are excellent for the reader who wishes to facilitate inner knowing and to clear old programming, as well as for individuals leading classes and wanting additional exercises and techniques to add that stimulating experiential touch.

As we begin to enter the world of new spirituality, there is so much to explore. We feel we have to know everything, so we often find ourselves rushing from here to there, topic to topic, gathering all the information we can. Later, after we have heard many stories about many subjects, we become more selective. We are ready now to go deeper into our quest for what will establish our individual approach. At the point, we are ready to dig ourselves ONE hole fifty feet deep. Our inner exploration is in process one step at a time.

Until this quiescent nature begins to stir, few people find such joy and well-being in their lives. Each quickening adds to the delight of the inner presence, claiming its place within daily life. Fresh new experiences, creative insights, and deep awareness generate "aha's" that move us nearer to the light and love that is our true nature.

Indeed, when we remove the facades behind which personality exists, each of us is mystical and magical. Too often we do not realize the wonder of our own nature. But for those who didn't hear it whispered into their ear when they were infants, they can now be empowered and loved into action.

Join others who delight in sharing the good news: *Each life is part of a divine design, and love is needed as we link ourselves together to light up the world.*

The wonderful title says it all. Discover and celebrate your "mystical magical" self!

Carol Hara

1

Ye Are Gods

*The seed of God is in us.
Pear seeds grow into pear trees,
nut seeds into nut trees,
and God seed into God.*
— Meister Eckhart

From the day we were born, we have been taught to believe that we are only human. *Only human?* This implies that our physical bodies are all that we are, when in fact we are gloriously designed beings made up of several nonphysical bodies. Each of these bodies plays an important role in our life. All our power is rooted in these invisible bodies. Our physical bodies are simply tools our souls use to learn the rules of creation while we dwell in the Earth School of experience.

Essentially, we are souls made in the image and likeness of God, with the ultimate goal of becoming co-creators and companions to God. As souls, we voluntarily came here for the experience. We had a definite plan with specific goals as to what we wanted to learn and accomplish. At the end of each life span, we return home with our newly gained knowledge. Then, as both judge and juror, we review that life, evaluating our successes and failures. Once the evaluation is over and our knowledge is assimilated, we begin laying plans for our next earth trip. It takes many lifetimes to achieve our lofty goals.

We have been told that we only live once. This is true only as it pertains to the physical body. Death does not touch the soul, which is who we *really* are.

We have each lived many lives on our path to greater knowledge and perfection. The Bible and many other ancient writings contain multiple references to reincarnation (see Appendix II). The familiar phrase "What goes around comes around" is a rewording of the biblical quote from Galatians 6:7, "Whatever a man sows, he shall also reap." This is just one of many well-known Bible verses referring to multiple incarnations. It is believed that the average person has lived hundreds of different lifetimes.

In Matthew 5:48, Jesus admonished us to "Be perfect." Yet we are aware that some of us are born in great wealth and with every opportunity to succeed, while others are born in poverty and sickness. Their lives are a struggle from beginning to end. Obviously, one lifetime is not enough for us to achieve perfection. Life without reincarnation would not be fair. Actually, we are fortunate to have a second chance — more if we need them.

When problems occur in our lives, friends solemnly advise, "It is God's will," implying harsh punishment from a loving God and suggesting that we are powerless to do anything about the problems. In essence, we have been taught to believe we are powerless victims of circumstances, and those beliefs have effectively kept us from becoming all we can be.

The good news is that this can only affect us if we accept it. In truth, we are not powerless at all. We are simply suffering from a series of false concepts and erroneous beliefs, which are temporarily preventing us from living our lives to the fullest.

Know Ye Not That Ye Are Gods?

In Psalms 82:6, the Bible clearly states, "Ye are gods, indeed, ye are sons of the Most High." It also declares that we were "created in the image and likeness of God ... as co-creators with God." It seems that we have forgotten our true heritage.

The truth (which we seldom hear) is that each of us is a child of God with unlimited creative capabilities. We are, in fact, gods and goddesses in the making, still growing, reaching out, and discovering our abilities by trial and error. We have the innate ability to create the desires of our hearts. The trouble is nobody told us that we could or should use it. Consequently, we no longer see ourselves as God's co-creators. We have forgotten how to play the game.

As evolving souls, we experience all kinds of conditions, problems, and adversities in our efforts to learn the laws of the universe. Since God is love, the most important of these is the Law of Love. This realization is the real key to successfully creating our deepest desires.

Those who believe themselves to be only human have to work hard for a living. On the other hand, those who understand their true heritage can create their desired circumstances and opportunities, which allow them to accomplish things with ease.

The Law of Love

In the beginning, God created us to be His companions and co-creators, working within the Law of Love. For a very long time we faithfully adhered to this law. Then, over many centuries, a few of us began to create selfishly, without concern for others. Eventually, more and more of us began to create selfishly. We began to see ourselves as separate from God, and we began to be self-conscious. Yet God never looked upon our selfish creations as mistakes or as "sins" but as a part of the learning process.

In our many long walks on earth, we all have experienced being king and slave, wise person and village idiot, victimizer and victim. We have run the gamut in a variety of roles. We have done it all for the experience. There is no reason for guilt over our so-called blunders. If we learn something, no experience is wasted. However, we do need to make amends when we have hurt someone. Now, as we look at our lives from the perspective of our soul's purpose, we will realize that all our adventures are for learning, growing, and living in joy on our chosen path to greater wisdom.

Creating

We all know, however dimly, that we create our own reality. Each one of us is exactly who, where, and what we have chosen to be, based upon all the decisions we have made along the way. God created us to be joyous, loving, and unlimited beings, yet we seem to have lost that knowledge in the activity of learning. Somewhere along the way, we wandered off the path and became blithely unaware of our heavenly heritage.

Now that we have entered the twenty-first century, we are finally ready to make a giant leap in consciousness, moving from our present commonly held beliefs to new and greater ideals. Let us reach for the mind-boggling concept that we are much-loved gods in the making with unlimited potentials for spiritual growth and creativity. Let us realize that our selfish creations were simply regarded as part of the overall learning process.

As a planetary people, we are finally ready to remember who we are and why we are here. Our ultimate goal is to become mature, knowledgeable co-creators, working with God and joyfully choosing to create within the Law of Love. We are coming out of the darkness and emerging into the light.

Cosmic Clock

The Cosmic Clock is ticking. It is time to realize that we are great spiritual beings who have lived many lives, learned many lessons, and are ready to graduate into our full potential. The major lesson remaining is fully accepting our divine heritage. We must cease thinking of ourselves as "only human," denying our creative potentials, and begin to reclaim that heritage. Let us learn to live again within the laws of love, joy, and harmony.

As we begin to acknowledge ourselves as creators instead of victims of circumstances, we can use our abilities to transform our present conditions into far more pleasant ones. Let us decide now to apply the principle of love in our lives and again make our dreams come true.

We can and do create our lives and circumstances every single day. However, since we do not remember the rules of the game, we often create the very things we do not want. Together, let us again learn the rules of the game and create *exactly* what we want, *every* time.

2

The Truth About You

*You shall know the truth and
the truth shall set you free.*
              —John 8:32

Before you can create your reality purposefully and intelligently, you need to understand thoroughly all that you are.

Although you were taught to think of yourself as only human, the truth is that you are a soul. You are a spiritual being who lives and works through your earthly body in much the same manner as you enter and exit your automobile. Your earthly body is the smallest, most condensed part of the total you. Surrounding and dwarfing your physical form are several nonphysical/invisible bodies, which make up the rest of you. You are born and reborn again and again until you have mastered all your lessons.

If you saw the movie *Cocoon*, you may recall the lovely female, Kit, who came from Antares. In one scene she happily peeled off her physical body-like "costume" and danced around in her shimmering lightform. Your lightbody (aura) is located outside your physical body instead of the other way around, as seen in *Cocoon*. However, the idea of human beings having a semi-transparent body is accurate. The simulation of Kit's lightbody in the movie was a delightful example.

As a spiritual being, your earthly body is surrounded and interpenetrated by an electromagnetic energy field that extends outward from around eighteen inches to thirty feet or more from your heart center. It is a large, oval-shaped unit composed of several nonphysical bodies, which make up the total god part of you known as your spirit. *Aura* or *lightbody* are names commonly used for your spiritual body. All the wisdom, knowledge, and experience you have gleaned through your many lifetimes, plus all the talents and abilities you have developed are stored in the aura.[1]

Your Lightbody

Your lightbody is made of the same electromagnetic properties as the magnetic field encircling our planet Earth. In fact, your auric field is an integral part of the magnetic field of Earth. Although invisible to the naked eye, both of these fields are well known in scientific circles. However, the human aura has a variety of names. The well-known biologist Rupert Sheldrake calls it a *morphogenic field*; neurophysiologist Jose Delgado describes it as a *mind field*; Dr. Harold Burr of Yale prefers *life field*; and Russian scientists declare it to be a *bioplasmic field*. Your local doctor might call it an *electromagnetic field*.

For centuries, artists have pictured this field as a halo of light surrounding people considered to be saints or holy ones. This may indicate that in more peaceful times many people were able to see and describe the radiant light around such spiritually advanced ones as Christ, Mary, Buddha, and others.

A special process known as Kirlian photography has produced replicas of this phenomenon. People with clairvoyant vision can perceive both size and colors in the auras of others. The degree to which they see depends on their individual abilities. Many people can sense another's aura without physically seeing it.

The auric field varies greatly in size and color from one individual to another. For example, a person who is highly evolved spiritually may have a large, bright aura extending as much as twenty or thirty feet from the heart center. On the other hand, one who is materialistic and selfish in nature might have a smaller, less illumined field extending no more than three feet and clearly showing the lack of spiritual development in that person.

Your aura surrounds, interpenetrates, and supports all of your bodies, including the physical, completing the vastness of all that you are. It is within this whole/holy body that you truly "live and move and have your being" (Acts 17:28).

Your Body's Vehicle—The Real You

1. Physical body
2. Etheric body
3. Emotional body (Astral)
4. Mental body
5. Intuitional body (Causal)
6. Buddhic body
7. Spiritual body

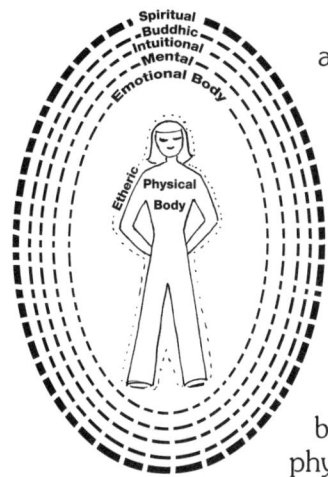

Note: The spiritual vehicles sketched here are shown here in layers for clarity only. In actuality, they completely interpenetrate the physical body and one another.[2]

You Are Greater Than You Think

The truth is that you are a beautiful, god-like being created in the spiritual (not physical) image and likeness of God. You leave your physical body with ease every time you go to sleep and frequently when you meditate, faint, or daydream. You are a spiritual being, a god in the making, a soul using your physical body as a vehicle for interacting with others. You are here to gather information and experience while on your quest for mastery over all of your bodies.

Regardless of your race, nationality, education, or religious preference, you are here by your own choice, walking on your chosen path back to God. At the soul level of your being, you know exactly why you are here and where you are going. At this level, you always know what to do, although you may not be consciously aware of it. As the saying goes, "the soul knows." So trust yourself and listen to your gut instincts, those deep, inner urges that come from your soul.

This is important in creating your reality. Remember, someone taught you to believe that you are a helpless victim of circumstances with little control over your life. In essence, you were taught to believe that you are powerless. That belief has very effectively kept you from becoming all you can be. The good news is that this belief can only affect you if you accept it. In truth, you are not powerless at all. You are suffering from a series of false concepts that are temporarily preventing you from living life to the fullest.

If you have no concept of yourself as a child of God and no understanding of your spiritual greatness, you will have no faith in yourself as the creator of your personal world. Without this knowledge of your god/goddess potential, you will remain in the role of the helpless, hopeless victim. Many of your fellow beings act out this role every day.

We are a planetary people steeped in low self-esteem. We have been carefully taught to doubt our abilities, our potentials, and ourselves. We have been coached to look to authority figures for answers to all our problems. We have been deliberately denied all knowledge of our true spiritual heritage. These limiting teachings began only a few years after the last disciple died. The concept of being "born in sin" was added much later. (*Author note:* St. Augustine introduced this concept of "born into sin" late in the fourth century.) Because of this truth-tampering by misguided religious leaders, we have been taught to believe we are defeated before we begin.

Knowing who you really are is a very important step in being able to believe in yourself enough to dare to be a creator. Train yourself to trust your instincts. If you do not believe in yourself, who will? Now you can prove to yourself just how great you are.

Learning to Recognize Auras

Although most people do not easily see the complete aura, you may catch glimpses of radiating light or energy waves emanating from the head and neck area, similar in appearance to heat waves rising off a hot surface. You may have noticed this light around the head and shoulders of a spiritually developed person who was speaking, singing, or performing. This heat-wave type of light or movement can sometimes be observed around animals, trees, plants, and even rocks. It is the manifestation of the life force or God-spark found in all living things.

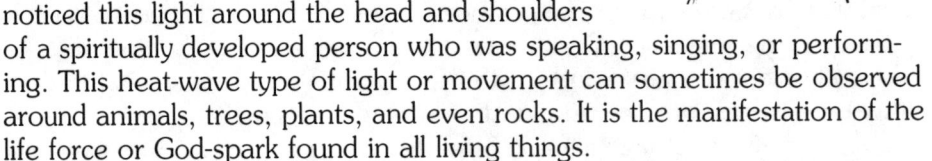

To practice seeing this phenomenon, have someone stand against a light background, such as a cream-colored wall, rather than against a dark or multicolored backdrop. Perception is most likely to occur as you are sitting comfortably and totally at ease. The deeper your relaxation, the more likely you are to see "the light." Remember to watch for a glimpse of aura at the first opportunity, and witness this spectacle for yourself. Be careful not to strain to see, but relax completely, using a soft, slightly out-of-focus gaze.

Another method for recognizing the aura is to look at yourself in a mirror. Do this just about dusk, before turning on any lights, or in a darkened room with a very soft light. Begin by staring into your reflected eyes for a few minutes, being careful not to strain. Again, you want to use a soft gaze. Keep yourself as relaxed as possible, sitting down, if necessary. Remember that you are looking for something akin to heat waves, fuzzy lines, or light areas, especially around the top of the head. Once you find these, continue to look around the neck and shoulders where the emanations may also be stronger or brighter. Eventually, you may be able to see the whole body aura, but that usually takes practice and great serenity.

You may be pleasantly surprised at what you can see. You might also wish to practice this with a friend.

Another suggestion is to hold your hand out in front of you when you are in a slightly darkened room. (Dusk is a good time.) Gaze with a soft focus and slowly move your hand back and forth. Watch for glimpses of a pale light that seem to flow from your fingertips. Often this will be dark blue, purple, or possibly tinged with other colors. Occasionally, the light may appear to be white or even colorless, but it will give you a glimpse of your aura and its energy flow. A plentiful supply of energy flowing out of your fingertips or from the center of your palms may indicate that you are a natural healer.

How Your Aura Affects Others

As a rule, the size and color of your lightbody varies from moment to moment in perfect synchrony with your thoughts and moods. Great fear, for instance, will actually cause the aura to shrink. In fact, you may have experienced feelings of tightening into a small ball or pulling into yourself when you felt frightened or threatened. On the other hand, you may have noticed that prayer, meditation, devotion, and warm thoughts of love and appreciation caused your magnetic field to enlarge and brighten. As you express more love and caring to others, your aura expands.

Hearts

Like Attracts Like!

The quality of your aura may be sensed as impressions radiating from you. Some people are more keenly aware of this than others, yet all of us sense these emanations to some extent, even to the point of picking up another's thoughts and attitudes. You may have noticed that close relatives and friends are often in such near harmony that they easily sense one another's thoughts and feelings.

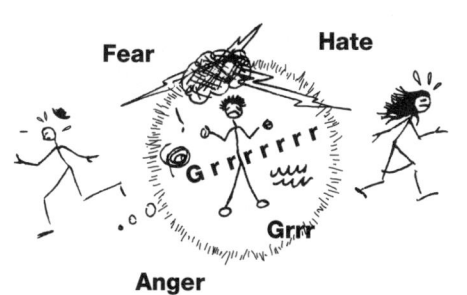

Fear **Hate**

Anger

Have you ever felt an instant dislike or distrust toward a person for no apparent reason? Have you instinctively moved away from someone without knowing why? You were probably reacting to the contents of that person's aura. It is not at all unusual to sense another person's dark moods, pain, anger, or negative energies, although such things are invisible to ordinary vision. The vibrations you feel radiating from a negatively focused person can be extremely depressing or downright repulsive. The energy field just described is the storage area for all our conceptual, creative endeavors as the illustration at the bottom of page 9 indicates.

Whatever is seen or felt in the auras of others indicates what they are manufacturing in their lives, since the creative thought first takes form inside the aura. This is how others can "read" you or "see" your future. They simply tune in to what you are thinking and creating in your mental body.[3]

What you put out mentally is what you get back physically. This is spiritual law in action.

Have you ever noticed that shortly after you make a statement such as, "I can't understand why anyone would _____ ," you find yourself involved in a situation that eventually furnishes you with the answer? Be careful about the things you ask for; you will undoubtedly get them, but perhaps not in the way you intended.

With the universe as your teacher of life and the Earth as your school, nothing ever "just happens." You very carefully select all of your life's events and circumstances, whether you are aware of it or not. At night, while the physical body sleeps, you, as soul, slip out of your body and astrally travel back "home." There you choose the events and lessons you need next, with the help of your guides and teachers in nonphysical realms. Although you are not always conscious of this, it is done in direct response to your need to learn, your desire to know, and the basic beliefs you hold about yourself and your world. All these work together in composing an integral part of your training as a young god or goddess on the path to ever-greater perfection.

As humans, many of us are just beginning to understand that the universe is a safe and loving place. As a loving, nurturing parent, it supports us in everything we do. Within the safe and caring environment of this God-Mind-Universe, we are constantly learning the lessons of cause and effect.

Whatsoever a man soweth, that shall he also reap.
—Galatians 6:7

Others can feel our thoughts and feelings, as these are constantly radiating from us as vibrations. Most often, they are expressed in word form, but they grow and expand into thought forms that eventually return to us in physical forms such as people, conditions, events, opportunities, or problems in our lives. Only in this way are we able to see, experience, and understand the results of our mental and emotional creations. In time, we learn that we do reap what we sow. Eventually, we discover that the consequences of love are far more rewarding than the consequences of hate, fear, or anger. From this, we grow into a greater realization of how to play the game of life. We slowly move from a sense of separation, victimization, and competition into knowledge of the oneness and interconnection of all beings and all things. We begin to perceive at our deepest levels that we truly are gods in the making; as such, we happily embark on a marvelous adventure of living life joyfully.

3

The Process of Creation

Speak the word only and it shall be done unto you.
— Matthew 9:29

Since we were made in God's image and given the power to create (Genesis 1:26), we need to understand that we construct our lives, our bodies, and our circumstances in accordance with Cosmic Law. Whether or not we believe in this process, the truth is that our *every* thought creates an effect of some kind in our lives.

How Thoughts Become Things

A thought, once conceived, first produces an undulation similar to that of a musical note. This, in turn, creates a vibrational imprint that begins to take form in the mental vehicle of the thinker. However, when there are strong emotions accompanying the thought, the form often takes up residence in the emotional body. Concurrently, the thought produces a living shape, known as a thought form, which is stored in the appropriate body of its maker.

Thought Forms[3]

One purpose of this is to facilitate the learning of skills and the accumulation of knowledge needed to live and perform in this world. Another is the ability to send telepathic messages, via thought forms and symbols. At the same time, this thought wave radiates from the originator and enters the mental or emotional bodies of others within range, resonating in a manner similar to a tuning fork. Following the universal concept that like attracts like, this wave can stir similar patterns and emotions within others of similar minds, leaving an imprint in all of the responding bodies. Those having no similar frequencies remain unaffected.

Over time, as we repeat a particular thought, the original thought form expands and strengthens. The thought maker's personal attitudes, feelings, and strong beliefs add their powerful vibrations, thus feeding the form. In addition, any words spoken about the matter trigger further emotions, actions, and reactions. Gradually, the combination of these forces begins to evolve and develop into a familiar habit. The longer the habit is reinforced the more firmly it becomes fixed. The total collection of these mental patterns eventually molds and creates the thinker's distinctive mind-set, attitudes, and character. The thoughts we entertain gradually alter even our faces. Sour thoughts eventually become sour faces and happy, optimistic thoughts develop into cheerful expressions. We truly become the accumulation of our thoughts.

Thought Form Construction

One could say that the human mind works in a manner similar to that of a computer, creating a symbolic record of every thought and storing these on a memory disk within the consciousness of the individual. Just like files on a computer, some of these stored thoughts may need to be deleted from time to time.

As the mind is busily engaged in the thinking process, it forms nebulous shapes that are in complete accordance with the mental concept. The attendant emotions add the appropriate colors to the form, such as red for anger. The more attention given to the subject, the stronger and more powerful the resulting construction becomes. The thought form contains both energy and force provided by its maker and immediately begins to take on a life of its own.

According to universal concepts, thought forms tend to attract to themselves anything and everything with a similar vibration but repel those that have no semblance. In this way, they gather more energies of the same caliber; eventually they return to their maker as manifested things, conditions, problems, or events. These unfold in our lives in such a way that we can see and experience the results of our thinking. However, since the results of our thinking may take weeks or months to manifest into physical form, we have a difficult time realizing that we create the circumstances around us. Instead, we tend to think someone else is to blame.

Thoughts that flash quickly in and out of the mind produce only momentary forms because they are given little attention or energy. When we give a great deal of attention or an additional emotional charge to a thought, it becomes a seed taking root in fertile ground. Our every thought produces an effect upon our lives and the lives of others. Therefore as the creators, lords, and masters of our thoughts, we are totally responsible for all that we have brought or will bring into being.

Thought + Emotion + Belief + Word = Effect

The one other ingredient to be factored in is expectation. No matter how much we may want a thing, or how carefully we follow the above formula, our failure to believe or expect that it can happen to us will ensure that it will not happen. If there is the faintest doubt that we truly deserve to have our desires, that old belief of "can't win" or "don't deserve" can and will slow or halt the momentum of that desire from manifesting.

Some Common Thought Forms

From the illustration, it is easy to see that even a simple thought like a question takes on an immediate shape even as we wonder. The structure forms in our aura and can become quite large, as shown in the five-foot question mark. Clairvoyants, who see beyond natural vision, can see and understand these figures. We may be able to see these when we are in a slightly altered state of consciousness, which is a deeply relaxed condition, similar to daydreaming.

Question in the Mind   **Question in the Aura**[2]

Every thought creates a form, however temporary. If the thinker is vague or unsure, the shape quickly dissipates as he or she switches from one idea to another.

When the thinker is clear in thought and intent, the form is sharp and distinct. It is a definite, recognizable object with both the energy and force to accomplish its intended mission. Once a thought is created, each repetition of the thought with its accompanying emotion will continue to strengthen and renew its force. In addition, each verbal repetition will add even greater power, especially when done often and/or emotionally.

Amazing as it seems, it is from the creation of just one little thought form that all habits are begun. Our potential habits need only to be fed regularly by our thoughts and feelings to evolve into a permanent thought pattern. In this way, we create our reality with just one thought at a time, day after day after day. Choose with care.

- **Intent to Know: Variations:** The patterns are produced by an intent to know or to understand. These thought forms are pointed and directed toward a probable source of information. This intellectual probe is yellow in color since mental activity appears in yellow tones. Varying shades will occur in accordance with differences in subject matter and in any added emotional content. Each emotion has its own distinct color.
- **Vague Thought:** Vague, unclear, or indecisive thinking tends to produce fuzzy shapes and forms as seen on your right. These assemblages have little power to impress or perform since there is no clarity of intent, purpose, or direction involved.
- **One Pointed Thought:** The sharpness of this image depends upon the concentration and clarity of the thinker. In this case, the extremely sharp, clear edges denote a very intent, disciplined, one-pointed focus and unwavering perseverance of the thinker. In the mind of someone who has less clarity of focus and intention, the image would have the same general shape but the edges would be soft, fuzzy, and less pointed.
- **Jealousy:** You can see how the saying, "green with jealousy," originated. Our language is full of descriptive phrases depicting ancient knowledge and ability to see the aura and its contents. This figure, similar to the form of an intent to know, represents a determination to watch over and guard the object or person the instigator considers to be his own personal property. The color is green, tinged with yellow and muddied with the brown tones of selfishness.
- **Grasping Affection:** Here we have just a hint of a hand shape. The thought form has slim tendrils with tiny hooks of greed or possessiveness. The color is pink to show affection, tinged with the brown tones of selfishness.

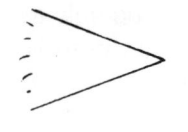

The Process of Creation

- **Greed:** Intense desires and grasping intentions to own a person or thing are variations of greediness, thus taking on the general shape of a claw-like grasping hand. The greater the greed, the more pronounced the hook-like endings are on the fingers, giving the appearance of grappling hooks.

    Colors vary with the type and intensity of the emotions involved. Greed for drugs, alcohol, and low passions produce a thicker hand colored a dark, reddish brown.

- **Fright, Fear:** Similar to an explosion, fright scatters out quickly from the head of the thinker in small streaks and tiny, moon-shaped figures in shades of red and gray. Gray, being the typical color of fear, may vary in its shades. Generally, the darker the tone, the greater the fear expressed. Fear can also be a gray, shapeless glob hanging in the aura long after the original fright is gone.

- **Irritation:** Mental creations have a cumulative effect upon both the thinker and those around him. The tenor of the thinker's overall mood tends to set permanent patterns in the mental body. Notice the spots on the man sketched at left. This man is constantly irritated. His whole aura has become dotted with red, measles-like spots of anger. These marks of annoyance are fast becoming a permanent collection in his electromagnetic field. Once created and established this pattern will quickly react to the slightest provocation from any source, keeping the him constantly agitated. This man has literally created his own private hell. Remember, just because he can't see it does not mean it is not there.

- **Slow Burn:** There is a saying, "I was so angry, I saw red." The reason becomes apparent in the thought form evoked by a slowly emerging anger. This semi-controlled rage gives the appearance of small red flames rising out of the hair. These are often in shades of red and brown, reflecting the depth of anger.

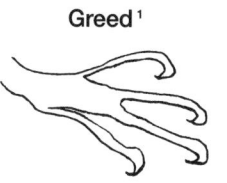

Greed[1]

Fright, Fear[1]

Irritation[2]

Slow Burn[2]

17

Those flickering flames may remain around the person's head for hours before "cooling down." Remnants of these sparks continue actively vibrating in the aura for days, making their creator even more susceptible to repeated outbursts of anger. Since these irate energies can radiate long distances, they attract other anger-prone people. Then, since like attracts like, each one attracts and stimulates the other's anger; tempers flare, harsh words fly, and numerous problems arise in each one's relationships.

- **Resentment:** This appears much as the "slow burn" except the reddish-brown flames are smaller and closer to the head. These tend to remain as a long-lasting, built-in attitude.
- **Exploding Anger:** Exploding anger scatters out from the head in shades of red, black, and sometimes yellow or orange, leaving a hole or blank space in the center. Remnants of this form will continue to vibrate in the aura for days and can easily be aroused again. At the same time, these forms are busily attracting more energies of the same kind, causing the person to become more easily provoked and angered. Each repeated explosion forms a more deeply embedded pattern of behavior.

  Uncontrolled anger literally becomes a habit. Unless the maker curtails this tendency, the anger form will continue to expand until eventually it will have mastery over its creator. Then "the tail will wag the dog."
- **Gratitude:** Thoughts of gratitude and appreciation appear to me as a stream of happy little bubbles floating upward from the head of the thinker, eventually making their way to the intended benefactor. Their silvery color may be tinged with the blue of devotion or with the pink of love and joy. They may sometimes seem to be a mixture of both, creating a rosy lavender hue.

Exploding Anger[1]

Gratitude[2]

Love and Affection

It has been said that "Healing flows on wings of love." This is sometimes seen as gentle, undulating waves of pink radiating toward the chosen person. The result is an immediate warm glow of happiness in the body of the receiver, which is both uplifting and healing. If this same loving energy were sent with the intent to heal, the vibration would be similar but the energy would be more directed to healing.

One or more persons sending love can uplift, inspire, and harmonize a large group of people just by sending waves of love and blessings into their midst. Either way, the thinker/sender is fully responsible for all he creates.

- **Protective Prayer:** Prayer is a message with a wide range of possible meanings and colored accordingly. Since this is usually a loving message, it tends to be pink, but may also be blue (devotion) or green (healing). Prayers are mostly seen in the shape of a circle with a pair of wings on each side, appearing to carry the prayer message held in the center.

    These forms fly to the intended target and hover there doing the work of protecting, healing, or whatever was sent, for at least a twenty-four hour period, depending on the intensity and clarity of thought. Eventually, they will fade away if not regularly renewed.
- **Healing Prayer Forms:** Because the energy of love is such a powerful force, it not only heals but inspires, uplifts, and energizes the recipient. Any love thoughts sent are healing to both the sender and the recipient.
- **Radiating Love:** Love is usually a bright, rosy pink radiating evenly on all sides of the person's aura similar to rays from the sun. This emanation has the power to cheer up all those in immediate range of the instigator's aura. If a strong, directed thought is sent with the love thought it can fill a whole room with its pink glow. Whether it is seen as such or not, it can instantly be felt as uplifting. People quickly gravitate to those radiating love.
- **Love Thoughts:** Love thoughts take on a variety of forms, mostly small suns, moons, bells, or flower blossom-like shapes. Occasionally they may be seen in geometric designs as well. The colors are in loving shades of pink, rose, and lavender. They may also appear in gold, denoting high spiritual ideals, or in a variety of pastels, depending on the type of thoughts and intentions.

- **Sending Affection:** Here the rosy pink waves of love and affection are sent and returned. Often the pink is studded with tiny silver stars, or flecked with golden sparks. As this moves, it may actually bend the sender's aura outward as the love waves move toward the magnetic field of the loved one, filling him or her with both the color and vibrations of love, joy, and happiness.

Sending Affection [2]

When two people are in love, their individual auras often blend into one big pink bubble, generously studded with flecks of silver or gold, giving the appearance of tiny stars. Seeing my teenage son and his girlfriend in this star-filled bubble, I understood why the old fashioned term for falling in love was "sparking."

Floating Thought Forms

Most of your mental creations and thought accumulations tend to remain around you, sticking closely within your aura. Unless you are well disciplined and taking conscious control of your thought processes, these forms are constantly acting and reacting on your overall thinking and feeling nature. At times, you may be keenly aware of the pressure and constant suggestions they assert. You might even feel that "the devil" is tempting you, but it is only your own negative thought forms you have created through repetition.

Since these are your own creations, only you can exert control over them. If you like them keep feeding them, if not, you need to take conscious control over them. Send them away immediately and deliberately replace the unwanted ideas with positive thoughts.

Floating Forms [3]

Most people have a number of wandering thoughts that escape and float freely about in the atmosphere. Perhaps you can recall incidents of walking into a room to pick up something only to find yourself wondering what it was you went after. Then, upon returning to the place where the idea originated, you suddenly remember. This is a clear example of a mental construction suspended in the air exactly where it was created.

Floating forms can be found almost anywhere, especially in public places. You need to realize that you can easily pick up these thought forms as you pass through the area where they are hanging. This is even more noticeable if you stop to linger. Have you ever wondered where a particular idea came from? Well, now you know.

Much of what you assume to be your thought may not be yours at all, but a suggestion left hanging in the air. This is especially true when the idea seems to come from "out of the blue" or is totally different from your current train of thought. This description also fits the pattern of intuitive input, so question the newfound idea. If it feels good, keep it. If not, you need to be warned that when your mind is open, unoccupied, or non-discriminating you can be adversely affected by these unwanted floaters. Remember, too, that you may pick up depression, anxiety, and many other undesirable moods and emanations from those in close proximity to you, especially when you are out in a crowd. This is one of the reasons why sensitive people have difficulty being in large groups or visiting certain places. Sometimes just casually walking past a bar, you may be surprised to feel the low, depraved, and ugly vibrations seeping through the doors.

The next time you walk into a building, pay close attention to how you feel. What kind of reaction do you have? If you do this in several different places, such as a church, library, store, or a funeral home you will receive an astounding education in the wide variety of vibrational effects. You may also be surprised to realize how easily you can identify them. Furthermore you may suddenly realize why you come away from some people or places suddenly feeling drained, tired, or depressed.

Directed Thought Forms

A directed thought is one aimed toward a particular person or group and can reproduce itself in the minds of those with similar ideas and inclinations. It has the power to affect others to some degree, depending on its clarity and the amount of energy expounded. (Prayers are good examples of this, with group prayers being stronger in energy and effect than solitary ones.)

Once sent, the thought form speeds to its targeted person and remains there until the person is receptive or the mind is relatively unoccupied. It then performs whatever it was intended to do, provided the receiving person harbors similar vibrations. A hateful thought sent to a loving person will be repelled just as negative and positive magnets repel. In fact, even an intention that is gentle, loving, and healing cannot be effective unless the intended recipient is open to the idea and willing to be healed. The soul can reject the healing energy if the illness is a necessary lesson to be learned.

- **Affection:** Here is a good example of a loving thought form deliberately sent out to another. As with all directed thought, this will affect the sender, the targeted person, and the world at large. Fortunately, the message is one of love and affection freely given with no hooks or strings attached. The color is clear pink inside with a deeper, rosy pink on the border. However, if the sender's mood were tinged with selfishness there would then be some telltale shades of brown.

  Affection[1]

  On the other hand, let's suppose we sent an angry, drop-dead type of thought to a gentle, loving person. What would happen? First, the form would go directly to the targeted person, then finding no similar vibration to connect with, it would promptly return to the sender adding its undelivered anger to the original anger. This is why Jesus said, "Curse not."

  When both sender and recipient are of like vibration, the thought form will activate and evoke a similar response in the recipient. Then, finding fertile ground, it will settle into that person's aura, adding to his own collection of similar thoughts. Realize there are all kinds of telepathic communication.

- **Directed Anger:** This angry thought construction is sharp, red, and jagged like a dagger or lightning bolt. When one or more of these are purposely aimed at a person, they have the energy and power to move swiftly to their target. On finding a compatible frequency, they will remain there doing what they were sent to do, hating and hurting, affecting the recipient to some degree, depending upon the amount of similar energies residing there. Again, the Rule of Attraction is at play. We also find that directed forms will return to the sender multiplied, so, we need to be careful what we send.

  Directed Anger[1]

  This cloud of hate is colored gray, brown, and black, with dark, angry red lightning streaks flashing toward its target. The person at the receiving end of this will definitely feel its effect and is likely to return the compliment. In which case, both parties will be ensconced in hate.

  In the case of rage sent to a peaceful person carrying no taint of anger, the thought form, finding no suitable home, will swiftly rebound to its sender and remain there.

The Process of Creation

During misunderstandings, disagreements, and arguments both persons can release much hate and anger. These torrid outbursts cause wild and ugly vibrations. Looking like daggers and lightning bolts, these forms fly through the air, bounce off the walls and ricochet around the room for hours or even days after the original disturbance. This results in the whole room feeling uncomfortable, especially to sensitive people, often repelling them. Meanwhile, other irritated, frustrated, and angry people are attracted to the spot.

Hate and Anger[1]

These forms fill your house with angry vibrations that cling to the walls and furnishings unless cleansed in some way. The simplest way is to burn purifying incense such as sandalwood or frankincense, taking it into each room with intent to clear out all dissension. Then deliberately fill the rooms with prayers of blessing, peace, and love to replace the anger.

- **Jealousy and Anger:** This figure is green, tinged with yellow and muddied with shades of brown for selfishness. The cloud-like shape is puffy with pointed red spikes varying from small, red darts to long, sword-like forms, depending on the intensity of anger. These darts shoot out from the sender toward the hated person and can actually be felt by the recipient to a some degree depending on the strength of the sender's vibrations and the sensitivity of the receiver.

Jealousy and Anger[1]

Radiating Love[2]  **Radiating Anger**[3]  **Radiating Gloom**[3]

Race Consciousness

A directed thought always affects the sender first, then the targeted person. From there it goes to the local group mind, then to

23

race consciousness and eventually reaches world thought. In other words, this thought form hangs in the aura of Mother Earth. There it contributes to what is called the race mind or collective unconsciousness by either creating a new group thought form or by adding energy to an existing one. For example, each prayer, contemplation, or intent of peace and harmony not only affects the thinker but also adds to the overall collective thought form of tranquility. This occurs both in the immediate area and in the total mind of humanity worldwide. On the other hand, each thought of hate, anger, or vengeance adds its energies to the local, negative cloud of hate and malice as well as to the total climate of world thinking.

Either way, the originating thought remains as a permanent record in the originator's spiritual vehicle. It becomes a part of his own personal entourage, affecting him as well as those persons encountered and, of course, adding to the group mind of humanity.

What most people do not seem to understand, or want to believe, is that each additional thought form of hate, anger, or negativity actually attracts natural disasters such as violent weather, disease, crime, or war. The Law of Attraction is always in effect and works on many levels.[2]

Low hanging clouds of smog and pollution are simply an outward manifestation of the accumulated negative thoughts in an area. Because of this, we often long to leave the city and escape to the country or the mountains where the air is purer — in more ways than one.

Angry, argumentative, hate-filled creations not only settle in the buildings in which they originated but also tend to move steadily downward, into the lowest areas of a town. Then, following the Law of Attraction, these creations attract more of the depressed and depraved until the whole area slowly dissolves into decay and slums. This, in turn, invites crime, violence, and disasters of all kinds — and it all started with a thought.

Rain or Rainbow

↪ The Process of Creation

Strong thoughts, sent intentionally, can influence many people at once for good or ill. If well focused, one can stimulate strong chords of emotion in others. In fact, this is one of the major causes of mob violence. Once started, this feeling can sweep through a crowd like a tidal wave, evoking a surge of responsive feeling, sweeping all undisciplined minds before it, resulting in group hysteria. Hitler was an expert at fanning people's discontent into burning fires of hate and war.

The Effect of Your Thoughts

Have you ever noticed that one person's anger, even when undirected, can permeate a room full of people, setting them all tingling with various shades of irritation and annoyance? This occurs quite frequently in business offices and other public places. The result of this kind of thinking can put a deterrent on the productivity of everyone in the vicinity unless it is deliberately counteracted in some way, or someone makes a funny remark or broadcasts positive thoughts.[3]

- **Happiness:** Love, joy, and happiness are often expressed as waves of undulating pink light. These vibrant energies tend to radiate from the person into the surrounding area. Those nearby can feel and enjoy the glow of happiness that emanates from them. It is like a ray of sunshine, touching everyone's aura and causing people everywhere to literally "lighten up."
- **Lovers:** You have heard the phrase "the whole world loves a lover." In this case, there is a double dose of love and joy. Two auras are joined in a pink bubble with tiny, sparkling star points of light. The love energies are transmitted like a busy broadcasting station for the world to enjoy. These waves of love are powerfully uplifting and can travel long distances, causing everyone within range to feel lighter, brighter, and happier.
- **Depression:** Depression is often spoken of as "the blues," but it actually manifests as a shapeless blob of dull, bluish gray, shading from light gray to tones of black. The darker the mood, the deeper the color.

Happiness [2]

Lovers [3]

Depression [1]

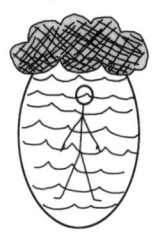

- **Continued Depression:** The actual thought form of depression usually has no distinct outlines but gives the general appearance of a low-flying storm cloud. It looks and feels gloomy. The possessors of these doomsday atmospheres are totally enveloped in their own "pity party." In time, the gloom expands to cover greater more of their minds and auras. Friends and family soon begin to avoid these gloomy folk simply because their presences cast a melancholy pall over others, making everyone around them feel depressed or repelled.
- **Prolonged Depression:** Prolonged depression is another emotional thought form that quickly builds upon itself in the aura of its creator. The cumulative effect soon fills the mental and emotional bodies with the grays and blacks of "gloom and doom" and often become the direct cause of physical illness. Eventually, this kind of deep melancholy can lead to suicide if allowed to go on uncontrolled.
- **Accumulations of Hate and Anger:** The things you think about over a long period of time not only radiate but eventually come out in your speech, tending to pop out unbidden. All too often, these are a subconscious buildup of ideas, emotions, and feelings, which burst forth from inner sources and explode spontaneously. Although you may regret your words, the truth remains that if you had not harbored those thoughts in the first place, they could not have emerged unbidden.

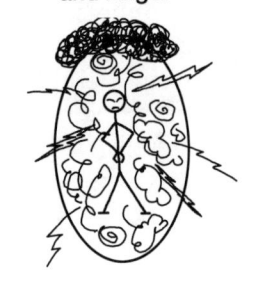

Eventually, having spoken your unguarded words, the thought forms move into manifestation as things, conditions, or problems in our lives. This process of reaping what you have sown allows you to experience the results of your thoughts and feelings, should you pause long enough to recognize and admit what you have done.

Unfortunately, rather than admit you have done it to yourself, the temptation is to place the blame on other people. It is far easier to point to the person that your thoughtless creation returned from and say, "He

The Process of Creation

did it to me." This kind of reaction often leads to thoughts of revenge, which will cause even more chaos in our lives. Frequently, this becomes a vicious cycle — you are constantly fighting and defending yourself against an unseen foe that is actually a product of your own mind, a reflection of your own fear, and a mirror of your own soul.

Thought Forms Collect in Your Aura

As a thought takes on form, it appears in your electromagnetic field to continue doing what it was created to do, love, hate, heal, or whatever was chosen. Wielding a constant force, it affects its creator while attracting like energies from the universe. In this way, it remains alive for varying lengths of time depending on whether or not the original idea is fed by repetition or emotion on a regular basis. Unfed forms will eventually fade out from lack of attention.

For example, a person with a wish for strong drink manifests a simple thought form with that idea. As the idea is repeated and indulged, the desire is added, and the construction grows. It becomes a habit. The more it is fed, the larger it becomes, attracting others with similar desires and drinking habits. In time, the original form further develops, attaching firmly to its master. It expands with every drink until its size almost matches that of the body that nurtures it. (This can be seen by some as a grotesque figure, frequently referred to as a "monkey on his back" because it actually attaches and grows along the spine of its owner.)

A Tale of Addiction[3]

Here is a cartoon of a little desire that grew into a habit, then broadened into a compulsion so compelling that the drinker (or the drug addict) lost all control over his consumption urges. The once innocent thought form has become a monster and taken dominion over its former master. Meanwhile the dethroned creator may whine and say, "I don't know what got into me." or "The devil made me do it." But who created that devil?

It is quite possible to become a victim of our own creations without ever realizing that we are the ones to blame.

Boomerangs

The thought forms we create invariably act like boomerangs; what goes out from us comes back, multiplied by the universe. If our thoughts are kind and loving, they will create pleasant things in our lives, but if they are angry, critical, or self-deprecating, the result, eventually, will be illness, poverty, hardship, and other problems. Our angry, nasty words and thoughts will invariably attract to us angry, nasty people and unpleasant, difficult situations.

Dwelling on our fears or thinking about the things we do not want will continually attract them into our lives and affairs. Our mental and emotional attention to things that we do not want is the attracting force that brings these things into our lives. As Job said, "That which I have feared the most has come upon me." There is no way we can escape the consequences of our thinking.

This, my friends, is the process of creation. Our every thought and word produces results, whether we are aware of it or not. Whatever occurs in our lives, we have created it.

One of the difficulties in accepting all these ancient teachings is the timing. For instance, if we said, "God D--n it" and were immediately struck by lightning, we would have instant understanding of why this happened. Luckily, for most of us, there is a time lag between our thoughts, spoken words, and the manifested results. Without this delayed reaction time, there would be a lot of fried bodies.

If we think of our words as boomerangs, which will eventually come back, we will be very careful about the words we speak.

In the Beginning

When God spoke the creative word, millions of years ago, the results were instant because we were all living within the Law of Love. Now when we speak, the manifestation is delayed, taking hours, days, months, or years. This is partly to protect us because we are still in the early stages of learning just how we create our reality. It is also partly because we vacillate, saying first one thing and then another with neither clear intention nor real understanding of what we are creating with our spoken words.

The delay tends to support our erroneous belief that things *just happen* to us and that we have nothing to do or say about life's events. Consequently, we often fail to connect the causes we set into motion with the results that we experience, regarding the results as luck or accident.

In time, as we gain greater understanding and control over our thoughts and words, we will be able to create quickly, even instantly. As it now stands, the present time lapse is fortunate for us since it gives us time to reconsider our hasty words as well as time to make needed corrections. Graduation time is upon us; the pace is picking up. The waiting period from spoken word to complete manifestation is becoming shorter and shorter.

As humans growing into our godhood, we are just beginning to understand our role in creation. This growth, like that of any child, takes time before coming into full stature. Similarly, we, as souls, young gods in the making, have taken many lifetimes to develop our talents and learn mastery over our mental and emotional bodies. Now we are swiftly rising to our greatest potential and coming into our full power. No longer are we living in illness, poverty, and blame, no longer being victims, but moving into our cosmic heritage as companions, coworkers, and co-creators with God. This is what the "New Age" is really all about.

Major Lessons

The major lesson left for us to learn, understand, and integrate into our lives is that we are gods in the making. We alone create our world and all our circumstances by our beliefs, attitudes, thoughts, words, and deeds. We are responsible for all we create.

There are no accidents, only lessons. Situations that seem to be errors are often questions answered and lessons that help us to learn and grow. Tests frequently follow these incidents to make sure we have acquired the needed wisdom.

As we become wise enough to acknowledge our role in creating situations, we are also ready to take the first step in making better decisions and instigating positive changes in our lives and in the world around us.

If we can create it, we can also change it.
Do It Now.

4

The Laws of Creation

All that we are is the result of what we have thought; it is founded on our thoughts; it is made up of our thoughts.
— Buddha

We each create our lives and all of our circumstances every single day. The problem is that since we are not aware of the process and how it works, we usually manifest the very thing we do not want. The more we worry about or fear a thing, the faster it comes into our lives. Then, we tend to blame others for what happens, not realizing that we have done it to ourselves.

It is said that the Bible is the most popular book in the world, as well as the most important. Now, wouldn't you suppose that the most important information would be on the first page, first chapter, and first verse? If so, you would be right. On the very first page, in the chapter of Genesis, we find the "secret formula" or the spiritual laws governing all creation. Here we discover the exact method used to bring an idea into physical form.

Sometimes truth is hidden in the most obvious places where it is overlooked by unquestioning minds. Only when we have developed our mentality beyond the mundane and trivia are we able to comprehend and apply the deeper meaning and mystery lying beneath the surface of apparently ordinary words. Such is the case in the Laws of Creation as found in the opening verses of Genesis.

> *In the beginning God created the heavens and the earth, and the earth was void and without form.*
> —Genesis 1:1

To restate: God had created the heavens and earth, but nothing was yet in physical form. There was only the thought form held in the mind of God. Any clear picture held in mind is highly creative in nature.

God said, "Let there be ..., and it was so.
—Genesis 1:3

The picture held in mind manifested into reality when God spoke (commanded) it into creation. Words, sounds, and tones are vibrations that bring creative ideas into form. Be careful what you say and how you say it for your words are creative.

God looked and saw that it was good.
—Genesis 1:4

In some versions, God pronounced it good. In others, it was perceived as good. Either way the point is that God always beholds His creations as good. This step completes the creative process as an intention for good.

In other words, when God created the universe, He did not use force. He did not use hammer and nails. He simply:

- Held a clear idea of what was desired, and
- Spoke the words, "Let there be."

And it was so. God completed the process by pronouncing it good.

God created our planet, our solar system, our galaxy, and our universe by thought. For you and me to create consciously, we follow the same formula then pronounce it good.

Clear Idea + Firm Intent/Command = Manifestation

Thoughts Are Things

We live in a thought-created universe. The original pattern for our universe was created within the mind of God. All variations added since have come from the mind of man. We are co-creators with God, whether we are consciously aware of it or not. The thoughts, hopes, and dreams of each one of us add their influence and contribute to the whole of our planet. Moreover, each of us is held accountable for our part in this great creative drama.

Whether we realize it or not, our whole world is made up of thoughts that have solidified into physical forms. Starting with God-created forms such as our planet in all its beauty, Earth is constantly being modified and added to by humankind's mental creations. Buildings, bridges, books, music, art, war, crime, things of great beauty, and things of great ugliness are being added, all in accordance with the thoughts held in the mind of man.

Now, having created the universe, the next step was

Let us make man in our image, after our likeness and let him have dominion ... over all the earth.
—Genesis 1:26

In this instance, "our likeness" refers to the angels and other spiritual beings in attendance around God at that time. This verse further emphasizes our likeness to God. Notice that we were not fashioned as slaves, underlings, or victims, but as spiritual beings, co-creators, having full authority over all the earth. We really are gods in the making.

God took man and placed him in the garden of Eden, to cultivate it and to care for it. ...
—Genesis 2:15

Part of our role as co-creators with God is to be responsible stewards of our earth, our bodies, our personal talents, our abilities, and our possessions. Originally, we were to use these wisely and lovingly, for the benefit of all beings. We were created to be the loving caregivers of earth, and whether we are aware of it or not, we are held fully accountable for the quality of our stewardship. We are truly all in this together and what each one does, thinks, or vibrates affects the whole.

All too often, we fail to take good care of our bodies and our possessions, but even worse, we thoughtlessly rape and pillage Mother Earth, poison her with chemicals, and carelessly dump our trash everywhere. Most of us like to think that we do not tear up the earth with bulldozers and we do not create tons of trash and pollution. However, as long as we buy from or work for companies that do these things, we are also a part of the problem. Whenever we purchase things in plastic, Styrofoam™, and other non-recyclable packages, we are contributing to overall damage to our planet. When we buy poisonous cleaning products, or spray our yards with chemicals, we add to the total destructive process. We are responsible. The same principal applies to failing to recycle all that we can.

It is a spiritual law that when we neglect to honor, cherish, and give thanks for the things we have been given, we set ourselves up to have less and less. (See the parable of the ten talents, Matthew 25:14–29.) To ignore or break spiritual laws is to cause our own suffering. Blaming our lack of prosperity on other people, rather than on ourselves, only compounds the problem.

> *Eat freely ... but do not eat from the tree of knowing good and evil.*
> —Genesis 2:17

This is saying, "Take freely whatever you want, but do not partake from the tree of knowing good and evil". That is, do not make judgments or negative comments about anything God has pronounced good. To condemn those things is to contradict God.

> *God ... brought the animals to Adam and whatever Adam called a living creature that was its name.*
> —Genesis 2:19

Whatever you label or name a thing, person, or situation, that is what it will be to you. You have created it by your spoken word. Call something good, as God did, and it will be good for you. But, for someone else, the same thing could be harsh, difficult, or even painful simply because of their negative spoken word. This is spiritual law in action.

As St. Paul reminds us in Romans 8:28, "All things work together for good." The universe was created in this way. You make trouble for yourself when you make negative judgments about people and things or focus your mind on wrongdoing.

> *As a man thinketh in his heart, so is he.*
> —Proverbs 23:7

We become the sum total of the thoughts we have and hold in our minds from day to day. Our minds steadily build and create according to our overall thoughts, feelings, and attitudes. We bring these thoughts into concrete manifestation with great accuracy and precision. We get exactly what we deserve by way of our words—no more and no less. There are no accidents. All is according to God's laws.

That which I have feared the most, I have brought upon me.
—Job 3:25

Job was recognizing that he alone had brought his fears into reality, which was very astute. The lesson given here is that we can and do cause our own problems through our ignorance or misuse of God's laws. Since one of the laws is the Law of Attraction, we are constantly attracting to ourselves the kinds of things we think about most often, along with the feelings (and resulting vibrations) we have about it. To compound this, many of us mentally dwell mostly on the things we fear. Since emotion adds power to our thoughts, and fear is a strong emotion, then the stronger the fear the quicker the dreaded event arrives at your door.

The law or the reason is not punishment, but a needed lesson. Fear works as a giant mental and emotional block that stops all forward movement, causing us to take circuitous paths of avoidance. There is no better way to overcome a crippling fear than by being directly faced with it and forced to find a workable solution. This done, the needed lesson has been learned and can never again stand in the way for the principles have been mastered, and mastery is the name of the game.

Whatever a man sows, that shall he also reap.
—Galatians 6:7

A final admonition comes in this spiritual Law of Cause and Effect given to us by the Master himself. We cannot avoid the consequences of our thoughts, words, and deeds. What we say and do to others returns to us multiplied. We may attempt to blame someone else for our problems and claim that "X" did it to us, but "X" was only the channel through which our own misdeeds came back to us. No one can escape God's laws.

Although this is not found in the Bible, it does seem to be a legitimate law of creation, having to do with the emotion of resistance, defense, struggle, or pushing against a dreaded thing or unwanted event. In essence, the strong, creative mental power focused on your resistance toward a thing or your concentration on prevention of an undesirable situation amounts to a negative use of your mental powers in a way that brings about the thing most dreaded. (This is how you make most of your creative errors.) What you worry about, talk about, or give your attention to will receive the full force of your creative energies and quickly manifest in your life.

Problem Perpetuators

In our society, we have numerous people who make it a practice to:

- Think about the problem,
- Study the problem,
- Analyze the problem,
- Research the problem,
- Report on the problem,
- Write about the problem,
- Protest the problem, and
- Organize committees to fight the problem.

These people are not problem solvers as they suppose; they are actually problem perpetuators. With all that energy focused on the problem, it can only increase (the Law of Attraction at work again).

Worry

Another common facet of resistance we need to consider is worry, a much overworked trait of society. To worry is to concentrate on the problem. Worry is going over and over the problem without coming to a conclusion. Most worriers are very good at this, practicing their art for days, weeks, months, and even years. The effects of worry are the same as those of resisting: what you worry about is what you attract into your life. It is merely a matter of time.

Worry Wart Mom

Breaking the Laws

The spiritual laws govern all creation. When we ignore or break these laws we run into difficulty, not so much as a punishment for wrong-doing, for God does not punish, but as a necessary lesson in the correct use of our creative abilities. The truth is that you can never be a victim unless you yourself choose to play that role by giving your power away. Fear is a good example of giving power away. Whatever you fear or give your creative mind-energy to, you create.

Fears

- The person who fears being robbed attracts the robber.
- The person who fears rape attracts the rapist.
- One who fears or focuses on an accident attracts the accident. The one fearing or contemplating murder attracts the murderer.

Remember that if you can create and attract what you do not want, you can also create and attract what you do want. It is strictly a matter of where you place your mental focus. Good creating is simply a matter of being able to concentrate exclusively on what is wanted rather than on what is not wanted.

Most folks find this difficult because of old mental habits of focusing on the negative. You need discipline and practice to turn around that process. Usually it takes about three weeks of diligently repeating the new pattern of thinking before the new replaces the old.

Although the principle of "Like Attracts Like" is a spiritual law on spiritual planes, the saying, "opposites attract" applies to the physical plane, especially to people. Often this is a matter of a karmic payback in accordance with attracting what one has sent out. In truth, no one can "do unto us" unless we have agreed, at some level of our being, to be "done unto."

It is well known that we learn the quickest from our mistakes. Our biggest problem is that when we err, we tend to judge ourselves harshly. Then we allow ourselves to be hurt or victimized because we have been taught by religionists that "God is gonna getcha" if you make a mistake.

It is erroneous to say, "God is love" and then, "God's gonna getcha." These are two contradictory statements designed to create confusion. A truly loving God forgives his children and offers them another chance to learn rather than punishing them for a mistake. Recall the story of the Prodigal Son, taught by Jesus. (This story is actually a teaching of reincarnation; leaving home, making mistakes, returning home, being forgiven by a loving Father, and welcomed with open arms.) Think about it.

     Jesus made it quite clear that the kingdom of heaven is within us, within our hearts, and within our minds. If heaven is within us, then so is hell. We create our own world, our own heaven, or our own hell by the things we think, say, and do. When we have suffered enough, from our own misdirected thought energies, we eventually learn to think and act in more loving ways and thus create our own heaven on earth. As Jesus said, "Love one another." This is the law. This is the "bottom line."

5

The Prison of Limited Thought

Life was not meant to be a struggle,
To be harsh, dull, and dark,
But as a game to be played with laughter
And enjoyed to the very last spark.
—Author

If you could catch a dozen fleas, put them in a jar then close the lid, the fleas would first jump up against the sides and the top, butting their little heads repeatedly. Surprisingly, in a matter of minutes, all this would cease for they would have learned their limits. At this point, you could safely remove the lid and not one would escape because they each had become conditioned to the limits of their present world.

The same principle also applies to elephants. If you have ever wandered around the circus grounds observing the animals, you may have noticed that the large, mature elephants were tied with only a rope and stake. However, the younger ones were fastened with a heavy chain with a sturdy pole deeply embedded in the ground. Seems strange, doesn't it? Yet, this is a necessary procedure for all young elephants until they come to believe there is no escape.

Once the young elephants have learned their limits, they can be tied with an ordinary rope to a small, easily removed stake. For, just like their parents, they have become conditioned to their boundaries. They know when they have reached the "end of their rope" and will no longer attempt to move beyond those limits.

Many of us, as young children, have been trained in much the same way. From infancy onward, we have been carefully conditioned to accept the boundaries of whatever our relatives considered right, wrong, proper, or improper. Innumerable limitations were impressed upon our minds as we grew to maturity. We have been carefully instructed as to what kind of things and which types of people are acceptable into our personal world. We were told what we could do, could not do, be, or have. Everything in our young world had to have the stamp of approval from family, teachers, and society. If we went to church, more rules and restrictions were added.

Although some of these restraints, such as safety measures, were wise and necessary for our survival, many were based on unfounded fears. A great number were prejudiced and manipulative, designed to keep us obedient — for example, "children should be seen and not heard" or, "spare the rod and spoil the child." (Many of our current child abuse problems are closely connected to such harsh, control-type teachings.)

We were also exposed to many dimly veiled threats such as "the boogy man will get you if …" Or "Santa won't come if …," "Mommy won't love you if …," "God's gonna getcha if …." All of these and more were used to manipulate and control children through fear. Sadly, many of these tactics are still being passed down from generation to generation as a good way of training children.

In addition to all this, most of us have been very carefully trained to doubt our talents, our abilities, and ourselves. We were thoroughly trained in the "Thou shalt nots" and "Don't you dares." Then there was the all too familiar, "You are too young for this … and too old for that." My parents used that trap repeatedly. There was no way out.

We were warned against trusting our own ideas, gut feelings, or intuitive guidance. At the same time, we were encouraged to always ask permission and/or advice from our "superiors" rather than be self-reliant. (Is that control, or not?)

Poverty Teachings

To add further to these manipulative measures we were often reminded of how hard life is. "Money doesn't grow on trees." "You have to work hard for a living." "There isn't enough to go around." "Money is the root of all evil." "We can't afford it." "You don't deserve it." Moreover, if we spoke of our dreams and the wonderful things we hoped to do when we grew up we were often laughed at or told, "You can't get there from here." Talk about discouraging words!

That isn't all. Parents who mean well often teach their children to be "people pleasers" as an integral part of being well mannered and considerate. This means, "Go to the end of the line and wait." It also teaches the child that he or she is not worthy to be anything but a servant and/or last on the list. Most of us have been carefully trained to feel inferior, unworthy, inadequate, or incapable. Many of us have also been taught to believe that we can't trust ourselves to do anything right.

Overcoming this kind of basic training is difficult even under the best of conditions, because from birth to the age of seven, our minds are extremely open, taking in all we see, hear, and feel. Then, after the age of seven, any new idea that does not fit comfortably with our pre-programmed framework is usually rejected without question.

To compound the situation, most of us are totally unaware of the true nature of our childhood programming. Much has been forgotten. The disempowering teachings now lie deeply buried in our subconscious minds and have become a permanent part of our basic belief system. Because of this, these concepts, unless we consciously change them, will continue to exert a constant, limiting influence on us.

Like the flea and the elephant, once we have been conditioned to a particular set of rules, beliefs, taboos, and limitations, we tend to remain within those mental boundaries. We seldom dare to venture beyond them, as we are so convinced of the solidity of the mental ropes that bind us.

We Live in an Abundant Universe

Contrary to what we have been taught, the universe has an endless supply of money. God created a world overflowing with abundance. When the American billionaire Ted Turner donated one billion dollars to the United Nations, he remarked, "The world is awash in money."

Most of our perceived limitations are from false teachings, erroneous convictions, or both. We tend to believe in our limits, the lid on the flea bottle, the rope tied to a stake, and the restrictions imposed on our thinking. We can change all that!

Each one of us has our own distinctive gifts, our own unique place, and a definite purpose for being in this world. It is up to you to find your place and do what you came here to do, with or without an expensive education. You are here to use your precious gifts in your own special way. You are to be a loving, joyous, and powerful being, happily using and sharing your gifts and talents and becoming prosperous in the process.

Poverty Is a Learned Condition

Success, prosperity, joy, and a sense of fulfillment are the natural results of following the desires of your heart. Instead of listening to our own hearts, we tend to listen to those in authority; consequently we settle for the first job that comes along, whether we like it or not.

Poverty is a learned condition, a false belief. We act out of our learned fear of not enough or that we may not get another chance.

Consequently, we compromise ourselves, take a position we are not particularly suited for, then wonder why we are lacking in joy and abundance.

Since hardship and lack are learned limits, the only reason we accept this in our lives is that we are still in the prison of our limited beliefs. We have accepted the societal programming that tells us that life is hard. Out of that belief, we continue to create hardship and poverty. It is just that simple.

Accept other people's limits and sure 'nuff, they become yours — to keep.

This book is about moving out of your old, limited beliefs and retraining your mind in such a way that it becomes a positive tool for achieving the things you want. Then you can deliberately create a prosperous and joyous lifestyle.

Life Is Meant to Be Joyous.

6

Understanding Your Belief System

It shall be done unto you according to your beliefs.
—Matthew 8:13

Before you begin to create the things you want in life, you need to have a clear understanding of the following:

- Your **Basic Belief System**,
- Your **Subconscious Mind**,
- Your **Conscious Mind** or intellect,
- Your **Will Power** which directs and empowers the mind, and
- Your **Super Conscious Mind** or intuition.

These factors are not always in agreement with one another. What you think you want (intellect) and what you believe you can have (basic belief system) are often in direct opposition to one another. Consequently, each one cancels the other. Such seemingly minor differences of opinion can cause you major problems simply because they go unrecognized.

Your Subconscious Mind

An excellent example of the power of your subconscious mind is seen in those who go on stringent diet and exercise programs to lose weight. As long as they are determined in their efforts (will power + intellect), the pounds obediently fall away, but as soon as the conscious mind (intellect + will) relaxes, the telltale scales move right back to the pre-diet point. In each case, the battle of the bulge is constantly being fought only to be lost many times.

Whenever the conscious and subconscious minds are in disagreement, the subconscious mind always wins.

Why? The subconscious mind is holding a belief about the amount of weight that is comfortable and safe. The subconscious belief may be that to be slim and slender is also to be weak and vulnerable. On the other hand, the belief may be that bigger is better, more powerful, and therefore, a greater protection from assaults, either real or imaginary.

Some people actually enjoy feeling that they can "throw their weight around," possibly because this gives them a sense of power. When this is their conviction, there will only be minor fluctuations of weight, despite all efforts to lose. Their basic belief is that *extra pounds feel "safe."* Therefore, unless the hidden belief is changed, diet and exercise programs will be effective only as long as the conscious mind is successful in overriding the subconscious.

Your subconscious mind works like a computer in its capacity to record and recall everything you see, hear, think, and experience. Your subconscious mind forgets nothing. All information, true or false, is stored without understanding or judgment as to its validity. The subconscious mind simply records everything as true.

Your subconscious mind is a vast memory bank that is the basis for all your conscious decisions. The sum total of all the information stored there is your basic belief system. Your beliefs are a composite of all your attitudes, feelings, and assumptions about who you are. Most of these concepts were instilled while you were very young and unable to discriminate truth, judgments, false beliefs, and the limited opinions of others. Because of this, your conscious mind is often totally unaware of these underlying influences. Yet, these convictions constantly color the way you see and experience your world. The fears, prejudices, and limited viewpoints from your childhood actively influence your adult decisions unless they are deliberately changed.

> *Everything you see, hear, and experience becomes a part of **who you are**.*

God originally designed your mind to accumulate facts to facilitate learning so that you do not have to learn how to read or write all over again each day. However, because this is a free will universe, the mind is not designed to filter out truth from fiction or useful information from useless. Therefore, since the subconscious mind does not discriminate, you need to choose carefully what you wish to see, hear, and do. Unfortunately, many fail to use that option.

Meanwhile, every idea you have ever heard from friends, family, teachers, books, and news media is duly recorded. Your memory banks hold all the old movies, television programs, commercials, and whatever else you have been exposed to while awake or asleep. This is particularly true when you fall asleep with the television on. You may find yourself lured into buying things you neither want nor need simply because of the commercials that have entered your unguarded mind. Think of all the hate and violence, sex and sarcasm being broadcast into your home every day. This is especially true in homes where the television set goes on the first thing in the morning and blares until the last thing at night.

In other words, any thought or thing you have ever seen or heard is stored in your memory banks. Unless you have consciously denied its validity by saying, "I don't believe that," your mind has accepted and stored it as truth whether you consciously remember it or not.

Decisions Conform to Your Basic Belief System

You will not say or do anything outside the limits of your basic belief system unless you are under great duress. It makes no difference whether the information is correct or not, your decisions are based on the beliefs you hold. It is important to review your beliefs and correct or update those that no longer apply. For example, "Never speak to strangers" is good advice for a child but inappropriate for adults in the business world.

Your beliefs, whether right or wrong, sensible or foolish, are permanently stored until you make a conscious choice to change them. Regardless of what you believe, your subconscious mind will always work to prove you right — even when you are wrong.

The principle of your subconscious mind relentlessly working to prove you right can get you into some pretty strange situations, since it can work both for you and against you. For example, if you hold the belief that it always rains on your picnic, your subconscious mind will arrange for you to spread your tablecloth in the only place around where rain will fall that day.

The Power of Your Beliefs

A good illustration of this is the old saying, "If you don't have faith in your doctor, he can't heal you." Perhaps you can recall some of the stories you have heard about a doctor telling someone that he or she will never recover. Some accepted the statement without question, fulfilling the gloomy prognosis. Others, either more stubborn or having more faith in themselves, not only refused to accept the verdict, but were determined to regain their health through sheer will power — and succeeded.

Much of what you create in your life today comes from your basic belief system that is often damaged early in life. If childhood experiences have given you the impression that you are unloved or unworthy, you believe this to be your truth. As you accept criticism and abuse as your reality, this pattern becomes set in your minds and you attract or recreate that scenario. Each occurrence further embeds the pattern of unworthiness.

Poor Self-Esteem

Poor self-esteem, however created, is the basic cause of almost all illness, unhappiness, and poverty. For example, when I was young, my parents wanted me to be perfect. Their idea of perfect was for me to sit still, speak only when spoken to, and to do nothing unless I was told to do it. Since this was impossible for me, I was always in trouble. On top of that, nothing I ever did was good enough. If I made an "A" in school, I was told it should have been an "A+."

Although there was decent food, clothing, and shelter, there were no expressions of love, caring, or approval. There was no hugging, kissing, compassion, or even an occasional pat on the back. My parents merely tolerated me. If there was a problem, well... I got myself into it and had better get myself out. I truly did not know what love was. The message I received from my parents was rejection. So, at age eighteen, I left home quite certain that my parents were genuinely glad to see me go. I later realized this was not totally true, but it was what I felt and believed at the time.

I was convinced of my unworthiness as an individual. In due time, I was married to an alcoholic who treated me with the same criticism and rejection as my parents. Having known nothing better, I accepted this without question. My way of life became one of disdain, disapproval, and poverty. After the children came along, I often called myself "Adelade, the Unpaid Maid," for this was exactly how I perceived myself.

Adelade, the Unpaid Maid

Out of my low self-worth, I created and accepted bad luck, poverty, pain, and drudgery in my life. I never questioned whether I deserved better. Once the idea of my unworthiness was established in my mind, it persistently produced its own results. Later, when I "hit bottom," I knew I had to change my life or drown in my own sorrow. It was a challenge to change my old belief system from poverty and pain to pleasure and prosperity, but I did it!

It took many months of struggle in my private "prison of limited beliefs" before I was able to recognize and work through the many false beliefs I held about myself. Finally, I began to understand just how easily old belief systems can perpetuate erroneous thinking and hold us in our old limiting patterns. This is not to say that old habits can't be eradicated. If I, in my great ignorance, could do it with a little bit of help in seeing my errors, you can do the same — and most likely, a lot quicker and better. This is good news because eventually we must face and transform our false concepts if we are to create the happy, prosperous, and wonderful world God meant for us to have.

Nothing Happens by Accident

In my desperate search to find a way out of my misery, I discovered the concept of reincarnation. This answered many questions my religion had left unanswered and helped me to understand the old question "Why me?" The ultimate answer is the Law of Cause and Effect, more commonly known as karma. Once I comprehended it, it was relatively easy for me to move into a new understanding and a happier attitude as I moved out of anger, resentment, and blame. Now I am creating my life, as I want it to be.

This book is the culmination of all I have learned through study, research, and good old trial and error in cleaning up my life. Was it worth it? Yes, I can happily say, "It worked for me." It is my sincere belief it will work for you.

Abuse

Low Self-Esteem Is Formed by Abuses

When a child is born into a situation of poverty, disease, and hardships, it appears as though there has been a grave injustice. As we grow up in unhappy circumstances, we may feel we were cheated of loving parents and a happy home. I certainly did.

I now understand that we choose our family, conditions, and environment before being born. I also realize that hardships are chosen to develop a special strength or to learn a specific lesson.[1] This is especially true of children who suffer with physical problems very early in life. Many famous people have had a difficult childhood, which as adults they claim forced them to excel. Everything happens for a reason. Each soul knows why it came. The physical personality is the one that forgets.

> *The Golden Rule:*
> *Do unto others as you would like to be done unto.*
> —Luke 6:31

This is a Biblical law and when we break it, we suffer the consequences of that decision until we learn how it feels to be treated in that manner and decide never to make that mistake again.

Common Mental and Emotional Abuses

- **Criticism:** Excessive criticism strips away self-confidence, leaving us feeling helpless and totally disconnected from our Source. Consequently, we feel vulnerable to those around us, both wise and foolish, who are quick to tell us what we should think or do. Has this happened to you?
- **Labels:** Derogatory words contaminate the mind of a young, impressionable child, causing him to believe he is valueless and undeserving of anything good. He is defeated before he starts. Thus, at an early age, he starts to judge himself as worthless and becomes a victim. Then what he believes, he repeatedly attracts.

Poor self-worth is based entirely on other people's opinions. Too many of us look to others for advice and confirmation instead of trusting ourselves.

Low Self-Esteem
Resulting Patterns and Beliefs

When children are addressed in terms of contempt, anger, or criticism over a period of time, great damage is done to their self-esteem. Shaming children for bedwetting, thumb sucking, or other imperfections they are unable to control does tremendous harm. Damage is also levied when children are teased, criticized, or publicly embarrassed. These labels tend to stick in the emotional body causing long-lasting impairment of the child's self-image and further disconnection from their basic soul-knowing.

- **Always Wrong:** This results from layers of unworthy feelings. One of the most commonly held traits of mentally abused people is their strong belief they are not good enough or they are always wrong. These people continually belittle and berate themselves with accusations of stupidity, wrongdoing, clumsiness, and the inability to do anything right. When plans go astray, they are the first to say, "What did I do wrong?" They are so accustomed to being criticized or blamed that it never occurs to them that it might not be their error.
- **Self-Critic:** This is the outer expression of self-disgust, self-deprecation, and self-hate. These attitudes are a direct result of constant censorship in childhood. Such training brings harsh self-judgment and faultfinding habits. Often these children, when expecting criticism from others, will hastily make disparaging and sarcastic remarks about themselves to prevent being censured by others. This self-hate attracts not only more criticism but also many forms of poverty. The basic attitude of "I don't deserve" renders them unable to accept the "good things in life."
- **Criticism of Others:** Those who live with harsh judgment and criticism quickly learn to find fault, first with themselves, then others. This is partly a means of self-defense and partly a way of overcoming their own feelings of inferiority. By negating others they temporarily make themselves feel a bit better. At the same time, they unwittingly set themselves up to attract more criticism.
- **Self-Destructive Habits:** Self-destructive people have great difficulty accepting good things for themselves. If they are given something nice, they will promptly manage to damage or lose the gift. This may seem to be an accident, but it is the person's own negative belief about himself as projected by others. Scolding does no good, for they have no conscious awareness of why the mishap occurs. Punishment only adds to the well-ingrained inferiority belief.
- **Illnesses, Accidents:** This is a desperate bid for the love and attention that one feels cannot be had in any other way. The person attracts accidents or diseases from a subconscious belief or need. It is a cry for help and a symptom of self-hate.
- **Over Defensive or Defenseless:** People who feel weak and defenseless are prone to attack others verbally as a means of sounding strong, thus warding off aggression. Regardless of their reasons, their damaging words return to them, bringing more discord. Although defensiveness may deter aggression, it also repels potential friends.

RESULTS: There are many different patterns of behavior caused by labeling. Even when we have forgiven the people involved, the programmed pattern remains. To remove the old thought forms we must do some conscious cleansing followed by deliberately replacing it with a new attitude.

PROBABLE CAUSE: Receiving harsh criticism as a child can be the result of one's own criticism and harsh judgments in the past, now manifesting to be recognized, evaluated, and changed into love and peace.

LESSON TO LEARN: There is a need to understand how harsh words wound the soul and bring this into balance by deliberately being kind, gentle, and nurturing to others.

Other Contributions to Poor Self-Esteem

- **Shame Manifesting as Self-Punishment:** Those who feel guilty or shameful will invariably create their own punishment. This applies even when the act itself was trivial. It is not uncommon for children to assume guilt or take on blame for something they did not actually do. They may even feel guilty over an event that never really happened.

  RESULT: Self-punishment for shame or guilt may show up as chronic illness or being accident-prone until the debt is paid. The results of self-punishment may go on for years before the truth is known or there is forgiveness.

  PROBABLE CAUSE: Being critical and judgmental toward others in a previous life brings those conditions into this life as lessons.

  LESSON: Remember the Golden Rule. Practice loving kindness. Learn to think, speak, and act with respect for all living things. Repeat until these become ingrained soul qualities.

- **Rejection, Abandonment:** Whether by death, divorce, illness, or deliberate departure, when a loved family member leaves the home, each child left behind automatically assumes the blame. Each will complain, "My ____ left me." The child sees this as a personal rejection, regardless of the reason for the departure. The child does not understand and believes that he or she has done something wrong to cause the loved one to leave.

Understanding Your Belief System

RESULT: Strong feelings of rejection and abandonment cause the child to expect to be rejected. This perpetuates the problem and tends to effect all the child's relationships in a negative and often painful way.
PROBABLE CAUSE: Abandonment, desertion, and not "*being there*" for others. Too many parents become workaholics and believe that money and things can replace love and togetherness.
LESSON: Practice *being there* for friends and family, express more love, nurturing, and support for those around you. Realize that love and companionship are more important than *things*.

- **Neglect:** When a child is ignored, criticized, and generally denied love and nurturing care, the child will assume he or she is *bad* and may grow up believing there is something terribly wrong with him or her. Like Adelade, the child feels unloved and unwanted. This affects the child's belief system, warping his or her whole outlook on life until the lesson is learned and corrected.

  RESULT: Unworthiness issues. With this belief, he expects to be ignored, rejected, unwanted, and thereby repeatedly attracting that treatment from others.
  PROBABLE CAUSE: That which was done to others comes back to be experienced and balanced.
  LESSON: Learn to treat others with tender, loving care, as you would like to be treated.

- **The Loner:** When a child feels abused, neglected, or unloved, the resulting emotional damage stunts the natural desire to reach out to those around him or her. The child then comes to believe that he or she is damaged goods; therefore, unworthy of love and affection. These negative beliefs then attract more and more incidents of disapproval, rejection, and isolation, which in turn manifest as many unhappy events and great loneliness.

  RESULT: Self-sabotage. Those who feel themselves to be unworthy often come close to achieving the desires of their hearts many times, only to sabotage themselves at the last minute. These people will consistently manage to thwart all their efforts to succeed, with no conscious

51

> realization that they are doing this to themselves. They then tend to blame others for their failures. This behavior pattern will continue to repeat in various forms until the basic beliefs are deliberately changed.
> **PROBABLE CAUSE:** Usually the situation you suffer from is the same as what you have done to others. The Golden Rule cannot be broken without unhappy consequences.
> **LESSON:** Realize what you do to others will always return home to roost. Experiencing the pain and suffering teaches understanding and tolerance. Move to undo what was done and begin to be a more caring, loving person.

If any of the above descriptions fit, remember we are always reaping what we have sown. Those who have abandoned others in the past have to experience the pain of being rejected or abandoned. Those who have hurt others need to experience that pain in order to understand. To learn our lessons we need to recognize this as a teaching, not punishment, and forgive ourselves and all others involved. Then we can use our new understanding to practice showing love and kindness for others.

Recent scientific studies now conclude that children who are held, hugged, and given plenty of love and attention actually grow more brain cells and are measurably smarter than those who are neglected mentally and emotionally.[2]

Fears

- **Unexplained:** Unexplained fears are those which show up in early childhood for no apparent reason, such as an unreasonable fear of heights, falling, flying, fire, knives, and so on. There may be fears of sudden loud noises, or even the sound of thunder. Along with these may be strong dislikes and minor idiosyncrasies that seem to make no sense. Such is the case with my dislike of basements, dark places, and even dark days (known as Seasonal Affective Disorder Syndrome or S.A.D.S.).

  It seems I spent considerable time, in one life, in a dungeon somewhere in Europe, and this is a bleed-through memory. Not a fear, but a distinct dislike with no present-day explanation—yet the uneasiness is very real.

RESULT: Careful research has shown these past-life traumas fit neatly into present life fears. A typical example would be a very young child having frequent nightmares of being surrounded by flames and at present having a seemingly groundless fear of fire. (These dreams may continue into puberty.)

PROBABLE CAUSE: In my many years of teaching and working with dreams, I have found that nightmares are of great importance, usually showing us our fears. They may also come as warnings of impending disaster to be avoided or reminders of past-life accidents to avert. (Many people dreamed of the *Titanic* sinking and canceled their reservations.) Children often have recurring dreams of traumatic experiences that are later found to be a vivid replay of their past life's violent death. Painful and shocking events cause the soul-memory to "bleed through" into the present lifetime as a kind of warning mechanism, reminding them how they died last time so it does not happen again.

LESSON: Once it is explained to the child that those dreams were only a memory of another life, the nightmares cease, and the fears are greatly lessened.

- **Plausible:** Trauma or a lack of love often causes fears developed in childhood. This can causes a deep sense of insecurity, laying the groundwork for all kinds of fears. These may be as simple as having a single, working mother struggling to provide for needs; a fearful mother; or one who is unable to express love for various other reasons. Also, there may have been one or more tragedies such as an accident, fire, flood, or other natural disaster in the present life. Local killings, gang wars, or prolonged stays in a hospital can leave one feeling lost or abandoned.

  RESULTS: Feeling shy, insecure, uncertain, and even incapable. There may be hesitance in making decisions and procrastination out of self-doubt or lack of confidence in one's ability to do well. A child may be fearful of being criticized or embarrassed when making mistakes.

  PROBABLE CAUSE: You may have been the source of a lack of love, safety, and security for those depending on you, whether as a parent or political leader. Irresponsible, runaway parents or leaders are certain to reap this type of lesson as they fail to perform with honor and integrity.

LESSON: First, realize you may have treated others in the same manner you are now experiencing. Acknowledge your mistake without moving into blame and remorse. Forgive yourself and then start balancing your debt by offering to others the ingredient missing in your present life, such as love, encouragement, and security. Give minimum criticism and maximum appreciation.

- **Fear of Failure:** The person who fears failure has lost all faith and self-confidence. Having failed in some small way and possibly having been criticized severely, he or she has lost hope and feels helpless, so makes little effort to succeed. Again, this is born of low self-worth, an aftermath of condemnation and victimization. We were all born with an active desire to achieve, but many of us lose incentive because of abuses and societal programming.

    Fear of failure is one of the most prevalent anxieties in our culture. Whenever we feel tension, anxiety, or anger, we are manifesting some level of fear. Often it is the fear of not being good enough, of ridicule, or of not measuring up to other people's standards. Our fears and anxieties can prevent growth and progress and totally immobilize us. We may waste much time and effort on avoidance and denial rather than facing and working through our dilemmas. Because fear is such a strong emotion, it quickly draws to us our worst nightmares—not for punishment, but for us to confront our problems. We must learn to face and eventually overcome that particular fear for it is part of our growth and evolution as souls.

- **Fraidy Cat:** When faced with new ideas or situations, Fraidy Cat is constantly declaring, "I don't know," rather than thinking things through for herself and making careful choices. This pattern of behavior actually affirms her fears, doubts, and ignorance about her circumstances. It also confirms her reluctance to make decisions, sending a clear message to her subconscious mind that she does not want to know.

    Putting off decisions is actually a choice to do nothing. (Let somebody else do it.) It is taking the easy way out, giving up her power to choose, and refusing to take any responsibility or action. All these choices reinforce her thought form of fear, helplessness, and vulnerability that so often lead to victimization.

RESULT: Procrastination, indecision, helplessness, and victimization. Holding fear beliefs attracts our worst fears without letting up until we have learned to take responsibility for ourselves and our lives by changing "I can't" attitudes to "I can and I will."
PROBABLE CAUSE: This can be shame based. You made a mistake and someone made fun of you, or perhaps you have made fun of others in the past and are reaping the results. You may have previously avoided making decisions and taking responsibility or this may be a childhood trauma where it was never permissible to make a mistake. Fear can be an old habit of thought brought over into this life to be conquered.
LESSON: Face your fears. Make a determined effort to overcome self-doubt. Deliberately make more choices and take responsibility for your actions. You need to carefully rebuild your sense of self-confidence, learning to trust yourself in matters large and small. Remember the power of prayer. Ask for help from your Guardian Angel. This is the self-mastery we need in order to become gods or goddesses.

Poverty

Poverty is often the direct result of low self-esteem and self-doubt, which becomes a "booby trap." Once established in mind, it creates a vicious cycle of a self-fulfilling prophecy. Parents or grandparents who experienced the "Crash of '29" and the Great Depression were saturated with ideas of lack and hard times and often passed these beliefs to their children and grandchildren.

Many of us have taken "vows of poverty" in other lives that have carried over into this life. Vows are sacred promises deeply etched into our soul memories and can still be influential as subconscious beliefs.

Resulting Pattern/Belief

- **Belief In Lack:** Many people harbor thoughts of scarcity, fears of insufficient food, money, or whatever for everyone, as well as beliefs that wealth is sinful, poverty is saintly. In addition, we have been taught that "Money is the root of all evil." (The correct quotation is, "the love of money is the root of evil." 1 Timothy 6:10) Last, there is, "I don't deserve it."
- **Poverty Pockets:** Poverty is, without doubt, one of the most damaging beliefs people can hold about themselves. Those who grow up in

need are literally taught to live, breathe, and act as paupers. These people are firmly fixed in the belief that there is never enough to go around. Lack is their accepted way of life. Once this idea of poverty is well established, it then influences all of the person's thought patterns, even years after the fact, unless the basic belief is changed. Meanwhile, constant talk about being broke, poor, in debt, or their inability to get ahead tends to strengthen their belief in poverty. These people are literally digging themselves deeper into poverty by repeatedly complaining about their lack.

Poverty is a state of mind, a belief in lack and a fear of failure. It is an absence of self-confidence in one's ability to do, be, and have. When one is poverty-minded, all thoughts about money center on the lack of it. It becomes a mind-set of permanent neediness.

RESULTS: Employers tend to offer those with low self-esteem less money than they would to those with more self-confidence. As a self-doubter, you will settle for less because you have been taught to "take whatever you can get," or that "a little bit is better than nothing." You wouldn't dare demand better because you honestly believe you do not deserve better.
PROBABLE CAUSE: Poverty vows or misuse of funds in the past. Possibly you were miserly or in some way failed to be a good steward over your belongings or another's belongings.
LESSON: Learn to be grateful and appreciative for what you have. Make positive statements about money. Think positively about money. Practice wise management of your abundance, which includes faithfully paying all your debts and returning good deeds. Begin to share, invest, and spend with wisdom. Remember you create your own abundance and there is much, much more where that came from.

Physical Abuse
Victimhood

There are many types of victimization, starting with mental and emotional abuses such as ridicule, threats, name-calling, and broken promises. Physical traumas include harsh punishment, ranging from slaps to beatings, child labor, child molesting, rape, and being deprived of food or sleep.

Resulting Pattern/Belief

Just one abuse can cause a child to feel like a victim, and after two or more, there is no doubt in his mind that he is a victim. Feeling defenseless and broken in spirit, he no longer tries to defend himself. The subconscious mind then creates proof of those beliefs repeatedly. Then when this child becomes an adult he will either repeat that pattern or retaliate by abusing others.

- **Ms. Victim:** She always feels that she is being misused and everyone is out to get her. She believes that whatever she gets, someone else will take away. As she assumes she "can't win for losing," she is a defenseless victim. With this strong mental image, she will repeatedly attract people who will victimize her in some way because that is her firm belief about herself. (If her self-esteem was in good shape, she would not allow others to victimize her, nor would she attract such people into her life.)

RESULTS: Once victimized, most people tend to wallow in the "poor me" aspect of what was done, talking endlessly about what happened and how wrong it was, reliving the trauma. The more you focus on a problem, the more similar situations you create for yourself. You simply can't afford to spend your creative mental energies so foolishly.
PROBABLE CAUSE: Neglect or cruelty to others. With early childhood traumas, there was probably some mistreatment of others in the past. No one suffers without due cause. There is always an agreement of some kind between victim and victimizer. Usually it is a pre-birth decision between them for each to learn a needed lesson or to bring both persons into balance. Again, all has been agreed upon at soul level.
LESSON: First, watch your complaints. Remember that your focus on a problem increases the problem. Begin now to switch your thinking to the good things in life; such as sunsets, birds singing, good friends, happy memories, and joyful things. Practice goodwill and gentle loving kindness to all beings.

Lessons of Victimhood

The lessons of victimhood are complex and often connected with low self-worth and negative thinking. Remember the Rule of Attraction keeps you repeating your lessons for as long as you continue to think and feel in terms of being mistreated.

A common challenge is broken agreements that leave you feeling betrayed and angry. The usual reaction is never to trust or speak to that person again.

Look at the type of problem you are attracting, especially the repeated ones. Consider what kind of thought or action would evoke this situation. Get a gut feeling for what needs to be changed. If your key thoughts create broken promises, start the change by being very careful about agreements you make with yourself and others. Pay more attention to your feelings than to other people's words.

Become acutely aware, alert, and clear about what is going on around you, especially when making agreements. Make a real effort to know and feel the intentions of the person speaking, especially those concerning promises of any kind. When uncertain, relax and think back to the situation and get in touch with those feelings as soon as possible afterward. (This is easy to do. The hardest part is to trust your answers.) If you felt good about the agreement, chances are it is a good one. If not, you may need to renegotiate. Your best policy is to feel out any new person or situation fully before making any agreements. Trust yourself to know what is best for you. This puts you back in power.

Be keenly aware of your situation and your surroundings at all times. Avoid abuse by deliberately taking more responsibility and control. Make firm decisions about what you want to do, be, or have in every part of your life. Have a clear intention as to your purpose and the results you want in order to overcome the old patterns of inertia. You especially need to come to full alert whenever anyone makes a date, a promise, or an agreement of any kind. As mentioned before, your best defense is a clear intent.

Plan Ahead
- Intend to know exactly what you want in your life.
- Intend to be clear about what the other person wants.
- Intend to know the exact meaning of all agreements.
- Intend to know the true motive behind the speaker's words.
- Intend to sense all deceptions, deviations, or ulterior motives. Stick to your side of any agreement made. Should you change your mind, notify other people involved.

Practice greater awareness and evaluation in all things. Even in casual conversations, mentally question whether the person is being totally honest with you. Use your feelings, insights, and impressions of what feels good and what does not. Learn to feel out anything not right. Trust your gut feelings to lead you in the right direction. And remember, this won't work unless you have clear intentions as to what you want in life.

Seeing Victimhood for What It Is

The idea of victimization is truly an illusion, an attitude, and a mindset of being used which sets up its own repetitive cycle. The truth is that victim and victimizer are in agreement. Both have chosen to participate. We are never victims of *fate*. We are, instead, the precise results of our own creative thoughts; creatures of our own design with no one to blame but ourselves. The missing link is the knowledge of reincarnation. With a true understanding of cause and effect, everything suddenly makes perfectly good sense.

People born in abject poverty are often people who misused their wealth in another life. Children left fatherless and/or in poverty are usually beings who neglected to parent and provide for their children and are now living the unhappy results of their own actions.

- No one is murdered unless he has been a murderer.
- No one is born blind unless he has blinded another.
- No one is abused unless he has been an abuser.

In war, captors neglect, beat, and abuse many prisoners. The Cosmic level notices such cruel treatments. Eventually, the abusers come back into homes where they will receive the same harsh treatment they so thoughtlessly gave to others. After the Hitler horrors of World War II, it is no wonder we now have such an upsurge of abused children. (Wartime is no excuse for cruelty.) As souls, we hold ourselves personally responsible for our deeds. Each time we fail to honor another person, animal, or anything in nature, we set ourselves up to receive the same treatment, until we finally learn the Law of Love and honor and respect all life forms.

Although we always reap what we have sown, it is not necessarily in the same lifetime. The man who rapes must return as a female to be raped in order to fully understand all the ramifications of his actions. In other words, we each set up our life experiments to teach us whatever we most need to learn. Let us realize we are here as students, that we come to Earth School to grow beyond our mistakes and misunderstandings. We can stop being angry and resentful about what happens to us once we really grasp the true purpose of why we are here. At that point, we can get on with our chosen goals, eventually graduating to higher levels of love and harmony in our lives.

In God's world, everything has a purpose. All is planned for our highest good. Once we truly understand this process, we will never feel victimized again.

Some Interesting Facts About Criminals and Victims

A few years ago, some ambitious people did an investigation concerning criminals and the victims they choose. The researchers carefully interviewed a number of prisoners to learn how and why they selected their prey. The study concluded that the unanimous "method of operation" used was to avoid those who were alert, who walked tall and proud, or appeared to be well able to defend themselves. Criminals selected only those who appeared tired, dejected, and defenseless. In other words, they chose victim-minded people

Since our facial expression, posture, and body movements clearly reflect our thinking, anyone with intent to harm can easily pick out those of us whose low self-esteem will not allow us to put up a good fight. In other words, without a good, positive self-image and sense of our worth, we can literally become a walking target.

Anger
All Anger Is Self-Anger
Although the abused person is understandably angry with the abuser, he is even more furious at himself for not acting in his own defense and allowing the trauma. He may feel he was not smart enough, big enough, or and strong enough to prevent being mistreated and now he cannot trust himself to prevent further injury. The result is one angry, resentful, and over-defensive warrior ready to fight at the drop of a syllable.

Buried Anger
Some childhood traumas are so severe that the youthful mind buries all memory of the incident. Yet, the wound is there and is often the hidden cause of what is called a "hot temper." This particular kind of anger may be deeply embedded not only in the mental body but also in the emotional and physical bodies. (These wounds are often stored in the

muscle tissues and need massage and other bodywork to release the physical trauma.) Counseling and hypnotherapy are very useful in the mental and emotional cleansing.

- **Mad Man:** The abused person may not even be aware that he is angry and defensive. He may not know the source of his frustrations, but the results of these emotions can be seen in his aura, hanging there like an ugly dark cloud with flashes of red lightning darting through it.

  RESULT: If you are one who is constantly frustrated, easily aggravated, and irritated, chances are you have a good load of buried anger. Although you may blame other people or situations for making you mad, the real problem is unventilated inner rage from abuses suffered when you were too young to understand or to fight back. Often there is deep pain beneath the anger.
  PROBABLE CAUSE: Annoyance, frustration, irritation, resentment, and hate are all shades of anger and as such, have a devastating effect on mind and body. It is well known in metaphysical circles that the true cause of cancer is buried anger and resentment which indicate a lack of peace within. Depression is also related to submerged anger. All this makes it doubly important to recognize the source of your anger and the need to make every effort to clean it out of your system. Seek out a good therapist or counselor to help you work out the problems. Meanwhile, there are many self-help books.
  LESSON: In such cases, it is important to look at what was done to you with the understanding you may have done this to others. Realizing everything happens for a good reason, seek to grasp the lesson, forgive yourself and any others involved and move on.

The Damaging Effects of Anger

It is often said that it is risky to drive a car when we are angry or upset for these conditions tend to create accidents. The principle behind this is that the thought forms and vibrations emanating from one who is angry and upset will automatically go out and attract more of the same. Given a bit of time, Mr. Mad Man will attract Ms. Furious in the form of a collision, confrontation, or fight — sometimes all three.

Mystical Magical You

We send out causes by our attitudes and emotions.

The above situation is actually created by both parties in order to give vent to their individual frustrations. Angry, irritated, and vengeful people consistently draw others of the same emotional vibration to them. Anger attracts anger. Hate attracts hate. Violent attitudes attract violence. On the other hand, gentle, loving people attract other loving people. It is Cosmic Law.

Some people draw accidents or difficulties to themselves through their strong emotions such as fear of an accident, fire, or robbery. This may seem to contradict the Rule of Attraction, but the basic truth remains, strong negative emotions attract strong, negative results.

> **PRESENT CAUSE:** Usually the angry one has been hurt, abused, or betrayed by a trusted friend or family member. It makes little difference whether the damage was physical, mental, or emotional. What does matter is the depth of the pain buried beneath the anger.
>
> **PROBABLE (PAST) CAUSE:** As always, we reap the results of our actions in our youth or in previous lives and the time has come to pay the debt. Blaming others only adds to the confusion. You have work to do to clean up the mess you have created.
>
> **LESSON:** Recognize your part in creating the problem and begin work on making things right with those you have hurt or angered in the past. Working through your own anger is an important part of your healing process. Forgiveness is needed all around.

Some Results of Buried Anger

- **Rebellion:** Hate, resentment, and rebellion often come from anger at life's seeming inequalities and unhappy circumstances. It is a way of striking back at society. Temper tantrums, angry outbursts, and brutality of all kinds stem from the same source; lack of love, honor, and respect at home. Children often misbehave from a simple need to be noticed. When attention is not forthcoming the child may become violent or try to get even in some way.

→ Understanding Your Belief System

PROBABLE CAUSE: Neglected children are often the direct results of their own careless parenting and failure to show love and honor in the past.

LESSON: Forgive and love yourself first. Then consciously begin to express love to all those around you. This not only corrects the error but also builds good, positive habits for the future.

- **Drugs and Alcohol:** This is an escape when life is just too difficult to handle.

  PROBABLE CAUSE: Extra sensitive people often feel the pain, depression, and harshness around them more readily than others do. They may feel unable to cope with life's problems, choosing substance abuse as an easy way to avoid responsibility. There may be a carry-over from self-indulgence or a misspent previous life where the lessons of discipline, respect, and responsibility were ignored leaving you with a definite weakness of character.

  LESSON: Escape is never the answer. We came here to learn. Discipline may be a much-needed ingredient, along with goal setting and responsibility. You may need to take a new look at your sensitivity and find good, wholesome uses for it rather than trying to bury or deny your talents. Take immediate steps to make the most of your sensitive nature by asking for insight and guidance to find your rightful place in this world. Try music, creative arts, healing, teaching, or writing.

- **Crime:** Children who know they are loved and appreciated seldom stray from the values taught at home. It is the unloved, unworthy, or rejected ones who have an unusual number of accidents and illnesses or will strike out and make their own laws.

  PROBABLE CAUSE: Being born into an unloving atmosphere is a good clue that you were probably unloving in the past. Non-loving people are born to unloving families to feel the uncomfortable results of such neglect. Consequent feelings of rejection or unworthiness may then become the underlying cause for poverty, rebellion, gangs, and crime. It all goes back to lack of love in a home that breeds anger, resentment, and general hostility that compounds the problem. This does not mean that your parents did not love you. It simply recognizes that parents, especially when busy, tired, or stressed, often fail to

> express love and caring in terms the child can understand. (Children frequently absorb more from the attitude and tone of voice than from the actual words spoken.)
> **LESSON:** Forgive and love yourself first, then reach out in loving ways to others as often as possible. Practice the art of caring, nurturing, comforting, and helping others. This will balance the scales and bring great rewards of love into your home and life.

Three Laws to Consider

In evaluating your overall life and its influence on your belief system there are some spiritual laws to consider.

1. *Universal Rules of Attraction*

Like attracts like, cause and effect or karma. You are constantly setting things in motion by mental and emotional attitudes that translate into vibrations. What you think and believe is what you get. For example, fear, which is a strong mental-emotional factor:

- Fear of being robbed attracts the robber.
- Fear of rape attracts the rapist.
- Fear of an accident attracts the accident.

The greater the fear, (strong emotion) the faster the results. In general, negative thoughts and feelings repel the good hoped for, while loving thoughts, the opposite of fear or hate, bring happiness in many forms.

Consider the possibility of a karmic payback; you may have victimized another person, creating a debt, possibly several of them. If you reacted to a karmic payback with anger, self-pity, or vengeance, you most likely began a mind-set of expecting to be done unto, which is self-perpetuating.

Ask yourself, "What is it in me, my attitude, belief, or mind-chatter that draws this to me?" You may need to clean up old attitudes of anger and defensiveness. When people ask "Why me?" as though they are being targeted for injustice, it implies their belief in victimhood; a conviction that things will always go wrong, and this belief perpetuates the problem.

2. *Law of Love*

Our whole universe operates according to law. No accidents, just many lessons and experiences, until we have learned to respect and obey

Understanding Your Belief System

the great Law of Love (most of these laws are covered in the Ten Commandments, Exodus 10:1–17). Jesus added an eleventh commandment, love one another. Ancient teachers advise us to "Regard all men equally, with love, honor and wisdom."

The soul knows these laws and keeps accurate records of all our deeds from one lifetime to another. When we refuse to live within these laws (ignorance is no excuse) we get lessons, difficult lessons, painful lessons, and repeated lessons until we finally get the message. Eventually, we must learn to love and honor all beings, starting with ourselves, for when we feel unworthy we can neither respect ourselves nor honor others.

Failing to honor your fellow beings brings karma to your door. There is a saying, "Man does not break the Ten Commandments, he breaks himself upon them." This is not victimhood, it is the Wheels of Justice grinding slowly.

3. Law of Chosen Lesson

Often this is a spin-off from the Law of Cause and Effect. After death, we, as souls, go back "home" to the spiritual planes where our life is reviewed in terms of what we set out to accomplish before entering the earth plane. God does not judge us, we judge ourselves. No one is harsher in judging our actions than we are. Many teachers have said that we review our mistakes and are reborn into circumstances that will allow us to learn the necessary lessons.

In a sense, we have agreed to give away our power in order to learn a specific lesson. Often this was preceded by some unloving act in the past that we have not forgiven ourselves. To atone for this, we agreed to suffer specific childhood indignities. In other words, on the soul level, we chose the people and situations needed to balance our debts and learn our lesson in love.

It is for this reason we find ourselves born into homes of poverty, disease, or whatever is needed to further our development. Our circumstances were carefully selected with our knowledge and permission before entering the earth plane in the hope of reclaiming our sense of godhood and self-assurance along with the acquirement of specific abilities.

To facilitate this, the home environment and parentage chosen were often deliberately lacking in the qualities we most needed to develop, forcing us to draw our strengths from within rather than from without. (When there is no one around to help us, we have to help ourselves.) We then develop the wisdom, courage, and self-sufficiency that were lacking.

These are some of the unseen and unsuspected gifts from the School of Hard Knocks. Ponder these for a moment to get comfortable with the self-healing concept of reincarnation.

To discover and understand your chosen lesson, look at the opposite side of our childhood environment and wounds. What was the missing ingredient? (For me, the lack of love and support taught me to become strong and independent.) Ask yourself what the lessons were in the traumas or missing ingredients. What was your greatest lesson? What strength did it evoke from within you? Move out of the cycle of victimhood by stopping long enough to evaluate your spiritual lesson. Once you recognize the gift in the lesson, you can easily move into a place of peace.

Blame Game

Although suffering from any source may seem to be an injustice from the standpoint of the *innocent* child, we need to remember that a child who has lived many lives is hardly innocent. Be assured there are no random incidents. Each is a carefully planned lesson or karmic balancing we have agreed to finish. This includes abuses of all kinds, including UFO abductions. All is in complete agreement with our stated soul-contract for this life. We may not consciously remember the details because many of us have lost our ability to contact soul memory. Much of this can be restored by working with your dreams and practicing meditation on a regular basis (try writing a dream question and watch for your answers).

Many of us, having lost our soul-connection, find ourselves angry and resentful at what we perceive as injustices from our limited physical viewpoint. As we hold bitterness and anger in our minds, we attract more wrongs, creating yet another cycle of entrapment. To change this, try picturing yourself as a player on a stage that allows you to work out your misunderstandings and differences.

See yourself paying off honest debts incurred, rather than as victims of a cruel god. With this higher overview, you begin to understand how to play the game of life.

When thinking in terms of defense and revenge, as "an eye for an eye" (Matthew 5:38), one may say, "That makes it right." Well, yes and no. In its true meaning, an eye for an eye was originally written in terms of making restitution, not taking revenge. In other words, the amount of damage or harm we have done to another must be paid back in full. The cosmic scales must be balanced eventually. Therefore, when we err, we must make full restitution for damages done to others.

On the other hand, when feeling victimized, remember the Bible also says "vengeance is mine" (Deuteronomy 32:35). Thoughts of revenge only make things worse. Thoughtfully consider what has happened and why. Carefully consider the Cosmic Laws just discussed, and decide how to respond. It is best to forgive all concerned, including one's self for the roles played. After that, plan to do some good deeds for others to help balance the scales. The Bible says "love covers all sins" (Proverbs 10:12). Try it; otherwise the wheels of karma could grind on and on.

Know Thyself

Your present life lessons are manifested as an item missing in your life that only you can supply. You chose to come in without it in order to realize its value. Now you must make the effort to find what was really never lost, just stored deep within yourself where you never thought to look.

Current Problem	**Probable Cause**	**Possible Lesson**
Abandonment	Abandoning others in their time of need. Failure to give love and support to others.	Learn to give of yourself. Be a friend. Reach out to others. Give encouragement. Love and accept others as they are. Be supportive.
Abuse, Wounds, Pain	Abusing others or yourself.	Accept, love, and honor yourself. Learn to comfort and nurture others and yourself. Enter a field of health care, teaching, or service to others.
Ridicule, Criticism	Inflicting the same on others.	Learn to give love, kindness, upliftment, and assistance to others.
Illness, Injury	Injuring or neglecting others or self. Possible misuse of strengths and power. Belief in illness.	Learn to heal others and yourself. Give comfort and nurturing to others.
Poverty	Stinginess. Greed. Selfishness. Misuse of money, strength, talents, or power.	Learn to share what you have with others. Practice appreciation, gratitude and bless all that you receive.

Current Problem	Probable Cause	Possible Lesson
Victimization	Failure to take responsibility. Not standing up for yourself. Lack of goals. May have victimized others.	Use your strengths, talents, and gifts wisely. Make and achieve high goals and standards. Assert yourself in positive ways.
Shame, Guilt, Low Self-Esteem	Lack of respect for others and yourself. May have been overly critical.	Learn to trust yourself. Build self-pride. Do things that make you feel good about yourself.

- **Abandonment/Rejection:** With this, you always expect to be rejected and you get what you expect. This old mind-set needs to be faced and deliberately over-ridden with new, firm intentions. The opposite of rejection is love, acceptance, and caring for yourself. This means appreciating all the things you do right, thinking noble thoughts, holding lofty ideals and living with the highest standards. It is earning love and respect, honoring yourself, acknowledging your own worth, and constantly validating yourself. It is saying something similar to, "I am healthy, wealthy, wise, and loving." Then, having learned to love yourself extend that loving attitude to those around you
- **Abuse:** The opposite of abuse is deliberately treating yourself with love, honor, and respect. It is loving yourself enough to give yourself the best of care, physically, mentally, and emotionally. It is important for you to learn to honor your needs, stand up for yourself, be an honorable person, and nurture your inner child. Intend to have a good, comfortable living and a well-groomed look, thinking and feeling pleased with yourself because you are worth it. (Remember you have a right to better treatment, a right to feel good about yourself, but you must first exercise that right.)

Your Growing-Up Years

To thine own self be true, and it must follow ... Thou canst not then be false to any man.
—Shakespeare

Understanding Your Belief System

For most of you, growing up was a mixed batch of experiences, some good, some bad, each contributing to your overall attitudes, beliefs, and self-esteem, usually resulting in very low self-worth. What you have learned to expect from childhood events you now tend to recreate in your grownup life, even when it is painful. Therefore, it is most beneficial to recognize those hidden beliefs and the causes behind them in order to change all that are keeping you from enjoying life.

One of the most common underlying beliefs is low self-esteem. You have been taught by means of other people's opinions that you are an inferior being. This just isn't so. Yet those labels become layers of unconscious armor, which repel all the good things you ask for, no matter how hard you work or pray for them.

Therefore, to succeed these beliefs must be removed, the attitudes changed. As the saying goes, "God does not make junk." In truth, you are a wonderful being, a godling, but you have forgotten this. You have been brainwashed into subservience through society's false concepts and teachings until you have come to believe you are worthless.

It is time to uncover the real you under the sludge. At the first opportunity, release the buried anger. Then take a symbolic bath. Set the scene with candles, aromatic herbs or salts and perhaps some incense. As you bathe, picture the sludge slipping away from your whole being and disappearing down the drain. Consider it gone forever. When you are finished, face yourself in the mirror, all clean and shining and say something like, "I am now alive, alert, and aware of the real me. I recognize my divine nature, my soul-connection, and my godliness. I accept myself as the god or goddess in the making which I truly am."

Begin to take calculated steps to get where you want to go in life. Concentrate on things that make you feel good. Stay away from those who criticize and condemn you. Choose new friends who are kind and happy. Think about who you really are, a god in the making, a brave soul with very high ideals on a path of learning, growing, and perfecting your skills. You are one who is gaining in wisdom, preparing to give loving service to yourself and your fellow beings while on the path back home to God. Give yourself constant encouragement and positive mental feedback. Congratulate yourself often. Celebrate your every success in some joyful way.

For your greatest growth, remember to trust yourself rather than listening to other people's opinions. Be wise enough to follow your heart-guidance, listen to your own intuition, and act within the Law of Love. You can never again become a victim of circumstance once you understand and act upon the above principles. You create your own world, on your own terms in accordance with the ideals of the god or goddess you really are.

The School of Life

We are all are pledged to learning our lessons like children in school, each in different grades and stages of growth. Any lesson not learned is repeated, with many variations, until the principle of love is finally learned.

The universe is a safe and loving place designed for the continued growth and evolution of humankind and Planet Earth. Like a loving parent, God sends us to school so that we may be properly trained to become wise coworkers in his Kingdom. The main lesson is to take full responsibility for all we say or do, with the ultimate goal of living in the Law of Love.

We can choose to learn quickly or avoid our lessons (usually by blaming others) for as long as we like, for we have free will. However, the rule is we can't move on to the next grade until our chosen lessons are learned and the test passed. Some people stay in the first grade a very long time.

When you are truly aware of your divinity no one can control or manipulate you.

Summary

The beliefs and attitudes we hold today are the result of all that we have seen, heard, and experienced in our lives to date. Some of these are held in conscious memory, but many, especially the more abusive and traumatic ones, are buried deep in the subconscious mind. It is these unseen, limiting beliefs that keep us from creating the things we most desire.

You are the Soul who chose your life and its lessons, and as such are always in command. You have free will to do as you wish. Your soul knows what you need and brings you the people, situations, and incidents required to help you clean out the old hang-ups that stand in the way of your progress. Realize that everything comes to you with but one purpose, and that is for your highest good and greatest growth as a child of God. Once you grasp the magnificence of this, you can know in your heart that God is good and all is well in your world.

When you approve of yourself and know in your heart that you are a good person you are in great shape. You have confidence in yourself, your desires, and intentions. With this combination, you have the best possible chance of manifesting your desires quickly and satisfactorily, for your basic belief system (your subconscious mind) would then be in total agreement with your conscious mind.

In the end, you and you alone are responsible for all your decisions, even when you choose to do nothing. In general, neglecting to decide is the worst selection of all, for it is better to make a poor choice, and learn from the mistake than to waste an opportunity by doing nothing at all. Life is precious.

Exercise

A Sample Life Review Exercise (From Author's Life):

1. Former life insight: Timidity, fear, shyness, dependency, and helplessness (from dreams and meditative insights).
2. Chosen childhood environment: Stark, cold, critical parents, who were unable to express love, nurture or support.
3. Reactions to home environment: Feelings of worthlessness, anger, resentment, criticism, pain, sense of injustice and victimhood to which I reacted defensively. (These thoughts and attitudes brought more victim-type incidents.)
4. What I learned: To be strong, independent, confident, and fully capable of making decisions, taking care of others and myself.
5. How I use this knowledge: Teaching, writing, counseling, healing, and supporting others at every opportunity.
6. Present endeavors: Learning my truth, cleaning up my life, and finding understanding and forgiveness. Watching my thoughts and attracting more love, joy, and abundance into my life.
7. My life today: Good and getting better every day. It is exciting with much joy and abundance. I am strong, healthy, and active, with many interests. I am happy, whether I am alone or I am with others. I am definitely not dependent on anyone.

When I began writing this chapter, I was still carrying many remnants of pain, anger, and victimhood. But after adding the above exercise and looking at the final results, things suddenly fit together and made better sense. Instant relief! I felt layers of old anger, pain, and resentments slip away. Defensive attitudes melted as I relaxed into a delightful sense of peace, good will, and completion. Now I wake each day feeling good. Naturally, I hope this will have the same cleansing and healing effect on you.

When you know in your heart that you are a good person and can approve of yourself and your lifestyle, then you are in great shape. You then have confidence in yourself, your desires, and your intentions. With this winning combination, you have the best chance of manifesting your desires quickly and satisfactorily.

This is a thought-created universe.
You create exactly what you think, feel, expect, and believe.

7

Changing Your Beliefs

A man's mind is like a garden, which may be intelligently cultivated or allowed to run wild.

—James Allen

The latest scientific research says that by the time a child reaches three to three and a half years of age he has already formed beliefs about himself and his world. Looking back at your childhood training and remembering the stories of the flea and the elephant (page 39), you can easily see the need to re-evaluate your early "programming." Where do you start? Before you can forgive, forget, and move past your traumas you need a clear understanding and acceptance of the overall purpose of them. Let me share an example.

Story of Two Brothers

As a friend of the family, I watched this story unfold. Two irresponsible teenagers, not ready for parenthood, conceived a child and entered a hasty marriage. All went fairly well until the first child was born. Almost immediately, there was discord and chaos. Soon after the second child was born, there was an angry divorce. Within months after the breakup, each parent had taken on a new, equally unreliable partner. Now these boys had four dysfunctional parents.

There was a lot of drinking, arguing, and fighting on all sides. The parents made and broke many promises. The father consistently failed to provide support and seldom came to see the boys, which caused many disappointments and hardships. Frustrated and angry, the mother became an alcoholic and matters deteriorated further. When the mother went to jail (D.U.I.), the children were moved in with their dad. (Another disaster.) Their grades suffered accordingly. When they reached their teenage years, the boys were angry and rebellious, making matters worse.

By the time they came to me, it was obvious even to them, that no one was going to "be there" or "do for" them. As friend and teacher I tried to point out that with so many unreliable parents, their chief lesson was to learn responsibility. I quietly pointed out that their only way out was to stand up for themselves, care for their own needs, and start taking full responsibility for their lives. The sooner they got started, the better.

I had to explain how we each choose our life circumstances with great care (just as we would select a college course) to learn specific lessons. God is a loving Father who allows us to rectify our mistakes through experience, which is the best teacher.

At this point, I stopped and waited, wondering how long it would take to soak in, if ever. To my surprise, the next day brought results. The oldest one called to tell me he had landed a job. Shortly afterward, the second one found a part-time job and both had begun working to take care of their own needs.

Accepting Our Lessons

When we understand the evolutionary concepts of our life and accept these as our chosen lessons rather than as unfair punishment, we can more easily let go of anger, resentment, and bitterness. Holding on to our traumas and self-pity only prolongs the learning process. With forgiveness, we quickly graduate and move on to better circumstances, being better persons for having that experience.

Old Concepts vs. the New

When we have been taught to believe certain concepts, especially at a very young age, those ideas become an established part of our basic belief system. Once that pattern of thinking is set, we have difficulty accepting any idea that does not fit comfortably within the framework of the old, well-known pattern. (This is especially true of religious beliefs.) We feel that old is safe and comfortable, but new is unknown, untried, and perhaps risky. So, at the very least, we have to think it over, sleep on it, and get used to the new idea. This process can be a matter of minutes, days, weeks, or even months unless deep inside, from one of our many lives, we recognize the truth of the new idea. Then we accept it quickly, like an old friend.

Occasionally the new information, which we instantly know to be right, hits our fine-tuned, clock-like mental network of wheels and cogs like the proverbial monkey wrench. It brings our whole belief system to a grinding halt. The newly found piece of truth does not fit anywhere within the framework of our old beliefs.

We may throw out the new idea simply because it doesn't fit, or we conclude that one or more of our old beliefs were based on false information. This starts a series of shock waves as our whole frame of reference begins to shift, crumble, and rearrange. It forces us to drop many old concepts. Then follows a period of painstaking rebuilding of a new, more wholesome philosophy of life based on higher principles. This is the process of evolution.

Burning Bridges

At this point, many people leave their churches and search for the truth with great vigor. This is a crucial point in the life of a young god or goddess in the making. It is similar to the youth who is no longer content to depend upon his or her parents and decides to leave home. It can be a time of great uncertainty and insecurity; at the same time, it can be a step of great growth and triumph.

Having made this decision and burned our bridges behind us, we find ourselves literally walking on water. The old bridge is gone and the new one not yet built, or at best, only partially built. Although we may be brave, we may also be very unsure of our foundation or our new direction. It is a scary business. We often feel forced to leave behind dear friends (who still believe the old way) because they are holding to our old concepts, making our new path more difficult. We find ourselves seeking new friends who embrace our newfound truth, share our beliefs, and encourage us on our new path.

It is an exciting risk, turning from the old and groping blindly toward a new and unknown path. Yet we are driven from within. It is a challenge we must meet, a higher path that our heart knows we must explore. So we push on to new levels of awareness.

Such an experience awaits all who are bold enough to cast aside the old beliefs of being only human and those who are beginning to accept the truth that we are indeed, gods in the making.

Escape from Prison

Since all our goals, decisions, and intentions are founded on our basic belief system, the lower our self-esteem, the more limited are our ideals and the less we dare to do. So it becomes vitally important to identify and clear out the old, limiting concepts that have held us in prison.

Be aware that when you are unable to love, respect, and honor yourself, you are also unable to accept love from others. More importantly, if you cannot love yourself, you are incapable of giving love to others. Oh, you might go through the motions and say the words, but the quality, depth, and feeling of real love is missing. Instead, there is a monopolizing kind of love/ownership, often tinged with jealousy and filled with fear of losing your prized possession.

Everyone knows at least one person who confuses possessiveness and ownership with love simply because he or she has never learned self-love. Even worse, most of us have been taught that it is wrong to love ourselves. It is all too easy to repeat the error with all relationships, compounding the problem generation after generation until you break out of the old mold of self-rejection and boldly create a life of self-love and acceptance.

Clearly, the art of loving yourself is one of life's most important lessons. Yet in spite of this, when things go wrong we all tend to move into blame and shame, berating ourselves with an abundance of "ought to's" and "should have knowns." We may even add a few cuss words to whip ourselves. This is not love. It is self-hate, a habit that must be eliminated if you are to be successful in life.

How do you begin to turn this self-denial around? First, you need to throw away the baseball bat that you use to beat yourself. Most of us have been very carefully trained to belittle ourselves as if it were the ultimate in good manners. Actually, it is a type of child abuse. Realize that as your parents were physically, mentally, or emotionally punishing you, you were learning to hate and chastise yourself. What a strange, warped society we live in!

This kind of thinking and behaving needs to be erased. You must let go of all the old, damaging programming you have discovered to date, then release old habits of believing you are unworthy. A most important rule in removing any old patterns is never to leave a void. Always replace the old with something new and better.[1]

If you could peek inside your brain you would see old habits—paths well-worn from constant usage. To create a new habit you must deliberately set a new goal and choose a new way of thinking. Then repeat the new thought as often as possible to carve a new trail. Otherwise, you will keep falling back into the ruts of old, familiar habits. Only repetition of the new thought will create a new mind-set and eventually, a whole new way of life.

Good Self-Esteem Is Important

When you believe in yourself and feel good about yourself, you are at your best. Your expression is pure you, coming from the soul, loving, harmonious, and uplifting. You are delightful to be near, a feast for the eyes, an inspiration to others.

Changing Your Beliefs

When you are not sure who you are, you doubt your worth. You are uncertain, struggling, and trying to please, but not knowing what to do or how to do it. You may feel flustered, confused, and awkward because of your false belief of not being good enough. Consequently, you try too hard and make simple work difficult. With anger and fear, you make foolish mistakes. Feeling a constant need to defend against all intruders, you are unable to walk in peace and harmony. Instead of making intelligent choices, you act in unwise ways, often reacting to threats and dangers not there. Out of your insecurity, you perceive harm when none was intended. Because of your self-doubt, your whole lifestyle becomes warped. These are doubts that you have based on other people's opinions.

This is a huge issue with many facets, all stemming from low self-esteem. Unless corrected, you will be unable to create efficiently. The basic tone of your thinking and feeling will not support your positive thinking efforts.

To tackle unwanted beliefs, start by realizing that your poor self-image is a learned behavior based on patterns instilled during your growing-up years. You lacked the wisdom to see the errors, misconceptions, and biased opinions of your so-called superiors. Today your subconscious holds this false programming as an indisputable fact. When you face a problem, your mind runs through its preset steps, giving the same erroneous results every time until you replace the faulty pattern with a new idea.

Measuring Your Self-Worth

Low self-esteem is a common barrier to your good fortune and well being. Almost everyone suffers this to some degree. How high or low is your sense of value? If it allows you to win as often as you lose, it is in fair shape. If success constantly eludes you, help is needed quickly.

One simple way to gauge yourself is to take an honest look at the way you handle compliments. For example, when you admire others your usual reaction is to tell them of your esteem as a way of showing your respect. In a sense, you offer them a verbal bouquet of admiration for who and what they are. It is a gift of love straight from your heart that you expect to be received graciously.

Now, for a moment, take time to consider how you behave when someone gives you a compliment. How do you react? Are you embarrassed? Flustered? Do you turn away from praise or make light of your abilities? Do you belittle your talent or deny your uniqueness? In short, do you have difficulty accepting praise? If so, you are refusing to receive love and honor from others simply because you do not believe you deserve it. If you stop to think about it, you will realize this type of behavior is questioning your friend's judgment. This could easily be regarded as a put-down or even an insult. Think about it.

Learning to Love Yourself

It is important for you to understand that if you are unable to accept your laurels with a gracious thank you, you are telling the world that you feel unworthy of honor and esteem. Obviously, you have much work to do in learning to love yourself. The best cure for this self-denying behavior is learning to love and accept yourself just as you are with no excuses, no exceptions.[2]

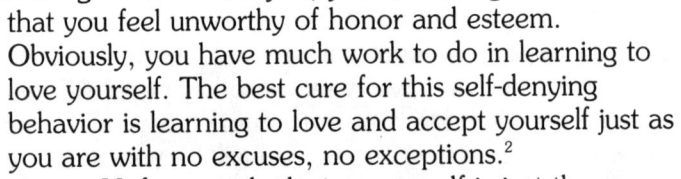

Unfortunately, loving yourself is just the opposite of what you have been taught, so you slough off all attempts from well-intentioned people to praise, honor, or thank you. You will allow all compliments to bounce off you without making a dent, just as effectively as armor repels arrows.

If you are in the habit of beating yourself up and putting yourself down, you can start correcting this by establishing a new habit of complimenting yourself every time you accomplish something. Repeat this as often as necessary until it becomes a new self-loving habit. This will replace the old habit with a new and better one.

At the end of the day, instead of berating yourself for the one thing you did wrong, make it a point to focus on what went right. Focusing on problems, disappointments, or failures only attracts more of those unwanted events. On the other hand, focusing on your successes creates even more triumphs, putting a whole new perspective on your life. As you recognize and nurture your worthiness, you gain new confidence in yourself and your abilities. This is exactly what you need to do. Reinforce your worthiness further by taking time out to do something nice for yourself every day.

To change old, limiting beliefs, remember you chose your circumstances for a reason. You had a purpose for this life. There was something here that you, as a soul, wanted to learn, understand, overcome, or balance. Lessons are included in just about everything you choose to do. Life is for learning. Earth is a school and you are the student god in the making, learning to create a wonderful world for yourself.

In this process, we experience incidents when we have erred. The usual habit is to label yourself as stupid. It is so easy to look back with the perfect vision of hindsight and judge yourself as wrong. Remember that the whole purpose of these encounters is to have meaningful learning experiences. Anytime you can look back and say, "I would never do it that way again," you have mastered that lesson, which is the whole point.

I Don't Understand All That I Know

As you realize at the highest level of your being that you have chosen each experience, it becomes easier to accept all things as steps upon your path to godliness. With that realization, tell yourself it is okay to make a mistake. Correct it and move on. Stop punishing yourself for those so-called "boo-boos." Then with your new, improved attitude, you can also forgive others for their role in this educational process of living. You may even laugh about those bloopers. Best of all, you move from *knowing the words* and moving past old traumas into a whole new understanding of what your life is really all about. You will be a new person who is wise, self-confident, and happy because you "got it."

Self-Forgiveness

Trivial though it may seem, this is an extremely important step in changing your beliefs. As long as you feel guilty about something, your subconscious will arrange to punish you in various ways, such as setting you up for failure or blocking your chances for success and happiness. This pattern of self-chastisement will repeat until you forgive yourself and establish peace. Why? Because the thoughts and beliefs you hold in mind are worn like an old hat that has become so comfortable and familiar you forget you are wearing it. In time, the hat/thought becomes a hardened thought form, like a helmet, which is far more difficult to remove. As the saying goes, "It grows on you."

The next step is to open up your closet of memories and make a deliberate effort to clean out all those moldy old guilt feelings and judgments that hold you in old patterns of unworthiness and defeat. However, you can't change them until you admit what they are.

Cleaning Your Mental Closet

To begin, take a piece of ordinary notebook paper and make a list of all the incidents you can recall

Mystical Magical You

that have feelings of guilt or discomfort attached. Leave a space between each incident.

Once this is complete, take a moment to detach yourself emotionally from the event; then from the standpoint of an older and much wiser adult, begin to re-evaluate each one separately. Write your new conclusions in the margin beside each.

Unchangeables are anything that when viewed through adult eyes can be honestly labeled as unavoidable. These are things that in retrospect you could not have changed under the prevailing circumstances. (We often think we could have done differently if we had only known _____ or done _____, when in actuality, we did the very best we could with the knowledge, understanding, and experience available to us at that moment.)

Lie down, close your eyes, and relax. Deliberately reenact the incident in your mind's eye, giving yourself credit for having done the best you knew at that time. Take a moment to look at the old scene in a new light. Chances are, from an adult point of view it wasn't half as bad as you remembered it. (We often chastise ourselves for failing to act on information that we did not have at that time, but learned about later—after the fact. Then we say, "I should have known." and punish ourselves needlessly.)

Formula for Forgiveness

For each problem, pain, or grievance, move thoughtfully through the following steps, looking at each incident as a lesson, not a problem. Try to see the point of the situation.

1. Ask yourself the following questions:
   - How did it make me feel?
   - What changes did it make in my life?
   - What did I learn from it? You may have learned one big lesson or several small ones. The main idea is to follow your heart and trust your inner knowing. Too often you are fooled or victimized because you failed to follow your feelings. (Even if you are unsure, think of what lesson you may have needed, some error in your belief, attitude, or thinking. Know there is something positive in this.)
   - How did this make me a better person? Perhaps you have become stronger, more aware, observant, and selective.
2. Ponder the positive aspects. Look for the good in this. Concentrate on the positive results rather than the difficulties involved. Remember that we learn great lessons from pain. However, there is nothing

Changing Your Beliefs

wrong in learning from joy. Actively seek the good, the gift contained in the event.
3. Find resolution, acceptance, and completeness. No more anger or guilt. There is no blame, no mistake — only experience. Forgive yourself and others. Make amends, ask forgiveness, call, write, or send a card/gift that says, "I love you."
4. Come to a point of peace within. Do whatever it takes to have peace and harmony about your situation. This could mean writing an apology, praying, asking for forgiveness, giving forgiveness, whatever seems appropriate. If the person is deceased, send a little prayer in his or her direction, asking your Guardian Angel to deliver it. Then bless it and let it go. Really, let go. Never go back to how bad it was.
5. Perform a small ceremony of final release and completion. Since rituals impress your subconscious mind, a small, simple ceremony will aid greatly in bringing about release and cleansing of old pain or guilt. (There are several suggested rituals at the end of this book in the chapter entitled Ceremonies and Rituals.)

When and if the old memory returns, remember the peace you made. Bless it again and move your mind to other things. You may need to repeat the procedure, should there be any pain left. This time, make a concentrated effort to clear out all remaining pain, anger, and sorrow using positive affirmations, prayer, meditation, incense, or whatever works for you. Ask for help in understanding and forgiving both the other person and yourself until you are at peace and have released any remaining anger, pain, or guilt.

Repeat this treatment for each additional trauma. You may want to record this in your journal. Follow your heart and do what feels best to you.

Reviewing and Cleansing Old Stuff

- **Honest Mistakes:** We have all had great ideas that backfired or just didn't work out as we expected, or made decisions which proved to be less than prudent. Regardless of the outcome, your intention is the crucial factor. If there was no desire to harm, treat this as a lesson, a needed experience. Forgive, bless, and release.
- **Accidents:** On the highest level of your God-self awareness, there is no such thing as an accident. Everything that happens is always carefully preplanned and agreed upon by you and all those involved in the

incident. Be assured there was a significant purpose or lesson, for nothing is ever wasted.

So carefully rethink your accidents, viewing each as a prearranged role you played with the permission and approval of all those who participated. Look at the changes that were brought about. Focus your attention on the good that came from it. Seek the deeper purpose until you know there is no need for shame or blame. Stay with this until you can honestly feel good about it. Then it is cleared forever. Celebrate. Reward yourself with a movie, a cookie, or whatever works for you. Rewards are self-empowering.

- **Purposeful Deeds:** The decisions we make and the actions we take in life situations stem directly from our deepest beliefs and feelings about worthiness. Low self-esteem frequently manifests in inappropriate behavior. You may become overly defensive, yelling, attacking, or blaming others, simply because you feel inadequate inside. You may overcompensate for your perceived weaknesses. If some of your past deeds fall in this category, you need not look at the act itself but at the underlying fears and opinions behind the action. Remedy these.

  Chances are you have nothing left to list here, but just in case you do, stop and ask yourself why you made your choice(s). Was it self-defense? Fear? Anger? Vengeance? You may lash out at another only because you know no other way to defend yourself from further attacks from thoughtless persons. In that case, your lesson may have been to discover how to stand up for your rights in a more dignified manner. Learn to confront firmly, but gracefully. Check deep inside to see if this concept has been learned. If so, mark this up as a success, a great lesson mastered.

  Were you people pleasing? Did you allow someone to talk or pressure you into doing something? Were you manipulated into action or goaded into a response? The lesson for you may have been to stop giving in to group pressure or relying on the opinions of others. You may have been teaching yourself to listen to your own feelings, follow your heart, think, and decide things for yourself. Remember to trust your feelings. Trust your inner knowing. Trust the god in you. Trust yourself.

  Search to see if this self-trust has been learned, for it is a hard lesson that often takes lifetimes to master. Even when only a modest advance has been made in this area, give yourself plenty of love and credit for your accomplishment. Pronounce it good. Pat yourself on the back and keep on asserting your independence.

The People-Pleasing Syndrome

The most common result of poor self-esteem is "people pleasing." When we feel unworthy and unwanted, the desire to be loved and accepted can drive us into unnecessary and unwanted servitude.

Unless you were born into a wealthy home, complete with servants (and even that is no guarantee of exception) you have been trained to defer your own needs and wishes to that of people in authority. You are last on the list. This has been taught as simple good manners, learning politeness, and respect for others. Generally, this is an excellent rule of society. However, it has been grossly overemphasized, going beyond respect to the point of constant self-depreciation in order to please others at the cost of displeasing yourself.

People pleasers often do for others until they become filled with resentment. At that point, they are actually doing themselves more harm (via accumulated resentment) than good. The negativity far outweighs the positive effects of the so-called "good deeds." When one person in a relationship does all the giving while the other does most of the taking, both are contributing to a highly unbalanced, dysfunctional relationship. Eventually, this unhealthy union must be brought into balance.

Common People-Pleasing Traits

Test your people-pleasing behaviors: how often do you do each?

N=Never   **S**=Sometimes   **O**=Often   **A**=Always

Traits	N	S	O	A
I do things I don't want to do in order to please someone else.				
I allow myself to be persuaded to do things that are not pleasurable to me.				
I set my needs and desires aside in order to satisfy others.				
I go along with the crowd against my better judgment.				
I fail to assert myself or defend my rights.				
I am afraid or unable to express my true feelings.				
I am afraid to ask for what I want.				
I am unable or unwilling to state my needs or rights in the face of other people's opinions.				
I put other people's opinions, beliefs, and desires ahead of my own.				
I do not trust myself.				

Break this self-defeating habit. Ask yourself the following questions.

- Does that person really mean that much to me?
- Is it really worth the effort I make to keep that friendship?
- Do I fear abandonment or rejection?
- Do I feel abandoned or rejected?

The High Cost of People Pleasing

People pleasers may have been people users. You could be balancing the scales from other lifetimes. If the shoe fits, tell yourself, "I got the message." Then forgive yourself, congratulate yourself, and move on to self-assurance.

- People pleasers allow others to take advantage of them because they do not love themselves enough to say no.
- People pleasers are invariably used and/or victimized by the smooth-talking users in our society.
- People pleasers are the doormats other people walk upon.
- People pleasers usually feel used and abused.
- People pleasers are often angry and resentful at being imposed upon or "talked into" doing something that turned out to be difficult, time consuming or just not pleasurable.

Whenever you are feeling angry, resentful, or used by another, you have probably been people pleasing, although you may not have been aware of it. If this description fits you, admit it now. The first step is to admit the problem. The second is to understand that this is part of your basic belief system. Third, you need to consciously work to change the programming.

Understanding Your Dilemma

People pleasing is a type of prostitution. In essence, you are trying to buy the approval and affection that your parents failed to provide. You please others at great cost to yourself, selling yourself short, doing without, and neglecting your own wants and needs to prove yourself worthy of love.

To change and heal this problem you must to understand why and how you came to believe yourself unworthy of love. It is good to write the reasons out in detail, preferably in your journal, which helps you get a good grip on your situation. Then decide what you intend to do about it.

Write out your new belief and intention. List some ways you can bring about the needed changes (like setting new goals, learning new skills, losing weight, avoiding "users," join new groups, making new friends). Do whatever it takes to make you feel good about yourself. Above all, you should treat yourself like a valuable person.

Sure Cure for People Pleasing

The next time someone asks you to do something, stop.

- Take time to think about it. (Pause to consult your schedule.)
- Ask yourself, "Do I really want to do this?
- Check your feelings carefully.
- Give yourself permission to do what you want to do.
- Dare to listen to your inner self.
- Take your power back. Stick with your decision.

- **Lesson for People Pleasers:** Remember, this is a learned behavior that can be changed. People pleasing may be a matter of not being decisive or strong in the past so you allowed yourself to be pushed around in order to learn assertiveness. You need to trust yourself and your feelings more often. It is a matter of being true to yourself and of honoring your needs. Claim your rights and remember if it doesn't feel right, it isn't right. Make plans to do something really nice for yourself on a regular basis to affirm your worthiness.
- **A Point to Ponder:** There is a vast difference between serving those you love because you want to and serving those who impose upon your good nature. If it feels like an imposition, it is.

Challenging People Who Challenge You

One way to help yourself stay out of the people-pleasing business is to name those "friends" who are always challenging, manipulating, using you, or just plain giving you trouble one way or another. To be prepared for the "battle" you need a battle plan. Write out the name, the challenge (what they do to provoke you) and your plan of action (how I will handle this person/situation). Keep it brief, loving, and positive and you will be prepared to defend yourself from falling back into old habits of people pleasing. Do it!

Here are a few categories:

- **Downers:** Try to make you feel bad, put you down when you are "up."
- **Manipulators:** Want you to do their dirty work.
- **Space Invaders:** Barge in, waste your time, spoil your plans, and leave you empty-handed.
- **Rug Jerkers:** Interrupt your fun, spoil your best efforts.
- **Weep 'n' Wailers:** Cry on your shoulder, take your time and energy.
- **Wet Blankets:** Make fun of you, find fault, rain on your parade, and generally downgrade everything you try to do.

The Final Touch

As a final touch, intend to deal promptly with any new problems as they come along. Write your problems and feelings in your diary or journal at the end of each day. Say a prayer and tell God your problem. If you are uncertain what to do, try asking your angels for guidance in finding the best solution. Then watch for answers. These may come through people, TV, reading materials, friendly encounters, or insights (pictures inside your head). Learn to work with your dream information; you may be pleasantly surprised.[3]

While writing in your journal, add plans for future behavior, changes in attitude, and new ways to handle old problems; this helps you to evaluate where you have been and make better selections for where you want to go and how to get there. The clearer you are about your intentions for your future, the greater your chances for achieving your goals.

Make it a habit to keep your closet of guilt feelings and skeletons cleaned up as you go through life so there is never again any guilt blocking your road to success.

The Healing Power of Love

Our society has promoted the teaching that boys, from a very young age, must not cry or show their feelings. Tender hearts are considered unmanly; traits of courage, strength, defiance, combativeness, belligerence, and aggressiveness are favored. Young men are encouraged to be tough, hardhearted, and quick to fight. Brute force, hostility, and warlike behavior are the expected norm. Males are warned that gentleness is a sign of weakness; they must be brave, strong, hard, argumentative, unbending, forceful, and highly competitive. Rough play, tough sports,

→ Changing Your Beliefs

anger, hate, and fighting at the slightest provocation is necessary to prove their manhood—all this in a society long exposed to a professed belief in the Ten Commandments and the concept that God is love and that we are to love one another. Yet we value and teach hate, revenge, and unloving behavior. Remember that all thoughts return to the sender; hate can be deadly.

Metaphysicians have long known what modern doctors are just beginning to realize: the basic emotional cause of a heart attack is the result of unexpressed love. The male habit of blocking all display of tenderness, love, and gentle emotions actually causes heart blockage and eventually, stroke, heart attack, or heart failure. Many females, competing in the "man's world" are also prone to be tough and hardhearted, showing little or no love, since it would be equated with weakness. Isn't it interesting to note that the United States has the largest percentage of heart attacks in the world? We have earned it by repressing love and tenderness to one another. Is it worth the price?

Along this same line, we can see that child abuse, even murder is on the rise in the USA. This is no surprise as hate, vengeance, and violence reign supreme in our movies and TV shows. Our so-called comedies are heavy with sarcasm and hateful, emotionally damaging put-downs. Even our cartoons are filled with vengeance and violence being passed off as humor. Situations such as these are an outward manifestation of our race-conscious attitudes and beliefs about our world and ourselves.

Hate is where we are. Meanwhile, the best prevention of heart degeneration is love. We need to show, give, express, and radiate love to the special people in our lives. Eventually we will be able to radiate love to all people, everywhere. Love is where we need to go.

- **Forgiveness:** The inclination and ability to forgive one another is an important expression of love ("Forgive us our trespasses as we forgive those who trespass against us," Matthew 6:9) Forgiveness is love extended outward.[4] It is a gift we need to provide freely to others and especially to ourselves, for we often treat ourselves far more harshly than anyone else. Forgiveness, like love, is healthy.

The vibrations that emanate from a loving heart and mind are gentle waves or circular spirals of energy, quite unlike the sharp edges of hate and anger. Loving vibrations radiate far beyond the thinker, like perfume on a breeze, pleasantly uplifting all those in the general vicinity. Most important of all, love is an expression of the soul, a quality all of us need to cultivate.

Self-Talk

Your mind and its mental chatter run continuously all day, stopping only when you fall asleep. This inner conversation can be a source of much difficulty and hardship in your life when it is negatively focused. Alternatively, it can create much love, joy, and beauty, depending upon your overall attitude. Obviously, you need to become acutely aware of the type and quality of your self-talk. Be conscious of the fact that your subconscious mind is constantly recording every thought you think and every word you say. Then, like a faithful scribe, it works diligently to prove you right by making those statements and beliefs come true. Your subconscious mind is your "genie in the bottle" that does as you command, even when you are oblivious of the process and are making foolish statements about yourself and your world.

Be aware that when you think of yourself in negative terms of being wrong, stupid, ignorant, clumsy, bad, and other derogatory names you are actually damaging your mental and emotional bodies. When you punish yourself with the "ought to's," "got to's," and "should have knowns," you are dishonoring and belittling your whole being. It is vitally important to change a self-debasing attitude that is poisoning your belief system. Deliberately replace the negative mental commentary with new, positive, self-loving statements about how great you are. Instead of beating yourself up and putting yourself down, a habit detrimental to body and soul, stop to realize the damage you are inflicting on yourself. Question why you are doing this. Are you still running other people's old opinion programming? Why?

Intend to look at each so-called problem as a lesson, a challenge to learn something new, which it really is, and see yourself as a student, wisely learning to love and honor yourself and all others. An effective practice for this is to picture yourself as shown on the facing page—seeing your physical body surrounded by all your nonphysical bodies. Think of yourself in terms of the complete, spiritual being that you truly are. Then visualize your Guardian Angel overshadowing you, guiding and helping you through every step of your soul journey.

This image alone can lift you into a higher place where you can begin to establish and realize a greater sense of your own worthiness.

As often as necessary, talk things over with your Guardian Angel. Use affirmations, visualizations, meditations, and whatever else is

→ Changing Your Beliefs

necessary to change your basic beliefs to the point where you can accept and enjoy your fondest dreams.

Remove yourself quickly from those who exude harsh judgments and words of condemnation. See them as venomous creatures whose ugly thought forms are poisoning the very air about them. Never allow yourself or anyone else to devalue your sense of worthiness. Surround yourself with kind and loving people as much as possible. Find new ways to nurture and love yourself with long, fragrant baths, flowers on your desk, or whatever it takes to remind yourself of your new, healthy, self-loving attitudes.

Knowing that everything has a purpose, intend to understand, learn, and grow from each and every challenge. It is imperative that you eliminate the old, harmful habit of blaming yourself for everything that goes wrong. If you make a mistake, let it be an okay thing — a lesson learned, a value gained. To berate yourself over every imagined error only adds to your overall stress and sets you up to make even more mistakes. Determine to be kind to yourself, making many complimentary mental comments about your performance during the day.

Bear in mind that it is never sufficient just to know things intellectually. To make any lasting change, it is necessary to practice and put into action what you have learned. So, make this a new, pleasant, and uplifting habit. Practice an ongoing, loving attitude toward yourself every day. When you master this, you will be able to generously give your love to others and receive abundant love in return.

Attaining a State of Well-Being

The ability to solve problems with ease and confidence, rather than becoming enmeshed in anger and self-punishment, is vital to your personal well-being. Consider all problems as a healthy part of your discovery process, like a child learning to walk. Make up your mind that the next time you

89

find yourself in a difficult situation that you will view it as a learning challenge. Instead of falling into the old blame game, take a deep breath and deliberately move into a patient, loving attitude about yourself and the circumstance. Determine to solve it in peace and joy.

Remember that emotions are reactions to what you believe to be true. How can we learn from unwanted emotions? We can ask ourselves, "What is my truth?" Then we need to listen for our soul's answer. Now is the time to journal your questions and answers, and see what you get.

Continue to probe your beliefs and feelings until you discover a meaningful answer. Once this is accomplished, immediately compliment yourself for "getting the point" and thank yourself for a valuable lesson learned. This allows you to be a winner rather than a loser. Continue this rewarding and reinforcing process that bolsters your self-worth, which is truly your most valuable asset.

Problems Are Messages You Need to Heed

There are times when everything seems to go wrong all at once. You usually plan (but perhaps don't remember) this event or crisis point by making some big, important new choice. Try not to panic, but stop and meditate about it. Consider the possibility that you may have been working too hard or you are all stressed out and just need a break. If so, make the time to recover your balance. Or perhaps you need to find something better suited to your nature and talents. If this feels right to you, ask your Guardian Angel to guide you to your rightful place.

Usually when things seem to pile up all at once, it is a clear signal for change. It could be saying that your basic belief, attitude, or whatever must be changed and you are being forced to make a decision to alter your habits or go elsewhere. What will you do? Is your lesson completed? Understand that if you quit, leave, divorce, or in any way run from an unsolved problem or unlearned lesson, you will only walk into the same situation again. It may be a different setting and different people, but the same lesson. Again, you cannot run away from your chosen lessons, so think carefully before deciding.

Take a good, deep look at what is happening around you. Feel out the situation. As you ask yourself these questions, pay close attention to your feelings.

- What is really going on? (Remember, your soul always knows the answer.)

Changing Your Beliefs

- Am I feeling restless? Fed up? Repelled?
- Is this a problem I need to solve?
- Is this a challenge to rise above?
- Is there something in me that needs to change?
- Is this a message saying it is time to move on to better things?
- Have I learned my lesson in this situation?
- Is it time to move on?

Be aware you may be telling yourself that you are in a situation or a job that is no longer right for you. It could be graduation time, especially if you are discontented with the old job or situation and are feeling eager to move in a new direction.

Generally, if you have been striving to clean up your old, limiting beliefs and changing your attitudes, it may be a clear sign you are ready to move on to better things. To be sure you make the right choice and the highest and best decision, stay away from other people's opinions. Listen only to your heart and follow your gut feelings.

It is helpful to know that most often your problem is your lesson. It comes to you because at this time in your life, you are ready to meet this challenge, solve it, overcome it, and bring it into balance. When you really grasp this, you can permanently move away from blaming yourself and those around you for your difficult experiences. It is all a part of growing up and moving into self-mastery. Be determined to look at your difficulties as lessons you have chosen to conquer. Look for the reward in the each experience. Pronounce it good, give yourself an "A," and move on.

Remember that life is for living joyfully.

8

Your Journal: An Important Tool for Growing

Man is the maker of his character, the molder of his life, and the builder of his destiny.

—James Allen

In the long process of changing old beliefs and writing out new goals and dreams, keeping a journal is a valuable tool for recording your thoughts, feelings, and goals. Your journal is a place to write of your struggles and triumphs as you clean up old beliefs and begin to create a new and better life for yourself.

Should you make a commitment to start a journal and faithfully write in it each evening, you will be pleasantly surprised at the progress you can make in one short month.

Most people stay so busy running about, they seldom take time to stop and consider what is going on in their lives. Rarely do they stop to check their feelings. Seldom do they record how they honestly feel. There is little wonder that they become so disconnected and stressed. It is good food for the soul to take some quiet time for frank and thoughtful appraisals about ourselves and the direction we are taking. Without this, we tend to drift along assuming or pretending that everything is fine. Then, too late, we see our ship of life heading for the rocks.

People often come to me with their problems, declaring they just don't know what to do. Yet once they start talking, I find that most people know exactly what is wrong with their lives and how to make the necessary corrections as well. All they really need is a safe place and an opportunity to put their feelings into words. Then even as they speak, their problems become clear and their answers apparent. I do not need to help except for perhaps a word of encouragement along the way. Writing in your journal produces the same effect without the high cost of a good counselor.

As you set up new goals and ideals for your life, your personal writing serves as a focus for all you are currently feeling and experiencing. The process of putting these thoughts on paper brings instant clarity to your situation. Most of all, writing in a journal helps you to look deeply into your life and affairs.

When you describe your day's events and express your deepest feelings, you come in close touch with your soul, which is who you really are. You are also more aware of the motives of those around you. Using your feelings as guidelines, your journal reveals your attitudes and allows you to see where you are going, what you are doing, the lessons you are learning, and the changes you need to make. Most importantly, this gives you greater awareness about your place in the world, which allows you to make better choices and exert more control over your circumstances. This is true particularly when you work with your goals in sight and in mind.

You could look at writing in your journal as your special time and place to talk to your best friend and counselor—you. Then, by taking a serious look at your life on a regular basis, you will be much more aware of the stream of events flowing about you. The more alert you are to the game playing and manipulations the better equipped you will be to understand the challenges. In this way you can meet the challenges head-on, rather than being caught unaware and swept away by surprise.

Getting Started

All you need is a loose-leaf notebook that will easily hold a year's supply of records. However, if you are a frequent traveler you may prefer something both lighter and more compact.

Some of you may want to use a computer or even a tape recorder. Just remember a recorder is no good if the information never gets off of the tape and onto some paper where you can see it. This is especially true for your list of goals, which you will want to refer to frequently. For most people, the act of writing and seeing thoughts in black and white brings clarity to mind. This is one of the primary reasons for using a journal.

Make yourself a promise that is not to be broken to journal every day. Keep your notebook handy, even when you travel. You may want to keep it on your pillow or bedside table as a reminder to make faithful entries, until this becomes a happy new habit.

Set aside quiet time each evening to look at your life situation and the events of your day in a calm, unemotional manner. Start thinking about new ideals for yourself. Keep your list of goals and desires readily available, possibly on a file card that can also be used as a bookmark. In the next few chapters, you will be setting many new goals and guidelines for creating your world as you want it to be.

Using a journal is as simple as writing in a diary, recording all the important events of the day along with your feelings about who did what to whom. Describe what you did, how you felt, your greatest concerns, and any decisions you made. Be totally honest and open, digging deep into your feelings in a detective-like manner rather than glossing over them. Your whole purpose is to get in touch with the deepest emotions of your soul and to list all the things that are bothering you, big and small. As you write, take special notice of prompting from your intuition.

The main object is to look at your life situation and the events of your day every evening. Review these in a detached manner, carefully evaluating how you worked, acted, and reacted in various situations with different people. Try to sense the underlying hopes, fears, and attitudes behind your choices and actions. Learn to weigh your actions in the light of the goals you have set for yourself. Evaluate in a gentle, honest, and loving manner. Nurture yourself with positive statements about your day. There is no need for criticism or punishment. Just look at your daily performance as an observer, assessing your words and actions and deciding which are commendable and which you would prefer to change. Pause now and then to consider where and how you can improve.

When you finish, you may find this is an excellent time to look over your goals and things-to-do list. Compliment yourself for each goal that you have already reached, then review your desires and intentions for those not yet completed.

Date your records, as the results of your goals and intentions can be instantaneous or take days, weeks, or even months. Some things may take a year or more, depending on size, complexity, and circumstances.

Reward Yourself for Each Goal Reached

Be very careful not to judge yourself harshly. Remember that every so-called mistake is another step in your learning process and should be understood and treasured, not condemned. Consciously intend to love yourself just as you are, realizing that the problem people and situations in your life are teaching you something you have chosen to learn. Accept these challenges as your personal lessons in life. Using your journal can be a ritual practice in loving self-evaluation and improvement, done with your most cherished hopes and goals in mind.

Summaries Are Important

After writing in your journal at the end of the day, write a brief commentary as a summary. At the end of each week, look back over your progress. Watch for synchronistic events, meaningful dreams, repeated situations, or comments. Again, write a brief summary for the week.

At the end of the month, repeat the summarizing process, remembering to comment on your progress and success with your goals. As you do this, you will find significant patterns beginning to emerge.

At the end of the year you can quickly look back over your successes and problem areas and once more summarize for the year. In this way, you have a solid background on which to base your new ideals and intentions for the coming year.

Using a journal will keep you in touch with your all-important, underlying feelings and attitudes — for these are the vibrations that will attract or repel the type of people and events you desire to have in your life.

Your continued self-search of your thoughts, your life, goals, motives, actions, and overall lifestyle will greatly aid in evaluating your progress and in understanding the "whys" and "hows" of the problems facing you. It also facilitates learning your lessons and overcoming difficulties quicker than ever before. In addition, it prepares the way for guidance from your God-self to come through with greater clarity.

Dreams as Guidance

As an added bonus, using a journal can trigger dream responses, making your dreams clearer and easier to remember. This is especially true when you write out a dream request or question about a problem. Your query narrows the dream content to that specific area, giving you answers or insights into the situation. A good clear question is your best tool for dream interpretation.

As you begin to work with your goals, your dreams will provide comments on the goals and the action that you have taken towards them. You may want to include your dreams in your journal or choose a separate notebook for this. Having worked with dreams for many years I find them extremely helpful in guiding me through one crisis after another. I highly recommend this practice to all who are serious about improving their lives.

You have everything to gain and nothing to lose by adopting the habit of using a journal. This is especially true for those who tend to be forgetful, unsure, or unfocused. It sharpens your perceptions and brings greater clarity.

Your Journal: An Important Tool for Growing

Remember that the balancing point in all creating is the Law of Love. When you are thinking, feeling, and living in a loving manner, your vibrations will invite beautiful, harmonious creations. On the other hand, a prevailing attitude of negative thoughts such as anger, fear, hate, or feelings of lack will draw negative conditions to you, regardless of your original intentions. Your soul-goal is to do all things lovingly, whether that is your physical ideal or not.

Do all things lovingly.

9

Decisions, Decisions

*Decision awakens the spirit of man,
The great decision comes first,
The great work follows.*
　　　　　　—Wilferd A. Peterson

People often speak of finding themselves in trouble as if they were taken by surprise. But folks don't just find themselves in awkward or unhappy situations. They put themselves there by an endless procession of poor choices based on old beliefs and fears, such as:

Poor Decisions
　　I don't like it, but I'll take it.
　　It isn't what I wanted, but...

No Decisions
　　I'll think about it (forever).
　　I don't know.
　　Maybe.
　　We'll see.

People-Pleasing Decisions
　　Whatever you decide is fine with me.
　　Well, what to you think?
　　That's OK, I don't mind...(much)
　　(Agreeing to something we do not want to do.)

Vacillating Decisions
　　Oh yes, I want it, but...
　　On the other hand...
　　I'm not quite sure yet.

Fuzzy, Unclear Decisions
It doesn't make any difference to me.
I think I like the red one, but the blue one is nice, too, or maybe the purple one.

Hasty Decisions
Saying yes when you really mean no.
Saying, "I'll do it," just to keep the peace.
Agreeing only because we feel pressured to do so.

Promises

What is a promise? Webster tells us it is "a declaration or assurance that something specified will or will not be done." Most of us make statements about what we will or won't do but fail to consider it as binding. As long as no written, legal agreement has been signed, most people believe it is okay to forget or ignore their spoken words. They say, "I didn't really mean it," or "I was just trying to be nice." Thoughtless remarks, little white lies, and empty agreements are actually promises, whether we mean them as such or not. Such careless words result in confusion of mind. (Remember those thought forms are always at work.) Unless corrected, our loose words eventually cause problems.

Not too long ago, when a person gave his or her word it was considered a sacred vow which could be depended upon. Anyone breaking that vow was disgraced. It was a matter of honor and honor was important. Today, many people have lost the meaning of honor. Unkept agreements are commonplace. Get it in writing. However, even that may prove useless. There are always karmic clouts (painful lessons) to pay for this, for in the eyes of your soul, your word is your bond, a contract or commitment to be fulfilled.

Remember that your soul knows and keeps track of these white lies, ill-considered words, and broken promises, even when you have forgotten. From the standpoint of the soul, these are your contracted obligations; although you did not make an actual promise, the soul sees this is as a binding agreement that must be kept. Your soul keeps an accurate record of everything and it is keenly aware that your chosen path is perfection. All flaws and misdeeds, however minor, must be set right and brought into balance before your soul can graduate from the earth plane.

It is a little-known fact that unkept promises (to you and to others) can bring about a variety of subtle difficulties including physical "dis-ease."

These sins of omission and incompleteness include all things left undecided, unfinished, or unforgiven.

Making excuses, pretending that you forgot, or saying you were too busy does not free you from your responsibility to honor your word. Many folks do not realize that failing to keep their word is equal to telling a lie. Whether little white lies or big black ones, they all leave a stain on the soul and sooner or later, you must make them right. It is imperative that we learn our lessons with honesty, integrity, and respect for the rights of others. We need to take responsibility for all we do or fail to do.

Blaming others or making excuses for your shortcomings does nothing but add to your personal burden of things left undone. Always, your soul remembers and holds you fully accountable. Procrastination and non-decision also fall in the category of unfinished business which hangs over your head, quite literally, as unfinished thought forms.

The Burden of Things Undone

Slowly, as these bits of unfinished business continue to multiply they circle and gather in your aura, cluttering your mental and emotional fields, bringing confusion, indecision, and absent-mindedness. This information overload causes decision making to become more and more difficult.

Meanwhile, as thought forms multiply, attracting more indecision and confusion, your problems grow in size and intensity. You develop a feeling of weightiness around your head and shoulders. You begin to feel heavy, sluggish, and depressed. It becomes a growing burden for the soul.

Until you bring them to a point of completion, you will carry these bundles of unfinished business for the rest of your life.

Could this be the reason why there are so many people who are bent and stoop-shouldered at an early age but others stand tall and upright into their nineties?

Unforgivingness

One of the burdens many of us carry is that of unforgivingness. Holding onto old hurts and grudges and refusing to forgive those we feel have "trespassed against us" only adds to our personal burden, further clouding our minds. It adds yet another piece of unfinished business to our burden of things undone.

Beautiful Morning

I clearly recall a long-ago morning, waking up to a perfectly beautiful summer day and feeling happy. Yet before setting one foot out of bed, I carefully gathered to mind all my unresolved problems from days, even weeks before. Suddenly I felt depressed. Mentally questioning the cause of my swift mood swing, I immediately realized that I had created this monster all by myself. How? By focusing on my problems, instead of enjoying the beauty that lay all around me. Now that, my friends, is the way to ruin a wonderful day.

Of course, we all do this to a greater or lesser extent. Often not consciously, we tend to carry our unresolved hurts, anger, and problems around with us every day because we have never stopped to think about them, much less try to resolve them. This is partly because we have been taught to bury our feelings, to people please, and to pretend all is well when it isn't. Obviously, this is a teaching we need to rethink.

Depression

A continued focus on painful events of the past can actually lead to clinical depression. Scientists are beginning to understand that the creative, mental/emotional cause of serious depression is a prolonged focus on negative events of the past.

Those who tend to wallow in self-pity over the pain and sorrow of old traumas need to remember that the soul came here to learn. Certain lessons can only be grasped by means of difficulties that were designed to teach us to be strong, courageous, and confident. We cannot know our own strength until we have been tested and have successfully overcome our challenges. We, as souls, choose to learn by selecting and living through a series of stressful encounters. Remember, absolutely nothing happens by accident. All has a purpose. The persons involved in our lessons were truthfully our teachers, not our enemies. Bearing this in mind, we need to make a valiant effort to forgive the past and find it in our hearts to be grateful for the things we have learned and the wisdom we have earned.

Your Own Little World

We often hear the expression, "She is living in her own little world." We accept this without question yet we seldom stop to wonder how.

Making a decision of any kind instantly sets up a complex and powerful sequence of events. Even a simple statement such as "I am going to take off ten pounds," amounts to a promise you have made to yourself. As such, this has far-reaching results no matter whether your resolution is in the form of a tenuous wish, a firm ambition, or a strong desire. The overall results are the same. The only difference is in the timing, since the strongest and most intense desires manifest with greater speed. This whole process, although unseen, unfelt, and unrecognized, is nevertheless a tremendously powerful force that definitely affects your mind, body, and life.

Try thinking of your body and its aura as your personal world, over which you have total responsibility and control. You are the spiritual essence that makes the choices, chooses the direction, charts the path, and gives the commands. You are the captain of your ship and the king of your physical domain. Your organs are similar to continents, each having a unique kind of culture, product, and specialty. Your bloodstream is similar to rivers and seas that flow from one country to another, bringing supplies. Your nervous system is a vast communication network, sending information through your world. When you make a decision, this news is flashed around your physical domain. Each area then prepares to do whatever is necessary to fulfill your demand. Silent forces are set into motion at your command.

Gaia

Since your personal world is part of a greater world, earth, your choices are duly recorded as a part of the mass consciousness of Gaia. (Gaia is the ancient Greek name for Mother Earth as a Living Being,

Mystical Magical You

complete with consciousness and intelligence. Native Indians have long known this but science is only now recognizing and accepting this concept.)

Gaia, in turn, is only one small part of our solar system, which is embodied and watched over by yet another great, living, spiritual essence. (Some people prefer to call these beings angels.) Our solar system in turn, is a small part of the Milky Way Galaxy. This great galactic being is an integral part of our universe. Both the galactic being and the universe being, whom most of us think of as God, are aware of your decisions.

Meanwhile, our universe was created in such a way that it is not only aware of your latest choice, but can and does act immediately in response to your command, to nurture and support your desire. Once your decision is stated, opportunities appear; ideas and insights come in through meditation, dreams, and "chance encounters." Other information comes through books, magazines, newspapers, and so forth. There is an endless barrage of help from innumerable sources, including angels. You ask for help or guidance and it comes. It pours out to you in great abundance, unless you countermand your orders. We use any number of things to countermand our desires by saying, "but," "too expensive," "can't have," "can't be done," "don't know how," "don't have time," and all those excuses we give when we are unsure of ourselves. These, and other similar remarks, will very effectively cancel your "order." The energies that were beginning to move on your behalf, will stop and return to the Source.

Each day you are creating your own little world and everything in it by the thoughts you think and the words you speak. You are also adding to the sum total of Gaia. Are you beginning to understand just how powerful you are?

You can also sabotage (but not cancel) your decisions by giving up, doubting your worth, doubting your ability, endlessly procrastinating, failing to follow through with your agreement, dropping or neglecting your project, forgetting your goal, or drifting to something else. Remember, the moment you say you want something you automatically release powerful forces to aid you in the completion of your edict. The more thought, energy, and emotion you give your desire, the faster it will come into your reality.

Conversely, the more energy you use in fearing you won't or can't have it or use in thinking about the lack of it, the more rapidly you will reap that fear or that lack. The energy has been set into motion and your thought is the director of that force. Having stated your desire and then having forgotten or neglected your purpose is akin to having unfinished business hanging in the air. More accurately, it is similar to abandoning your car while the motor is running and brakes unset. It can run amuck. The forces unleashed continue steadily and relentlessly pushing toward the completion of your chosen goal. You may find yourself feeling restless and uneasy, fragmented, dissatisfied, stressed out, and wondering what is wrong with you. Why? Because the energy which was to be commanded by you in the completion of your forgotten goal is now undirected. Like a misguided missile, it can cause you many unnecessary problems.

Decisions made but not kept are uncontrolled forces whipping around and about in your little world. They produce havoc in your life and affairs, buffeting your physical body as well as your mental and emotional ones.

Marital Agreements

Weddings are a good example. One of the hidden causes behind marital problems is broken agreements. Take a couple who has been living together quite happily. They decide to marry, which is a process involving promises. Before the wedding, in most cases, there were no real commitments or binding decisions other than to be together. Almost immediately after the vows are made the trouble begins. After the wedding the forces set into motion by the promises come into collision with other intents and commitments of both bride and groom and must be worked out. Often this is precipitated by a difference in understanding, expectations, or suppositions about the meaning of their agreements. (Business, political, and legal agreements follow the same general rules.)

Once you have faced each problem and corrected it through new programming, you may still have some details to work out. After that, it will never bother you again for you have mastered that area of your life.

Should the same problem come up again, it will only be a test to prove that you have truly mastered that issue. Like any lesson once learned, you are able to deal with it quickly through your wisdom and you will not need to repeat the problem.

The spiritual purpose for coming to Earth School in the first place is to achieve dominion over each of our nonphysical bodies. As a soul, you have carefully selected each of your challenges (problems) for the specific purpose of achieving this mastery. So your lessons are designed in such a way that any situation not brought to a fair and honorable conclusion will keep reoccurring until it is set right and brought into balance. (If not in this lifetime, then in another.)

You have heard the expression "a heart as light as a feather," meaning a heart totally free and unburdened with guilt or pain. The saying dates back to the days of ancient Egypt when Anubis, god of the underworld, weighed the heart of each dead person on a scale with only a feather as a counterbalance. If the scales balanced, it was said there were no misdeeds or unpaid debts (mental, emotional, or physical) weighing on the heart of that soul. It was then free to graduate to higher levels of consciousness. This principle, although ancient, still holds true today.

Remember, it is not what happens to you but how you react to it that counts, for every experience is a needed lesson, a chance to make higher choices. Bearing grudges just keeps the problem recycling until you overcome it in love. The sooner you face and clear your unresolved issues, the better you will feel on not one, but many levels of your being. Coming to the point of peace with yourself can be compared to a good thunderstorm, settling the dust (of half-finished thought forms) and clearing the air (of your aura). This allows you to have a heart that is carefree and light as a feather.

The Importance of Forgiveness in Cleaning Up the Past

Whenever you are hurt in any way, physically, mentally, or emotionally, the event leaves a kind of bruise in your auric field. This tends to fade away in time. You may even forget all about it as long as no resentment is held. Yet, the very presence of pain or resentment indicates a lack of forgiveness that can smolder a long time, gradually gaining strength. It attracts people and events of a similar nature like a magnet. Like a child with a sign on his back saying "kick me," the unforgiven pain keeps attracting incidents like that of the original bruise. The more defensive you become, the more powerfully the magnet attracts. The pattern repeats, relentlessly drawing variations of the unforgiven pain. You begin to feel used, abused, and victimized. It all seems so unfair. At this point, you do not understand that you are attracting these incidents for the sole purpose of cleansing them from your world through forgiveness and letting go.

Resentment is like a splinter under the skin, hurting and festering to draw attention to it so it can be healed. It wants to get your full attention and determination to do something. Aspirin and bandages won't help. You need to dig it out and clean it up. Failure to forgive the trauma eventually allows the wound to turn into a cancer-like growth in the body. Caring doctors who are aware of the mental/emotional background of their patients have long noted the high incidence of trauma, resentment, and anger in relation to the growth of cancer. The growth begins about two to three years after the stressful event.

We all need to understand that the overall lesson of life on earth is to come back to the Source. God is love. We were created in love. God created the whole universe out of love. When we move from love and caring into hate and unforgivingness, we also move into pain and suffering.

Dropping Your Burden Through Forgiveness

Everything moves in cycles of vibration. We set things in motion by our thoughts and emotions that manifest as deeds. In time, we reap the results. When we are kind and loving, we enjoy our cyclic return. However, when we dwell in anger and resentment this comes back not once, but many times until we recognize and clean up the negative thoughts. Now, you might say, "But, he did it to me first." To which I reply, "How do you know? How can you be sure?" Jesus said, "Love your enemies and pray for your persecutors" (Matthew 5:44). Accepting forgiveness is concluding the process, completing the circle of giving and receiving.

The Act of Forgiveness

Name the one person you are having the most trouble forgiving. Recall briefly just why you hate him or her. (One minute is enough; you don't want to waste your creative mental energies concentrating on the problem.) Then remember that at soul level you agreed to this experience for a specific reason and were a co-creator in it.

Mystical Magical You

Exercise 1:

Review the situation. What happened? If you had known then what you know now could you have avoided this incident? How? What may have been the lesson to be learned? Have you had a similar experience? If yes, name it or them. Why would you have chosen this lesson? What have you learned from it? How can you best use this knowledge in the future?

Exercise 2:

Find at least one good thing that came from this experience (the more the better). Now that you see the good in it, can you forgive yourself? Can you forgive the other person? Can you honestly thank him or her for being your teacher? Take a moment to do this; if you have trouble, call on Archangel Michael (with sword and scales) to cut you free from hate or anger. Now that it is over, how do you want to feel about this? (The purpose is for you to feel good about it.)

Intend to come to a place of harmony and peace about this event. Remember that taking offense is just as bad as giving it. You may need to forgive yourself as well as the other person(s). If this is difficult, remember the guidelines in the Lord's Prayer; "Forgive us our trespasses as we forgive those who trespass against us."

If this fails, try putting yourself in the other person's place. Consider their background. How were they treated at home? Consider the fact that all of us do the very best we can in accordance with our current understanding and basic beliefs.

If you still have a problem, remember your purpose for being here. Spend some time in prayer and meditation. Make it your goal to resolve this situation for the good of all concerned. (The other person may be just as hurt as you are.) Spend several days, if necessary. You may need to do some soul searching. You may also need to contact your former enemy and let him or her know you are ready to forgive and forget. This opens doors for both of you to give and receive peace. Resolve to come to a definite point of peace. Do whatever needs to be done, for it is important to your soul growth and your general well-being to bring this to a harmonious conclusion.

Once you have finished, write out what you gained from this experience. Then focus on the lesson learned and wisdom gained. Pronounce it good.

Train your mind to focus on the way you want to feel. Take conscious control over your emotions. Be grateful for the lesson learned, for this will leave you with a sense of peace and satisfaction that all is well in your world. By now you are probably feeling much better about it so celebrate your success: light a candle, buy yourself some fresh flowers or do something really nice, just for you.

Cleaning Up Your Past

Start with a clear understanding of:

- **Who am I?** A child of God, a soul, a god in the making, a spiritual being, and a co-creator with God. (Write your own version of this statement.)
- **Why am I here?** To bring all your bodies into perfection and become a master over the earth plane before moving on to even greater things.
- **What did I come to do?** Live in freedom and joy, experience life, and create the desires of your heart within the Law of Love. (We failed to do this once and fell into self-consciousness. Now we are working our way back to living totally within the Law of Love and harmony. This includes achieving control over each of our bodies, giving the soul mastery over our lives.)

Dealing With Undecided Items

Make a list of as many of your undecided issues as you can recall. Once they are written, many can be brought to a speedy conclusion with a firm, "Yes, I want to do this," or "No, I do not want this." (If other people are involved, you need to inform them of your new decisions.) Understand that most non-decisions stem from mixed feelings. Generally, you know what you want but hesitate out of fear of argument, of ridicule, or of hurting someone's feelings. Don't forget your desires and feelings; they are valid and important too.

As to arguments, ridicule, tears, or temper tantrums, be aware that these are manipulative actions practiced by people who want to have their own way. Don't be fooled. Recognize this behavior for the childishness that it is and treat it as such. They will cease the ridiculous behavior once they discover these tactics don't work anymore. Meanwhile, you need to love yourself enough to honor your own needs and desires equally with those of others. Intend to make your decisions from soul level. Anything less is self-destructive.

Promises, Promises
When Your Best Intentions Fail

Sometimes you say to yourself, "Tomorrow I will clean out the garage." You think you mean it, but deep down inside your really don't want to do that at all—in fact, you are dreading it. What happens? Your strongest emotional energy flow is dread. One part of you thinks you should clean the garage, but your most dominant mental/emotional energy is dread. The result? Delays, interruptions, and sidetracks occur because your deepest desire is to avoid the job. You get your real desire.

Dreading a visit to see your in-laws? Detours, flat tires, traffic delays, whatever it takes to keep you from getting there will occur. Your subconscious mind will fix it so you can't get there. (Remember, when the conscious and subconscious minds are in disagreement, the subconscious always wins.)

The next time you feel frustrated because things just aren't going according to your plans, stop and consider your real motives. Perhaps you have been kidding yourself again. Parts of these sidetracking events are really lessons in honesty. They teach you to be totally truthful with yourself about how you really feel so you can plan accordingly. Be more willing to admit your true, gut feelings about things. When you really dread an upcoming event, admit your reluctance.

Be articulate about what you do or don't want, and with the help of your partner find mutually enjoyable alternatives. Look for ways to vary the old routine or find more pleasant, comfortable ways to do what is needed. If the males in your group want to watch football, get the females together for some female-type fun so both sides are happy. If that fails, honor yourself and just say "no."

Promises: Self

List some of the promises you made to yourself in your journal, such as losing weight, making all A's and so forth. Leave ample space for your decisions beside each one. Make a concerted effort to either cancel these promises right now or make plans to bring each one into completion as soon as possible. Write out your new intentions beside each listed promise. Pronounce it good, pat yourself on the back, and make sure you keep those promises to yourself.

Promises: Others

Follow the same process with promises you made to others. Execute or cancel, but if you decide not to keep a promise be sure to inform the person(s) involved. This is the only way to bring this to completion, balance, and harmony.

Promises: Things-To-Do List

Write down all the jobs on your things-to-do list, including things started but not finished. Then take a good, thoughtful look at each one. Start with those things you really do not want to do and make a definite choice about each one. Mark off those you decide not to do, making a closing statement for each one and ending your mental contracts so they no longer hang over your head.

Look at what is left and put a star by all those you really want to finish. Put a square by each task that is difficult or distasteful. Consider hiring someone to do those jobs. You might be able to trade jobs with someone or hire an ambitious teenager.

From your star list, pick one or two jobs you can do right away and place them on your calendar for this week. Pick another one or two for the following week, being careful not to take on more than you can comfortably handle. Consider hiring someone to do at least one square-marked job per week, and you are off to a great start. Keep your pace comfortable, allowing for the unexpected. Do only as much as you can do in joy. Part of your problem may be in taking on more work than you can handle, which can quickly overwhelm you.

Continue moving in this direction until your list is smaller and more manageable before tackling the larger, more time-consuming projects. Be good to yourself, allowing finished tasks to unfold in a happy, leisurely manner. From time to time, recheck your list and perhaps say no to a few more chores. Consider more tradeoffs. Invite some friends to help you. As you do more decision making and clear out the cobwebs of overload, you should begin feeling much lighter and happier.

Once you understand how you have created your life up to now, you will see that you can change the parts you don't like. Remind yourself that you are a god in the making. Start making deliberate, positive decisions at every opportunity, even if it is only to choose to have a happy, harmonious day in spite of problems.

Realize that your past failures to act in a positive way to life's events were influenced by fears, a sense of inadequacy or low self-esteem. These reactions were based on past experiences that you have judged inferior. These attitudes can be changed.

A good rule is never to judge the present by the past. We grow and learn with every event, and all of our experiences can leave us wiser people. As you begin thinking in new, more positive ways your decisions, actions and lifestyle all change for the better. Since you learn best from your mistakes, make it a practice to re-evaluate your so-called failures and rename them as learning experiences. Feel free to ask questions, take classes, and read about or study subjects in which you desire more training. Do whatever you can to give yourself more self-confidence and make your life happier. Remember that you deserve it.

If you simply must make judgments, try using positive labels such as perfect, wonderful, inspiring, or delightful. When things are a bit difficult, remember to name them as good learning experiences, great challenges, or whatever positive description you like. Stay away from negative statements unless you want negative results.

Things Wanted and Things Not Wanted

Just as anxiety draws the thing you fear the most, hate is a strong emotional energy that attracts the thing hated in a swift and powerful manner. The same principle applies to anything you strongly dislike. The more you mumble, grumble, and complain about your dislikes, the stronger those thought forms become until it seems you cannot get away from their influence. Negative emotions attract negative events consistently. Loving folks always attract loving people and situations and bitter and angry persons attract bitter and angry people and events. It pays to stay in a peaceful, loving state of mind as much as possible.

Whatever you struggle with will produce itself in your life because you give it attention. Stop when you catch yourself finger pointing, berating, and pushing against things. Quickly correct yourself and put your focus on the solutions and happy endings instead. The point here is to watch your "don'ts," "shoulds,"and "nots". This includes anything you do not want to do, be, have, see, or hear.

Success Is a Feeling

Success is a state of mind. It is a positive, inner knowing, self-assured awareness that all is well. It is having complete confidence in your ability to achieve, which is often based on careful preplanning. It is knowing that you create your own world, feeling good about yourself and having faith in the beauty and the rightness of all things.

Failure Is a Fatal Attitude

Failure is a negative frame of mind that does not believe you can achieve what you want in life. It is the feeling of uselessness and victimization, a belief in your unworthiness and ineptitude, a firm conviction that you "can't get there from here" that ultimately leads you to defeat. In this state of mind, struggle becomes a way of life. When you find yourself in this mode, change it quickly. Make some positive intentions about who you are and what you want to do. Focus your creative energy on what you want.

Faith

Everyone has faith. It is a commodity shared by all. The difference is in where you place it. You can have faith in the rightness of things such as "All things work together for good" (Romans 8:28), or you can place your faith in failure, illness, and hardship.

Consider for a moment the biblical comment from Job, "That which I have feared the most, I have brought upon me." He clearly understood that his thinking had created his problem—not God or anyone else. It was his choice to dwell on thoughts of death and disease. Then, by feeding the fearful thoughts with his mental energy he brought disaster to his doorstep. Like Job, you and I have a tendency to create problems unintentionally by our unguarded thoughts. You need to be keenly aware of who you are and how you are directing your mental energies.

Worry Is Negative Goal Setting

Most people seem to think that worry helps to solve a difficult situation. This is not so. A good definition of worry is going around and around a problem without coming to a conclusion. Understand that whatever you focus your creative mind power upon significantly increases. Therefore, to ponder a problem is to magnify it. To dwell on your illness multiplies your poor health. Struggling against poverty creates more poverty; at the same time, it blocks decision making. The reverse is also true. When you think in terms of the good things you have and appreciate them, you also increase your prosperity and other good things without any effort.

We Always Have Choices

Power is nothing if it is not the power to choose.
—Joseph Weisenbaum

Every event in your life offers choices. The instant a new situation arises, you have a selection of options. In that moment, whether you are consciously aware of it or not, you make a choice to accept or reject, to succeed or to fail. Understand that unless you consciously, intentionally, and willfully choose to succeed, you are automatically selecting mediocrity or defeat by default. Any time you neglect to make a deliberate, positive decision, you just naturally fall back into old patterns of thinking. Your subconscious programming takes over and you literally become a victim of your own limited beliefs.[1] Most of your biggest blunders result from a simple lack of clear intentions about what you want to accomplish and visualization of your goal.

Generally, when you are tired or in a bad mood, you tend to make poor decisions. When you are happy and feeling good about yourself, you just naturally make positive selections. For best results, do your planning and decision making when you are happy and feeling good about yourself. If you wait until something unpleasant happens you may react.

Procrastination Is a Self-Defeating Habit

On the surface, procrastination seems to be putting off a decision until later. Actually, it is another way of not deciding. It is waiting for someone else to take responsibility, letting another person do it for you, taking no action at all, or surrendering your power of choice by just letting things drift into oblivion. Often it is a way of saying "no" without actually speaking the word. This kind of indecisiveness frequently stems from old childhood fears of being criticized, of making a wrong choice, or of failing to succeed. Rather than risk failure or ridicule, you make no decision at all. It is easier that way, and you deftly avoid all responsibility. At the same time, it is a practice that steadily robs you of the courage to do things for yourself and lessens your self-esteem. Ultimately, it paves the way to victimhood.

Carefully choosing and taking full responsibility for your selections (or lack of them) is yours and yours alone. Making deliberate, well-thought-out choices is an important part of fulfilling your dreams and creating what you want, rather than settling for what is left after everyone else claims their share. Failing to make a decision is relinquishing your power, abdicating your throne of choice, and allowing the person who is the clearest about their desires to have their way.

As a nation, we have abdicated our throne of authority and allowed politicians to decide things for us. As I see it, our country will continue to feed the rich and greedy at the expense of the working poor until we, as individuals, begin to stand up for our rights. We need to take full responsibility for our nonchalance and start making wiser choices, making our decisions known, demanding more information and accountability. This includes calling or writing our senators and representatives to let our voices be heard clearly and strongly. As a people, we must begin taking back the power we have so foolishly given away.

Procrastination Reality Check

The first step in eliminating a bad habit is to understand the causes behind it. Just what causes you to put things off until later? (Check those which apply.)

- ❏ Fear I cannot do it right.
- ❏ The task is unimportant to me.
- ❏ The task is distasteful.
- ❏ Fear of failure or embarrassment.
- ❏ It is not my job.
- ❏ I don't have enough time.
- ❏ I don't want the responsibility.
- ❏ I am afraid to commit myself.
- ❏ I would much rather do something else.

Not to Decide Is a Decision to Do Nothing

In the late sixties, there was a popular poster saying, "Not to decide is to decide." In other words, if you do not accept an offer, you have already decided against it by default.

Often when important major situations arise, we fail to make any decision at all, preferring to stop and think about it. My mom was a master at this. Whenever she had no ready answer she would say, "I'll think about it," which was her way of dodging the issue by making no decision. It was a grand stall, and always worked when I was young. Now as a grown-up I see many people playing the same game, especially those who were ridiculed or criticized for their mistakes or beliefs as a child.

Whether aware of it or not, most of us either procrastinate, fail to decide, or make our decisions based on old, childish beliefs about ourselves, right or wrong. When you catch yourself procrastinating or when you really can't decide, do yourself a favor and ask why. First, do you have the necessary information? If not, do whatever it takes to make an intelligent decision. If that doesn't solve the problem, ask what is it about the situation that you don't want to face. What memories does this evoke? What fears? Who or what is the real problem? What is stopping you from action? This questioning process is especially helpful if you have no trouble making decisions in other areas. Pin down the one area of difficulty. What makes this one different? Check your feelings and do some writing in your journal to gain clarity. Be totally honest in searching for answers. Once you understand the reasons behind your reluctance, you can solve the problem.

Make Clear Decisions for Tomorrow Today

Since you are always creating your reality, do some deliberate creating for a better life. Before you go to bed at night, make some positive decisions as to how you want the next day to go. Choose to feel good all day long. Choose to work with ease and harmony. Choose to be happy and successful in everything you do. Choose to have a wonderful day. Choose to be a loving person. Choose to live in love, harmony, and joy. Then go to sleep knowing you will have a wonderful day because you created it.

Knowing What Is Right for You

In the moment any new situation, suggestion, or idea comes before you, there is an instant, inner response. (Your soul always knows what is right for you.) Your feelings relay the soul message with a swift, clear signal that comes in the form of a sensation somewhere between your heart area and the pit of your stomach. This gut-level reaction is the voice of your soul (your intuition) communicating to you through your feelings. It may arrive as a bubble of joy, a feeling of delight, a sudden desire to accept; or it may feel like a rock or a heavy stone on your shoulders or in your stomach. Trust the rock. Trust your feelings. This is your own personal built-in guidance system, always at your service — if you choose to listen.

The trick, if you want to call it that, is to learn how to listen and pay attention to that sudden urge or feeling. Your signal comes with the speed of lightning, sometimes as a flash of insight. (Insight is like clairvoyance, a picture seen inside your head, which gives you instant understanding of a situation.) Like lightning, it disappears with great speed, making it necessary to be alert to catch the message in the moment of delivery. Make it your goal to remember the quality of that instant message.

Intellect vs. Intuition

Since your conscious mind has been very carefully trained to doubt any intuitive input, your conscious mind will attempt to negate or override the soul message. It will suggest that you can't possibly know that. How do you know? Where is your proof? Who is your authority in this matter? Your mind will give you many rational reasons for not trusting your insight or your feelings. Just recognize that this is your social training clicking into place, filling you with doubt. This is when you slip back into old programming and fail to trust yourself. Bad move. Very bad move.

However, you have now been warned. You know what to expect both from your intuitive, heart-felt inner knowing, and your socially trained nothing-but-the-facts intellect. From now on, make a strong effort to be aware of the intellect versus intuition battle. You need to recognize it for what it is and to make wise choices. You and you alone can decide which way you will go.

Prayer and the Holy Grail

The universe is a safe and loving place, especially designed to co-create with you and bring you the desires of your heart. As the Bible describes it, "It is the Father's good pleasure to give you the kingdom." Whenever you earnestly talk to God as a partner, stating your specific requirement, your prayer thought form actually takes on the shape of a cup or chalice. A true, heart-felt prayer, made in compliance with the Law of Love, becomes your Holy Grail, waiting to be filled by the universe. As long as your request is a clear, positive statement, you need not worry about how this will come about. You need only to wait in expectancy and gratitude, knowing that your wish will be granted.

Intention

An intention is very similar to a prayer except it is never done from the standpoint of begging or pleading as most prayers are. (Be aware that begging comes from a sense of disempowerment and lack rather than from a stance of positive co-creating with God, therefore going against the Universal Rule of Attraction.) Lack attracts lack. If you ask for something positive while in a state of lack and negativity, your order will be canceled.

The word intend means to make a firm, co-creative decision about what is wanted. It does not hope, wish, beg, plead, or ask a favor but states in positive terms, "This is what I want. I know that I deserve it and I fully expect to have it." This is said from a place of knowing you are a god in the making, deliberately working and co-creating with your Heavenly Father. Your clear intention makes a vital link between you and your desire. It acts as a bridge or highway to where you want to go. Your positive (as opposed to beggarly) prayer or intent, once stated, works as a framework, setting up barriers which repel or restrict all unwanted results. Only that which fulfills the mold designated by the description of your desired gift is allowed entrance.

For instance, let us say that you intend to have apples that are no less than three inches in diameter. Apples will flow to you on the universe conveyer belt. Your specification of size will act as a kind of framework or screen which allows all apples less than three inches to drop out while your preferred size comes right to your door. However, you may receive a variety of brands and colors unless you were explicit enough to ask for red apples. Then only red ones would come to you. Had you selected Red Winesap, then only that type, color, and size would come to you. Clarity is important.

The Only Way to Have Happiness Is to Choose It

Some of you may remember the old Sears and Roebuck Catalog that came in the mail, affectionately called the "Wish Book." Inside its glossy pages were many wonderful things to buy and you always had the choice of good, better, or best. Of course, the best would cost a bit more and we were tempted to choose the lesser so we could have more. It was a difficult choice, for times were hard and money was scarce.

Those days are gone now, but many people are still in the habit of choosing less than the best for themselves because of their childhood programming. Are you one of them? Many of those who came along later still had the spillover of poverty thinking from grandparents and other family members. Think about it. If there is any doubt, just make a new intention to always choose the best. Then add a statement like, "Because I am worth it!"

Aim for the very best you can be in all your choices because nothing heals low self-esteem better than the knowledge that you have done the very best you can.

Decisions, Decisions

In every event life puts before you, choose success. If it is a family outing, deliberately make a decision to have a pleasant one. Intend that all will go smoothly and joyfully instead of worrying about something spoiling it all. Remember that you are in charge every moment of the day. You are the writer of your life's script, the set designer, the director, the star, and the audience. Deliberately create a happy event. Make your choices at every turn of the road, intentionally stating what you want with clarity, knowing that you and you alone are responsible for what you produce. Generate more joy and laughter. Plan to have more fun. Choose to enjoy life. Intend to live with a full measure of health, wealth, and happiness. You will find it is much easier to construct pleasure than pain.

When you go shopping for some special item, determine exactly what you want ahead of time. If you choose to drive, start by mentally creating your perfect parking place. Firmly intend (not wish or hope) that you will be led to the right place to find your desired item at a very satisfactory price. You might also determine to shop in comfort and joy. Lighten up. Plan to be happy. Make your life fun. Then make it even better.

My Motto:

To walk in peace and harmony
And be the best that I can be.

10

Goal Setting

The greatest thing in the world is not so much where we stand as in what direction we are moving.
—Oliver Wendell Holmes

Each day you create every aspect of your life by the thoughts you think, the beliefs you hold, the words you speak, and the goals you set. Without clear goals, you can easily drift into mediocrity and dullness.

Most people do not actively set clear goals for themselves; instead they tend to drift somewhat aimlessly through their day. Being directionless, they are often jostled about by other people's goals. They react to the words and actions of others in a defensive and/or aggressive manner with varying degrees of pain and anger. This overly protective, reactionary behavior keeps them in an agitated, warlike state. This kind of stance attracts even more irritating and upsetting people and events. In turn, this leads to more and more militant behavior. The result is a downward spiral, which only becomes worse with the passing years.

Having well-thought-out intentions can easily prevent all of this aggravation. It is absolutely necessary for you to have clear, well-considered goals if you are to take control of your life and affairs. You will no longer react to other people's upsets and misplaced anger. It takes time, effort, and careful thought to delineate your ideals and purposes. But once written down, they stand as golden guidelines for where you want to go and what you want to achieve in your life.

Once you have clearly defined your goals and have them held in mind, good decisions spring forth naturally and easily. You will have created a well-marked path, a super highway with clear directions to guide you. Then with all doubts, sidetracks, and other obstacles removed, your way is clear. Your choices conform easily to the plans already set. Many small distracting matters find no place in your new, well-ordered world. Your specific intentions have set restraining parameters that automatically filter out unsuitable options and ideas.

Never Judge the Present by the Past

Making choices and decisions is a major part of the ongoing process of living. Each day brings hundreds, possibly thousands, of decisions to make until you reach the point when you no longer notice them. They have become habits. Seldom do you question or even consider changing the old routines. They have become too comfortable, and the mind enjoys the familiar.

It is just too easy to base present decisions on past performances. In areas where you have excelled, you are eager to try again. However, in the arena in which you have once erred, you assume that another failure is inevitable; therefore, you refuse any further challenges for growth in that field. Old memories about past failures color your belief system. There is a tendency to judge your present capabilities by past records, even when the original failure may have happened years ago. Generally, you won't even give yourself a chance to try again. Nor do you set new and more exciting goals. To keep from getting entangled in these old traps of limitation, question the motives behind your delays and refusals. Ask yourself, "Are they valid in terms of who and what I am today?" If not, rethink, reevaluate, and allow yourself to grow beyond your old limits.

To move forward you must let go of the past and drop old pain and prejudices — or let them return again and again. You can live in anger, jealousy, and hate or learn to live in love.

A good point to remember is that you cannot want something without having the potential of having it. So, get off of what "is" and mentally move forward to what you want. Start envisioning a brighter, happier life. Once you have clearly stated your desire, trust that the universe will bring you the opportunities and circumstances you need to fulfill your dream.

Planning for Success

In setting goals for your life, be aware that whenever there are problems, confrontations, or decisions, the person with the clearest intentions will "sway the day." Knowing this, you need to understand the importance of planning to take better control of your life. You need to make positive, deliberate decisions based on knowing what you want and having absolute confidence that you deserve to have it. (To doubt your worthiness is to sabotage your thinking and cancel your chances of success.)

The best way to be successful is to plan for it. As the old saying goes, "Plan your work and work your plan." Good planning and clear goals play an extremely important part in keeping you feeling empowered and in charge. The more you actively utilize your ability to choose what you want and to be clear about your desires, the more you will find things going your way. Your small conquests will lead to greater ones. Then as you begin to feel triumphant, you will become even more victorious. Success breeds more success. Start now to make plans for a great accomplishments and victories every day, year after year.

Goals Give Your Life Direction

Goals are thoughts and beliefs you hold in mind. These goals become the framework from which you create, consciously or mindlessly. Many people dwell most on what they believe they cannot have, often putting out angry, jealous thoughts toward those who seem rich, talented, and successful. As you have learned, this simply draws more lack and misfortune.

Without a positive goal or ideal, nothing much happens. Things just drift along, never getting anywhere. There must be a motivating thought or intention to produce a specific result. This becomes the framework for attracting the right people, opportunities, insights, guiding dreams, and synchronicities to help you on your chosen journey. Without a definite choice and commitment you have no direction and no help from your guiding angels. You work alone and unaided.

Remember that God is the power source activated by your thought. Together you bring things into manifestation according to your specific desires. For this reason, it is wise to take all matters of choice to God first. God is love and the Law of the Universe is love. It is wisest to work within the framework of love and goodwill. Then let your desires come forth in love and joy.

Guidelines for Goal Setting

For the basic framework, begin setting your goals by choosing a high ideal for your soul. This sets the framework for your whole life. All other ideals and goals follow that.

Example:

- **Soul Ideal:** Live a life of unconditional love. Attain the level of Christ Consciousness. Become the best teacher, writer, or artist I can be.
- **Mental Ideal:** Earn my Master's Degree. Read the Bible every day. Speak kindly to everyone I meet.

- **Physical Ideal:** Exercise daily. Watch my food intake; eat more fresh fruits and vegetables. Practice gentle-loving kindness in all relationships.

General high ideals set in place will help you make the best selections.

True and False Goals

Almost everyone is familiar with the story of Aladdin and his magic lamp. Just for a moment, pretend you have just found such a lamp and your genie has asked the magic question, "What do you want?" What would be your reply? Riches? Success? Health? Fame? Beauty? Most people look at these as prized goals, when actually, they are not really goals at all, nor are they clear.

Non-specific	Specific
Riches	I wish to have $250,000 in liquid assets and an annual income of $100,000.
Success	I wish to have a job that I love, which utilizes my talents and skills. I wish for everyone to respect and admire me for my hard work, dedication, and integrity.
Health	I wish to feel fantastic every morning when I wake up. I wish my body to be radiant, slim, and fit.

Actually, success and riches are only the by-products of our true, soul goals. Since each of us was created in the image and likeness of God, we all have a basic, indwelling desire to uplift humanity and to add to its betterment in some way. Part of our soul purpose is to make the world a better place than we found it, to add something to enrich it, and to give our special gift to the world. Usually this is done using our own unique talents such as music, art, drama, discoveries and inventions, inspiring leadership, and so forth. We all have some kind of gift to give. Unfortunately, this desire for good can be overridden by selfishly aimed willpower or by a strong desire for different, more earth-oriented goals. We all have the free will to use our talents constructively or destructively. The choice is always in our hands.

The most important thing we can do each day is to be happy. When we are joyful we radiate that cheer to all those around us, lifting everyone's spirits. Moreover, since our thoughts are creative we are creating delightful events for our future.

Our soul's purpose is directed toward expressing our own special, individual talents and abilities in a positive and creative manner. Should we each choose to listen to our hearts and do what we truly love to do (rather than surrendering our dreams for "security" and/or a paycheck) we are choosing a lifestyle of soul satisfaction. Making our decisions from soul level rather than from selfish motives gives us a wonderful sense of upliftment, fulfillment, success, and joy. These in turn create the happy state of mind that automatically attracts success, power, riches, health, and beauty into our lives.

Now, with this deeper understanding of goals, you are in a better position to determine your goals with wisdom and understanding.

Your Life Purpose

In our every deliberation, we must consider the impact of our decisions on the next seven generations.
—The Iroquois Nation[1]

When selecting the overall goals for your life, you are paving the way to a specific, well-thought-out lifestyle. Your aims are clear, setting directions and boundaries that provide a well-marked path to guide you in all the minor choices you make each day. These goals keep you on target by providing clarity about what is desired, as well as setting priorities for which things are most important.

Key Question:

- If you could do, be, or have anything you want, what would it be?
- What would you like most to accomplish?
- What are your plans/goals for accomplishing this?

It is best to motivate yourself by what you want, not by what other people think nor by what you have done or where you have been in the past. What you are becoming is far more important than what has been. Since all of your power to choose or do is in the present moment, give this all-important selection some serious thought. John Powell, in his book *Unconditional Love*, calls this a "life principle," a theme around which everything else revolves. It then becomes a reference point against which you test every decision before you adopt it as your goal.

Spend some quiet time in prayer and meditation. Intend to feel into the deepest levels of your being to know what it is that you have always wanted to do since you were very young. With great sensitivity, sort out the desires of your heart from the ideas and standards that society has imposed upon you. Carefully separate the false from the real. Do not allow matters of money or education to deter you from deciding what you really want to do. Remember that you want to follow your heart, find your bliss, and discover what you want most, then decide to do what makes you happiest. This is following your intuition.

When you think you have come to a decision, check your intuition. Make sure this feels good and joyful. (You may have to rethink this several times before getting it just right.) If it doesn't bring joy to your heart and fill you with enthusiasm, it is not right for you. Make up your mind never to settle for second best. Remember you are creating your "own little world" and everything in it. What kind of world do you want to live in? Plan carefully, for this is your life.

Once you are clear and sure, it would be good to write this purpose on the first page of your journal where it will serve as a constant reminder. In addition, you might make a copy on an index card to carry around with you. In this way, you are making both a decision and a commitment.

With your overall life goals set, you can fill in the rest of your life's framework based on your chosen purpose.

Laying Out the Guidelines

- **Twenty-Year Goals:** Long range goals are important. Look ahead to the next twenty years of your life and start planning what you would like to accomplish.
- **Ten-Year Goals:** Looking ten years in advance, write your future plans for that time frame.
- **Five-Year Goals:** Follow the same formula for five-year goals. You may want to keep these plans for your future in your journal to look over and update occasionally.

Now that your long-term goals are clear, ask yourself the all-important questions, "Do my chosen goals excite me? Am I enthusiastic about what they accomplish?" If not, maybe you chose less than the best for yourself. Stop and reconsider any questionable goals.

Setting Goals for the Year

- **Yearly Goals:** Write out what you expect to accomplish by the end of this year. (You may want to do this in your journal where it will be handy for referrals.) You may want to have one major goal plus several less important ones. You could make out an index card for each category, but put your main efforts, your full, creative mental powers on one intention at a time for a period of seven days. This gets it well launched and empowered. After that, continue to feed your main intention while proceeding to launch your next big goal.

    It is important to include ideas of spiritual growth, success, and peace in your goals. Don't forget those positive qualities you would like to develop within yourself, and, of course, happiness on a daily basis. Write these in your journal as well as on index cards that you can carry about with you.
- **Monthly Goals:** These can include bits and pieces of your yearly intentions divided into smaller increments plus some seasonal things such as vacation plans or current career goals. You may even want to write the most important of these on your personal calendar where you can see them every day.
- **Weekly Goals:** This can include parts of your monthly goals plus odds and ends from your ongoing things-to-do list. Remember that you want to include goals of success, harmony, joy, and general ideals of positive self-talk.

Setting Your Daily Goals: The Things-To-Do List

We all have our daily list of chores we need to do. These are usually small yet very important because they have the power to give us a real sense of satisfaction and achievement at the end of the day. As such, they contribute to our happiness and self-confidence.

As you begin to make your list, first ask yourself, "How does this fit in overall with my life goals?" If it doesn't correlate well, either eliminate or rearrange it to make it fit. Be sure to include time for fun and recreation every week, preferably every day. It is highly important to your feeling of self-worth and well-being. Remember that a happy person and a joyful stance are necessary ingredients for manifesting your desires.

You will find your greatest results when you make your plans at least one day in advance. Three days is better, especially for beginners. (The further ahead, the better. Your time range will shorten with practice.)

Mystical Magical You

Begin with a piece of paper wide enough for three columns. Place your chore list on the left, your intentions for each in the middle, and a space to record the results at the right.

As you write out your list of duties, pause a moment to think about what you want to happen. Decide how you would like this to manifest such as, "with good for all concerned," or "in peace and harmony." You can include being inspired with great ideas, having all the help and cooperation you need, and enjoying pleasant relations with all those you encounter. Beside each chore write your intent such as, easily, lovingly, and joyfully. As you do this, mentally send these positive thoughts out ahead of you, like little fairies winging their way to smooth your path. Remember that thoughts are things.

To further enhance your decisions and impress them into your subconscious mind, use index cards to write out your goals and intentions. Since these goal cards are small enough to fit into pockets, purses, wallets, or desk drawers, they will be handy to take out and review frequently. (Three times a day is a good rule; four would be even better.) This practice is extremely helpful for imprinting your newest goals, plans, intents, and ideals firmly in your conscious and subconscious levels of mind. Since your subconscious mind is always working to prove you right, give it a chance to work for you.

Add pictures, sketches, or symbols of your goal to help you visualize.

Color code your cards for different categories such as health, career, and so forth. Always allow a reasonable length of time for results. Too little time can create a built-in failure.

If you have the privacy or freedom you might place some of these cards or little reminder notes in areas where you will see them often, like your bathroom mirror or your dashboard. Self-stick notes would also be quick, handy, and easy to use. You could also pin notes or cards on bathroom or kitchen curtains or in other conspicuous places to remind you of your latest projects. You might even choose to sketch or cut out pictures of things you desire and place them in strategic places. Make a poster out of pictures or sketches of the things you want most. If privacy is difficult, try devising a catchy logo or a slogan to represent your idea or buy a small toy replica of the new car (or whatever) you want.

→ Goal Setting

Index Cards for Goals
(Suggested Outline for Cards, Goal Book, or Journal)

Date	May 3	**Category** Health	**Target Date** 6/15
Goal	I intend to take off 15 lbs. by June 15th.		
Intention	Accomplishing this with ease and joy.		
Steps	I will exercise 30 minutes per day, 5 days a week.		
	No fried foods at all. Lots of water. No soft drinks.		
	Light dessert once a week only. Plenty of fruits and salads.		
Motto	Every day, in every way, I'm getting better and better.		
See & Feel	Very successful. Pronounce it good 3 times a day.		

Additional Empowerment: Pick a special day, such as a new moon, to plant the seed thoughts to give your intentions extra energy. Say a prayer, do a ritual, burn incense, light a candle, or whatever works for you to make it a special occasion that will further impress your subconscious mind.

Personally, I like to make my intentions into little poems because they are easier to remember that way. In addition, when I am feeling extra frisky, I can sing them while I am working or driving my car. Sometimes, when starting a brand new goal or habit, I like to put on something special like a ring, necklace, or dangling bracelet to remind me of my new intention until it becomes routine.

The Importance of Preparing the Way

The following exercise, done several days in advance, gives your newly created thought forms time to gather force and direction, as well as the opportunity to attract the right people and circumstance to fulfill your desires. It also builds the bridges to where you want to go and what you want to achieve.

Make it a habit to go over your list several days ahead and especially on the night before your intents are to be accomplished. See your goals being worked out as you have previously pictured them. Feel yourself happy and overflowing with joy and a sense of goodwill in the outcome. You might even imagine yourself thanking your coworkers for their cooperation and having everyone involved looking happy and feeling good. Always program for a win-win situation. (You can't get much better than that.)

Then when the time comes to act, everything will fall easily into place because you have thoughtfully prepared the way in advance. Be sure to congratulate yourself for your every triumph. Remember each success breeds more success.

Get It All on One Page

You will need to get your major and minor goals plus daily chores together in one place. One possibility is a large calendar for goals and appointments plus a journal or goal book to record your progress each day.

A large desk calendar, 18 × 22 inches, gives you plenty of room to fill in details and provides an overall view. If this isn't feasible, get a poster, blackboard, bulletin board, appointment book, or whatever works best for you and place, draw, or paste a calendar page in the middle. Use your goal cards, "sticky reminders," and whatever you need as backups to reinforce your intentions.

- **Life Goal or Yearly Goal:** Using a colored marker, write your life goal or yearly goal at the top of your calendar in large letters so you can see it plainly.
- **Major (Monthly) Goal:** Starting with a new week or new moon, mark off a twenty-one day section for your major monthly goal in color. Write or print your goal clearly at the top of this section and include how you want to see it manifest.
- **Minor (Weekly) Goals:** In a different color, add a minor goal, along with your specific desires for how this will be accomplished. Repeat in a different colors for each minor or weekly goal. Place a star next to the most important things to be accomplished for the week.
- **Add Appointments, Classes, Birthdays, Etc.**
- **Add Daily Goals (Things To Do):** Decide which projects from your things-to-do list are most important. Once priorities are set, begin adding some of these into your goal book on appropriate days.
- **Happy Ending Goals and Affirmations:** For each goal or chore, always decide how you want things to go and make some positive

statements for peaceful, harmonious conclusions with cooperation and joy. See all things working out smoothly, efficiently and successfully with everyone feeling good. Write a descriptive word or phrase beside each to remind you of your specific intentions for each one.
- **Add Some Fun Time:** Plan at least one happy event for each week.

Beware of overcrowding your calendar. Add only what you can handle with ease, allowing some free time for unexpected events. Also, leave some spare time for rest and relaxation. Remember this is important, too. Give yourself plenty of time to accomplish your goals without feeling pressured.

Keep working faithfully with your goal cards. They are an excellent tool for taking your power back and getting your life under control.

Set aside some quiet time each day to look over your upcoming goals and intentions for the coming week. Picture everything accomplished in perfection, joy, and harmony plus whatever other qualities you would like to add. Prepare for the next day by rereading your plan. See it working perfectly, going smoothly. Picture clearly your tasks completed and your day peaceful, happy, and fulfilling. See yourself in a pink glow of love, joy, and harmony. Then each day restate your goal and do the action for that day. Act in joy and confidence that all is well in your world.

All this may seem tedious, but remember, all things are created mentally first. They become physical later. Your mental preparations will smooth your life so much that you will get more done than ever before. Things will literally flow into place. It is truly time well spent. And, in the process, you are changing your whole lifestyle for the better.

A Goal Book

Some experts recommend keeping a goal book. Divide a composition book into sections, one for each category of goals. It is recommended that you update your goals frequently, reflecting your personal changes and your growth. Work frequently in revising your personal goals. This is a joint activity between your outer self and your inner self, and you will receive inspiration to direct your life and goals from the powerful, internal source.

First, write your goals for the different categories. Secondly, visualize yourself having accomplished each one of the goals, in turn. Third, plan the actions for the day or week and decide what will be done and in what order of priority. At the end of the day or week, evaluate your performance and take corrective action, if necessary."[2]

Mystical Magical You ⌣·

To further the process of seeing your goal, you could follow up with visualization sessions such as the following one. (If you don't like this one, make up one that suits you better.)

Exercise:
Find a quiet, comfortable place, close your eyes, and relax. Take three or four deep breaths, inhaling deeply, then letting go of all stress and tension as you exhale. Do this at least three times, more if necessary to feel deeply relaxed.

Making Changes

Whatever you can do, or dream you can, begin it —
Boldness has genius, power and magic in it.
  —Goethe

To change something you no longer desire, first admit you created it, consciously or unconsciously. Know that if you can create it, you can also change or rearrange it to something more to your liking. Then declare, "I now intend to consciously create something better."

- State firmly, This is what I want. _____.
- This is what I would like to see happen. _____.
- List the steps or changes for your new scenario in detail.

Keep the steps clear and obtainable, starting now.

Limit your changes to only one area of your life at a time. Avoid the temptation to change your whole life in one session as this will most likely result in failure. Always set yourself up to succeed.

Back yourself up with some positive statements such as:

"I now choose to make my life light, easy, and joyful."

"I am now choosing a new and improved lifestyle."

"I am now moving in a new and wonderful direction."

Some Helpful Hints

Not everyone likes to work in the same way. If you are a very visual person, you may prefer to work with pictures. Once your ideal is chosen you can look for a picture that would be appropriate for your goal. If this fails, take a photo, find a symbol, draw a sketch, make a clay model or buy a toy to represent your goal. Then put this in a place where you can see it often. Or, you may choose to work with a goal book as described in the next section.

Let No One Rain on Your Parade

A little word of warning: make sure you keep your cards and signs out of reach and out of sight of those who may ridicule your dreams and goals. Allow no one to rain on your parade. You don't need disparaging jokes, discouraging remarks, or people who try to tell you this can't be done, because it can.

Plan Your Work and Work Your Plan

Bear in mind that it is more effective to choose only one new ideal and give it your full, undivided attention for at least seven days. This gets you off to a good, solid start and prevents you from becoming discouraged or overwhelmed, which could defeat your purpose. Choose only what you can comfortably remember and carry out. (You don't need any more unfinished business hanging over your head.) Besides, you can always add more later.

Meanwhile, be aware that you are constantly making choices. You can choose to live in love and joy. You can add prosperity or anything you want as long as you believe that you can have it.

If you feel uncomfortable with any decision, that is a sign that you are stretching too far too fast. Keep it comfortable and feeling good.

You can choose to live drifting aimlessly along, which keeps you learning slowly and painfully through trial and error. On the other hand, you can make a decision to live, learn, and grow the easy way, through the wise use of your mind power that brings you into a happier lifestyle. It is your choice.

You may want to resolve that from now on, you will be more aware of the kinds of decisions you make (or avoid) every day. Keep reminding yourself that you are the one and only creator of every event in your life. (God created you, but you alone create your world.) If you don't like what you now have, you can change it. Your fate is entirely in your hands.

Think of what you want as just another page in your daily living rather than a big deal. Don't make it difficult to get. Know that you easily draw your desires to you once you stop negating yourself. Focus with clarity. Say it and know it.

Start creating a joyous life for yourself right now. Bless each new day. Make it happy. See it as a brand new learning and growing adventure filled with love, laughter and wonder, just for you.

I create my reality in love, light and joy.
I choose to live happily ever after.
I love to live and live to love.
I abide in love and harmony.
I walk in beauty.
I live in joy.

11

Creating Your Heart's Desires

A wise man makes more opportunities than he finds.
— Francis Bacon

Back in the days when I taught an adult Sunday School class I had a student called Nell. She came stamping into the classroom complaining about an illegally parked car that was blocking her view at what she called a dangerous intersection. The next week she again complained bitterly about the same offensive car, saying, "He should get a ticket for that." This scene was repeated every Sunday for about five weeks until once again, she came marching in, angrily saying "That guy is still parked illegally. He still hasn't gotten a ticket, but I have."

Nell was a highly intelligent woman, but she had difficulty understanding how her wanting "that guy to get a ticket" had caused her to get one. How did it happen? She spoke long, loud and repeatedly with a good amount of anger as she focused on him getting a ticket. All the creative ingredients were there. She just didn't understand the process.

- Energy follows thought (and expands it)
- Thoughts are things
- What you think is what you get

Creating is easy. Nell wanted someone to get a ticket, but her driving emotional power was anger and her attitude vengeful. Remember that thoughts sent out look for a matching vibration. When a loving person receives a hateful thought it is automatically returned to the sender like a boomerang.

As gods in the making, our minds are constantly creating something in every moment of our waking lives, regardless of whether or not we understand it or believe it. The problem is that these creations are not necessarily conscious, well-planned ideas and decisions. Often they are more like thoughtless reactions with negative attitudes. We often allow our thoughts to run rampant like an automobile without a driver going downhill. The results of our minds wandering in an undisciplined manner are not always pleasant, yet they are in exact accordance with the tenor of our thoughts, words, attitudes, and emotions.

Obviously, our ability to create is excellent, but the quality of our production is in dire need of repair. In a single day we make a multitude of positive and negative statements about ourselves. Only a good computer, such as the subconscious mind, could keep an accurate score. This kind of unpredictable, ping-pong ball type of thinking can only bring a hodge-podge of results. What we need is some quality control.

Timing

Whatever you are experiencing in your life right now is what you have been attracting by your thoughts and emotions of the last few days or weeks. (Timing for Nell was about five to six weeks.) Your thoughts and attitudes of today are now building your future events. For some it is a matter of only two or three days. Others can manifest results almost instantly. Timing varies according to your spiritual development and understanding.

Since your world is formed by the sum total of your daily thinking, your first task is to find a way to channel your thoughts and words into carefully preselected directions. This will assure that your manifestations will be only that which you have chosen. Undeniably, the only way to effect this is to change the way you think on a day-to-day basis. This may prove difficult since the average person's mind-chatter is almost incessant and often completely undisciplined. Very few people are aware of the overall tone of their self-talk. Most have no idea how consistently they influence their circumstances for the worst by their fears and negative statements about themselves. The task of changing your old mental habits is formidable, but not impossible.

Let's think of this in terms of a plot of ground. Before you plant the seeds of the desires of your heart, the soil must be prepared. You need to clear out the rocks of old belief systems, the stumps of erroneous teachings, the rusty fences of old, limiting habits, and the clutter of negative thoughts. You must remove the weeds of self-doubt.

Just as a scientist creates the proper conditions in his laboratory to grow a particular culture, you need to prepare the right mental conditions to bring about a specific creative result.

Your Basic Stance

A stance is a position you take, a place in consciousness where you stand, a frame of mind, an attitude, and a way of seeing and feeling that colors everything in your mental world. It is the sum total of your goals, beliefs, and intentions. Reduced to its basic essence, it is the way your life field vibrates on a daily basis. Your personal vibratory rate is subject to change from moment to moment, according to your fluctuating thoughts and emotions. Once these emotions pass, you return to your basic vibratory rate that is based on the predominate tenor of your overall thinking and feeling. Everything entering your personal world comes to you by your use of thought and the universe's ability to give you what you desire.

- **Negative Stance:** Nearly everyone has had the experience of knowing someone like Nell, who just loves to complain. These people are great masters at grumbling, fault-finding, and blaming others for all their troubles. They do not seem to understand that their habit of criticizing and focusing their mental energies on what they dislike most is attracting the very things they do not want. With this attitude of aggravation, their basic stance is that of anger and resentment. People who think mostly in terms of struggle and problems can never seem to overcome their own self imposed limitations. Because of this, their creative thoughts will always bring negative results.

  Anything created from a stance of frustration, fear, poverty, self-pity, and similar negative vibrations will return in a like mode. The beautiful new car ordered in a state of deficient vibes may look good but turn out to be a lemon. The negative waves on which your desire is sent will return in some negative form. The Law of Attraction is always at work.

- **Positive Stance:** When you are happy and feeling good about yourself, your loving and joyful state of mind naturally produces positive, harmonious vibrations. This is exactly what you need to be radiating when you make your creative statements. Holding a joyful frame of mind is a basic requirement for achieving the best results from your creative endeavors.

Then, as you make your creative statement or request, your positive (rather than negative) vibrations permanently imprint your thought form with that special quality of energy you were radiating at the time. You can see the importance of placing yourself in the most peaceful, loving state of mind possible before planting your seed thought.

By the way, did you know that ancient farmers always sang when they planted their seeds? They knew the secret of pleasant, joyful vibrations and their positive effect on growing things — and songs are vibes.

Changing Your Thoughts

Wallowing in old hurts, unhappy memories, and self-pity causes negative mental states. Riding along with these thoughts is an attitude of judgment and helplessness. These unhealthy thought patterns attract even more negativity into your life. All of these are creations of mind — your mind. Only you can change it.

As you come to realize that you can and do create your reality according to the focus of your thoughts, you will also know this:

- The more you think, talk, complain, and relive your traumas and tragedies, the faster you create more of them.
- The more you struggle against loneliness, illness, poverty, and so forth, the more of these you draw to you by your attention to them.
- The clearer your intentions, the more easily they manifest, especially when you are standing in a place of love, peace, and joy.
- Goodwill and positive, joyful emotions add speed and power to your creations.

The Man with the Hose

It is known that the steady drip of water can wear away a stone. It is true that a steady stream of water can eventually carve a Grand Canyon. This is also true of your steady stream of thought creating a path to where you want to be, provided it is aimed in the right direction. It all starts with a simple statement of what you want. Each time it is repeated, the path becomes deeper and clearer. In time, it becomes an automatic flow to your stated desire.

You may want to begin by acknowledging that your mind-chatter is a powerful, unceasing flow of vital energy that is creating for you in exact accordance with your mental focus. You could picture this as a garden hose equipped with a fantastic fertilizer that promotes good, healthy growth wherever it falls. You, as the gardener, hold the hose. You can aim this life-giving liquid along a path of fear, poverty, and defeat, or you may just as easily direct it toward love, joy, and laughter. You are the director of the flow that feeds and multiplies the crop.

Don't even consider trying to fix what is wrong, for that is feeding the error. Selectively direct your energy only toward that which you want. Your attention should be one of awareness as to where you are pouring your creative mental energies. Remember, dear one, you are always a co-creator.

By the way, your dreams often will show you how your energy is flowing regarding the subject matter of the dream. Additionally, your dreams will give you vivid pictures showing your progress in manifesting your desired ideal.

Choosing Your Creative Goals with Care

Once your intentions, ideals, and goals are set via your willpower, they act as guideposts and guardrails. They will keep you on track even when you are engrossed by life's demanding experiences and have no conscious recall of your intentions. (They work for you unconsciously.)

Most people will speak at great length about what they do not want and yet be quite inarticulate in stating what they do want. What is your greatest ambition? Do you know exactly what you want? Is your goal clear? Take a few moments to think about it, and write down your greatest desires. Choose only those that will make you feel happy.

Health, Wealth, and Loving Relationships

Chances are you have chosen at least one of the above. If so, it is back to the drawing board of building an appropriate mental field or state of consciousness to contain this new way of thinking. (Remember you must have a matching vibration for what you want.)

In the Laws of Creation you learned this is a thought-created universe. Any longstanding problem you now face was either mentally constructed and accepted in this life or was brought over from a past one—not for punishment, but for healing. The longer you have had the problem the more deeply imbedded it is in the mind. Such deep-set mental conditions are often difficult to dislodge. Like an old building, no longer sound or useful, the old mind-set must first be cleared away before a new and better one can be built.

For example, let's take Mr. Poverty Pockets and throw him in the prison of limited beliefs. Do you think a few positive affirmations can undo twenty years of poverty thinking? Of course not. Even five to ten years of living an old mind-set can cause trouble.

To change this you must consciously and deliberately plan and build a new habit of thinking, a new state of consciousness that will match your new desire. It is the Like Attracts Like Law. The length of time needed depends on the amount of resistance held in the old habit patterns, the strength of your desire to change, and the amount of willpower you exert. Some people can let go of old "stuff" more easily than others do.

Moving from Where You Are to Where You Want to Be

Knowing that what you think is what you get, choose to dwell on happy things and stay out of the swamp land of misery. You cannot create happy circumstances from a grumpy state of mind. Universal Law simply will not allow it!

Remember the adage "No one can upset you unless you let them." So determine not to allow it. Realize that the company you keep and the thoughts you think are also choices you make for yourself. You can choose to think loving thoughts, choose to be happy, choose to be around positive thinking people. Choose to walk in harmony and beauty and your dreams will be fulfilled.

Going from How Bad It Was to How Sweet It Is
(Laying the Overall Foundation)

Happy people just naturally create happiness and pleasant events without even trying. Groaners and complainers automatically repel their desires and create problems by their ongoing attitudes. What you really need is to change your attitude from negative to positive. Nothing but good can come to you when you have a positive frame of mind.

To set the right foundation for receiving, begin monitoring your thoughts, your self-talk, the movies you watch, the things you read, and the kind of people you choose to have around you. Avoid complainers and doomsdayers. Stay away from negativity as much as possible. Instead, surround yourself with happy, positive-thinking people because you become a part of all you see and hear. In addition, other people's negativity can drain your energy and dampen your spirits. In other words, you cannot dance in a mud puddle of negativity without getting muddy.

To lay the groundwork for receiving what you want, give yourself plenty of positive feedback and learn to quickly acknowledge all the good things you do. Focus on beauty and happy things. Find more things to appreciate and your whole life becomes more pleasant. Your vibrational rate rises, putting you in the best possible mode to attract the finest people, conditions, and events into your life. When you are happy, you automatically attract more of the good things in life. Then the things you want fall right into your waiting hands.

Building a New Consciousness
(For a specific problem)

To reprogram your old mind-set you will need to create a whole new scenario to implant in your subconscious mind, then practice it faithfully until the new one is stronger than the old. This works best when you use all of your senses.

Health

Touch parts of your body that have been giving you trouble. Find yourself free of pain and disease or bruised, broken skin. Love yourself and touch your body with love. Send love and healing deep into the troubled area.

See yourself in vibrant good health. Spend as much time as possible participating happily in your favorite sport or activities. See yourself in the appropriate clothing and the perfect spot with ideal weather conditions enjoying moving about freely and easily. Picture yourself at your ideal weight, healthy, happy, and carefree.

Feel your body responding quickly to your needs. Bask in the sense of joy and freedom. Reach back to a time when your health was perfect. Relive that perfection, feel how good it was, and know it will be again.

Smell the flowers and other pleasant scents in the area. Inhale the fragrance with joy.

Hear happy sounds that accompany your activities. Hear people talking, laughing, and playing. Hear sounds of music and joyfulness.

Taste the cool drinks, the snacks, or special foods that go with these activities.

Add emotions, especially happy ones. Make your scenario fun-filled, happy, and appreciative. Keep it light and joyous.

You have the power to bless or to curse, so bless. Finding fault with your body and condemning your condition only makes it worse. Learn a new habit. Bless your body, send it love, care for it lovingly, and give thanks for every little improvement. Bless and encourage your body to be whole and healthy. Love yourself, all of yourself. As the saying goes, "Your body hears every word you say."

Spend a good fifteen or twenty minutes creating your ideal scene. Keep improving and updating this daily until you can totally feel this happening in, through, and around you. Joyfully practice this exercise in every spare moment until it literally becomes a part of you. Practice using all your senses to the fullest.

Fortify with Pictures

Help build a better picture of you, both physically and mentally. Use pictures from magazines, stick figure sketches, and photographs to build the new you. Collect appropriate pictures and place them on a poster, in a frame, on your desk, or anywhere you will see them often. Let them remind you of your creative project and reinforce your visualizations. Look at them often. This is especially helpful for people who are visual.

Positive Backup Statements

Back up your intentions with supportive Bible quotes such as

- "Ask and ye shall receive." (Matthew 7:7)
- "It is the Father's good pleasure to give you the kingdom." (Luke 12:32)
- "Thou shalt decree a thing and it shall be done unto you."(Job 22:28)
- "Speak the word only and it shall be done unto you according to your belief." (Matthew 8: 5–13)
- "The Lord is my shepherd, I shall not want" (for any good thing). (Psalm 23)

Add some of your own positive affirmations and statements about looking good, feeling good, and being healthy, wealthy, and happy. Make a few goal cards with affirmative declarations about the new healthy attitude now being mirrored in your life. Louise Hay has several books with ideas for changing your self-image, plus many positive declarations and affirmations for good health and well-being. Unity Church has an incredible number of affirmations, books, and tapes on this subject. Those people who learn best by hearing can make audiotapes of affirmations to go along with goals, intents, and decrees.

Self-Empowerment
Use every tool at your disposal, including avoidance of all your nay-saying friends and relatives. Surrounding yourself with supportive people is a very important ingredient when making major changes in your life. When these practices can be felt physically, mentally, and emotionally, you are then ready to move on with the creation steps that follow.

- **Prosperity:** Remember Mr. Poverty Pockets and his poverty consciousness. His whole mental world is saturated with lack, and from this standpoint of "not having" no mere words can change that vibration enough to receive abundance. Using the formula outlined above, create your own prosperity version using the touching, seeing, feeling, and so on. Add spending, with your prosperity in mind.

  Finally, follow up with practicing your new scenario until it becomes a part of your thinking and feeling world. Add pictures, back-up statements and your self-empowerment rules. Then you will have created a consciousness of prosperity.

- **Loving Relationships:** Stop to consider the fact that if you don't love yourself, no one else will. Then use the same formula for building a new consciousness to write out your own version. Read some of the recommended books listed in the appendix to help you. You can treat other long-standing problems in the same manner.

After following the process for building a new state of consciousness to replace the old, you are now ready to begin some serious creating. Let's practice on some small things first.

Start with Small Goals
Choose two or three minor goals, either from your things-to-do list or from the following small goals, to work on this week. It is easier to start with some small things and see results from these before launching on a major production. Here are a few ideas:

- **Parking Places:** Manifesting parking places is a good first goal for

143

beginners. When you decide to go somewhere, before you get into your automobile, include your desired parking place in your plans. Be clear about your preferred area. Right in front of the main door is a great spot. (Someone has to park there, why not you?) Decide what you want, intend to have it and expect it to be there when you arrive. You may want to repeat your intentions a few times in the beginning. After a few successes, one clear statement of intent will suffice.

- **Highway Entrance Ramps:** If you have already done parking places, try the same idea with ramps. My personal program was that there would be enough room for a tractor-trailer as I entered the merge point. After a few months of doing this, the hole was always there for me, even when I forgot to mention it. It has now become a permanent part of my life. Your personal programming can also become automatic when you practice it regularly for awhile.
- **Lost Items:** If you have already mastered the first two manifestations, you might put your efforts into locating a lost article. Ask to be shown where it is and to be led to the right spot. Then let go of the thought entirely and when you least expect it, you will find the item.
- **Elusive People:** Plan to rendezvous with someone you want to meet. If you have had difficulty in contacting someone, mentally invite him or her to call you. Focus on the face of that person and using deep concentration ask him or her to call you. Repeat at least three times. It works!
- **Some Quickies:** Just for fun, intend to "live happily ever after." Set goals to be a gentle, loving person, to do the best possible job, be the most successful salesperson, the finest teacher, artist, friend, or parent. You may want to run the fastest, climb the highest — the choices are endless. Aim at creating whatever will bring you the greatest joy and fulfillment.

Carefully Calculated Creating: The Process

This is a long, detailed process to give the beginner a clear understanding of the steps involved. A briefer outline comes later.

- **Selection:** Having written the desires of your heart, look them over and choose one. Carefully choose only one major, but reachable, goal. (Although there is a great temptation to choose many things you would like to accomplish, I strongly recommend choosing only one major goal at a time.) Work with this for at least a week (seven days of

↪ Creating Your Heart's Desires

creation) before starting another major goal. (Twenty-one days is best, especially for beginners.)
- **Reality Check:** With your goal suggestions complete, select one that feels important enough to be your first project and begin the process of bringing it into creation using the following guidelines:
  - **Feelings:** Ask yourself, "How does this feel?" Quietly sense your heart (or gut) reaction. If it feels good, you may proceed. If not, choose again. Test again before proceeding.
  - **Attainability:** It is important to select only that which you believe is attainable by you. Asking for a million dollars in tomorrow's mail would stretch your sense of credibility to the point of defeat. Make sure your intentions are reasonable and reachable. You do not want to set yourself up for failure.
  - **Deservingness:** You need to feel good about your desires or affirmations and about yourself. Your self-esteem has to be in good shape. You must know that you are deserving of what you want.
  - **Anxiety, Doubt, and Guilt:** Any kind of doubt, frustration, worry, anxiety, strain, or struggle is a sign of resistance. This can come from many causes, often guilt-based ones. Remember, "What goes around, comes around." Your buried guilt will keep you from your desires, punishing you until you have set the record straight, made amends, and balanced your scales. Then if your conscience is clear you may proceed and succeed.

You can reprogram anything by writing out your goals and then visualizing the results daily. I do this every day over my morning cup of coffee and nightly just as I drift off to sleep.

Writing Your Clear Decree

Once your ambition has passed the test of attainability and deservingness, you are ready to write out your aim completely and carefully. Be certain the desire is yours and not another person's idea of what you should do. Know beyond a shadow of doubt just what you want. Your desire must be strong and vivid. Clear aims and statements keep you on your chosen track, help you focus your thoughts, and bring about better choices and decisions.

In general, be as specific as you can be about what you want and still feel good about it. You may find that as you push your desires further and further there seems to be a point of balance. Up to that point, you feel good, beyond it, you become more and more uncomfortable. Always follow your feelings and stay within your comfort range. For example:

- **Automobile:** To want a new car is an indefinite description. To set your heart on this year's Toyota Camry four-door sedan in light blue is a good, explicit command. However, if you push for a Rolls Royce, you may feel you have gone over your edge of believability.
- **Prosperity:** Refrain from making vague statements such as "I want lots of money." Five thousand dollars may seem like "lots" to some but be a mere dribble for others. Prosperity can also be a vague amount. You need to state the amount per year or more to start.

    If you have trouble with this, rather than asking for a large amount ask that by the end of the year your present salary be doubled. On the other hand, you may find it far more productive to intend to find your right career, becoming highly successful in doing what you enjoy most. When you do what you love most, prosperity will automatically follow.
- **Home:** Instead of "I want a new home," be precise, what kind of house? How many rooms? One story or two? Neighborhood? Yard? School district? Proximity to your workplace? — and so on.
- **Doubt Free:** Stay away from concerns of whom, how, and where. Set no limits such as your boss, lottery ticket, etc. Just trust that the universe will find a way to bring you what you want within a reasonable length of time.
- **Make It Positive:** Carefully avoid all negative words, for example, not, but, if, when, how, never, can't, or don't. Rewrite your decree as often as necessary to make sure your desire is stated in the clearest, most positive, joyous, and upbeat terms you can devise. Then, rewrite some more to pare your statement into the briefest terms, making it easy to remember and repeat.
- **Intuition Check:** As you write, notice your gut reaction to what you think you want. Be aware of any clues that you do not feel deserving. (These usually start as a feeling in the pit of your stomach.) Watch for these signs and deal with them promptly. You don't want to deny them, but to expose these "I don't deserve it" feelings and clean them up. Jot down any pro and con feelings, as these will be helpful in understanding your emotions and analyzing your results.
- **Rhythm and Rhyme:** If you can find a way to make your words rhyme or put them to music, however simple, so much the better. Even a childish singsong style is good. Any rhythmic phrase that you

can say, sing, chant, or hum is a distinct aid in programming your desires. Keep it short and sweet; make it easy to repeat. I strongly recommend singing your decree as often as possible, in the shower, auto, anywhere you can. You might even whistle it while you walk or work.
- **Present Tense:** Always remember the saying "tomorrow never comes" and keep your statements in the here and now. Things you are "going to do" are in the future and may never arrive in your life. Speak in terms of the present.

The opportunity for my right job placement comes to me now.
I now have the funds I desire.

All "I Am" statements are powerful. When you use the words I Am you are actually calling upon your I Am Presence, your Holy Spirit, your God Spark. These are so powerful they must be used with care. See that the content is always positive for they work equally well in the negative, and that can cause you problems.

Example: An old habit of saying "I am sick and tired of..." can actually make you sick. The same holds true for "I am afraid of..." which is the surest way to attract what you fear.

You need to become keenly aware of making careless or negative "I Am" statements. When you catch yourself, stop and correct it immediately or you will find yourself undermining your positive intentions. What's more, you may create more havoc than harmony in your world.

- **Simplicity:** Before further action, carefully check your written desires for simplicity, and most of all, see that it feels good to you on your deepest levels.
- **Check for Harmlessness:** Be sure your goals are harmless to people, animals, and nature. It is best to have intention for the highest good for all concerned.

Thou shalt not hurt thyself.
Thou shalt not hurt others.
Thou shalt not hurt any living thing.

Quick Check Summary

Mystical Magical You

- ❏ Write your desire in full.
- ❏ Remove all negative words.
- ❏ Check for clarity and simplicity.
- ❏ Speak your intention aloud.
- ❏ Feel your body reactions to your decree.

Check Your "Feeling Thermometer"

Feeling	Feeling Result
❏ Excited and happy	Sure winner
❏ Happy	Pretty sure
❏ Somewhat happy	Needs work to win
❏ Good	Needs extra work to win
❏ OK	Need to motivate self or rewrite
❏ Perhaps wishful thinking	Rework, rewrite, build self up
❏ I'd love to have it but…	Take a good look at your but's.
❏ Uneasy, guilty	Go back to the Anxiety, Doubt, and Guilt section.

Get those "but's" out of your subconscious and onto the table where you can take a good look at them. Finish your sentence of "I'd love to have it but…" But what?

List all the reasons why you think you can't succeed. Pin them down as specifically as possible before going any further. Find the mental/emotional problem and fix it.

Final Checkpoint: Does It Make You Happy?

Look at your desires one by one. Feel out which ones fill your heart and which ones only tickle your senses. (Faint responses often indicate Other People's Opinions (OPO's) or preprogrammed responses from our society, advertisements, and so forth.) Choose to work only with those that fill your heart, separating the wheat from the chaff and adding clarity.

Then put your whole heart joyfully into the creation of that which you truly desire.

Right Stance: Love

- **Check Your Stance:** In working with your creative mind, the major point to remember is the Law of Love. We were made to be co-creators with God, and God is Love. In other words, to create exactly what you desire you must be in a peaceful, loving state of consciousness. Any other mind-set outside the Law of Love can damage your crop.
- **Prayer Power:** Prayer is co-creating with God. Without prayer, you are creating alone and without power. (We are not talking of the "beggar's prayer" from a "poor me" stance.) Stand up tall and state your desires with dignity and assurance that your needs will be met wisely, graciously, and generously.

    Whenever your connection to God is fully open, you receive plentifully. (Prayer and meditation keep the pipes open.) When you are in doubt or fear you clog the pipeline and you get a spoonful rather than a flood. The problem is not on God's end; it's on yours. Remind yourself, "The Father and I are one. We are working together on this creation and God is all-powerful."
- **Loving Kindness:** To do your best intending and attracting, maintain an attitude of gentle-loving kindness. Speak your intentions and decrees in the highest state of love, peace, and harmony that you can reach. When you are centered in this loving state, working with the Law of Love, you are creating and attracting with love. Since like attracts like, whatever is generated in this loving vibration will return to you lovingly and peacefully — in harmony and beauty.

Right Time and Right Place

- **Right Time:** Remember there is extra energy at your disposal at dawn, high noon, and sunset. In addition, a new moon is an excellent time to launch a new project. Take advantage of all available opportunities to help you.
- **Right Place:** You may want to make your prayer or decree in some special place where you feel most empowered, perhaps outdoors in a favorite spot, a sacred place, a church or home worship center. You

could make your decrees before getting out of bed, while you are still warm, relaxed, and comfortable. Remember that feeling good is important.

Your Spoken Word

Thou shalt decree a thing and it shall be done unto you.
—Job 22:28

When speaking your word of creation it is best for beginners to start with finding a comfortable place to sit and relax. You may want to provide yourself with some soothing music. Add candlelight, flowers, and incense; make it anything that would add to your state of peace and harmony. Deliberately place yourself in a gentle, loving state of mind. Thoughts of love, appreciation, and gratitude are extremely helpful in producing the desired attitude. You may also want to visualize yourself in a beautiful garden, up on a mountain, down by a stream, or whatever brings you mental and emotional harmony.

- **Speak:** When ready, speak your desire with great conviction, adding your feelings of love, harmony, and joy. Feel them bubbling up from deep within. See the vibrations radiating to energize your chosen seed thought. You might say something like, "I intend ___ and I do this in love and joy, for the good of all concerned."
- **Energize:** Now close your eyes and see your dream come true. Using all your senses, picture how it will look. Imagine how it will feel. Think of how it will sound and smell. Let your imagination go. Daydream all the wonderful things that could happen and revel in how great you will feel and how joyous you will be. See others joining in your joy. Give it all you've got in enthusiasm, love, and laughter. See it through to a happy conclusion. When finished, give thanks for your joy and pronounce it good. Maintain an attitude of gentle-loving kindness as long as possible.
- **Commit:** Be willing to do whatever it takes to lovingly attain the thing you want. Be ready to follow any hunches concerning your goal. Watch for opportunities and synchronicities. Follow your heart wherever you feel led to go, knowing you are moving toward your highest good. Take a step, then watch for confirmation or correction. Trust the process. Trust your feelings to guide you.
- **Affirm:** The universe is a magnet to my desires. I am charged posi-

tively and draw to me only the things I so desire.
- **Give thanks:** It is always wise to give thanks ahead of time for each and every one of your decrees. For example, "I sing with joy for my highest good."
- **Release:** Once you have spoken your word, bless it and release it to the universe, knowing you are a god in the making, assured of your power to create.

Expect a Miracle

- **Expect:** Let miracles happen. Do not let doubts enter. It may be wise to keep your intentions to yourself unless you are working with a partner who won't "rain on your parade." Keep open and expectant about achieving your goals. Remember your divine heritage and hold onto your vision in spite of all tests, distractions, and contrary comments from others.

  Whatever you do, give no thought as to how this will come about; just hold onto the idea that it is already yours. Expect positive results. Doubt and worry says you are not sure you can have it. It is an uncertain signal that can cancel your order.
- **Trust:** Know that you live in a safe and loving universe. Jesus said, "It is the Father's good pleasure to give you the kingdom" (Luke 12:32). Actually, all you have to do is decide what you want and accept it. The biggest problem is in accepting.

  Be not dismayed; know only good can come from this co-creation. Hold that thought. Remember the whole universe is working for your highest good and greatest happiness. Learn to trust this process.
- **Date:** Include a date on each of these, so you can see just how long it takes to attain some of your desires. Feel free to change, rearrange, or redefine these aims as you move along.
- **Repeat:** Repeat this routine to set up your smaller goals, at least the first few times while you are learning. Later you can just use the outline in the next section.

Keeping Records

There are several ways to write your goals, intentions, steps, dates, and general scorekeeping. Choose a calendar, appointment book, index cards, or computer. Find whatever works for you and start with that. Later you can add, subtract, or otherwise modify your recordkeeping. When you record your true feelings in your journal, you become much clearer in perspective about your situation. From there you can make much better decisions as you move toward your goal.

Another option is a special book of goals of your own design. This could be divided into sections of career, health, and so on.

1. In your journal, or on an index card (possibly both), write the final form of your goal.
2. Add date begun and leave a place for date completed. (Omit this step if a deadline makes you feel pressured.)
3. List any steps you plan to take to facilitate your goal.
4. Make plans to execute those steps as soon as possible.
5. Make a commitment to follow through on your goals.
6. Add some positive statements about your ability to achieve your goal.
7. Write, "I pronounce it *good*."
8. Picture yourself having and enjoying your goal. Repeat this as often as possible. Keep score on this.
9. Always give thanks in advance for your fulfilled desire.

Follow-Up

- **Cards:** Carry your index cards with you and look at them two or three times a day. Plan to spend at least five minutes each time in energizing your new creation. The minimum time is seven days, although the preferred time is twenty-one. (In a very short time, you will be able to do this anytime, anywhere.) This will reinforce what you have already started. It is your fantastic fertilizer. Use it.
- **Sing, Hum, Whistle Your Song:** Do this as often as possible. This further impresses your subconscious mind and keeps your creative juices going.
- **Journal:** Each evening, take time to look at your life in the light of your new intentions. Analyze them carefully and decide what you would like to see happen the next day. Write your feelings about what is going on in your life. Plan your day with the goal of having all things flowing smoothly. You may wish to set clear goals for some specific challenge you may be facing. Intend to see your whole life move into peace and harmony.
- **Nurture Your Goals:** Whenever you are unsure of what to do, say

"Let there be light," or intend to have greater clarity on the matter. Then wait for some new ideas, feelings, symbols, or the flow of events to guide you. Meditation is an excellent way to get insights and answers. Help is always there, but you have to ask.

Remember, whatever you send out comes back to you multiplied, so be sure to send nothing that could harm another. Send only that which is good, just, and loving.

A Simple Outline

The foregoing instructions may seem to be exceedingly lengthy, but please, do not be discouraged. I have deliberately gone into great detail in order to give you a solid understanding of the basic principles involved, especially the powerful imprint of your stance. Once you understand these, all you will need is a simple outline as follows. Trust me.

1. Selection
2. Reality Check
3. Writing Your Decree
4. Check for Harmlessness
5. Quick Check Summary
6. Final Check
7. A Stance of Love
8. Right Time, Right Place
9. Spoken Word
10. Expect A Miracle
11. Records
12. Follow Up
13. Walk Your Talk

From this point on, be sure you keep your thoughts and words in line with your declarations. Your daily speech and mind-chatter will negate or give added power to your thought forms, so be careful of making negative statements about your desire, yourself, or your abilities. You also want to keep your attitudes and actions in harmony with your intentions.

Carefully monitor your mind-chatter. Counter any negative statements with positive ones so as not to cancel your decrees. Learning to speak only that which you desire to have requires some active mental discipline. It means listening to what you think and say. Catch yourself in

Mystical Magical You

mid-sentence, if necessary, to negate any careless words. Then rephrase your thoughts in a more positive way. This may seem difficult at first, but it soon becomes a new, positive habit and is well worth the effort.

The only thing keeping you from all you desire is your own limited thinking. You have been taught for centuries that you can't get there from here. Now it is time to throw out those old concepts. Open the door from your "prison of limited ideas" and step out into freedom and prosperity.

Create a wonderful life for yourself. Bless each new day and each new adventure you experience. See every day as a brand new learning and growing experience filled with joy and wonder just for you.

Follow your heart.
Trust yourself.
Trust the universe and live happily ever after.

12

Nurturing Your Creations

Our life is what our thoughts make it.
— Marcus Aurelius

Y ou are the writer of your life's script, the director of the drama, the leading character in the play, and the producer of the show. You create it all from the standpoint of your mind.

Once you have birthed a new creative venture, you need to feed and nurture it to bring it into fulfillment. Whenever your thoughts begin to question your new goal (as they will) be prepared. Let no doubt enter or take root. Keep your thoughts and emotions in line with achieving your goals. Have in mind some positive, well-chosen statements ready to affirm your success. Hold a positive stance. Protect and support your new project just as you would an infant. After all, this is your baby.

In order to change your outer world, you have to change your inner one.

Adelade, the Unpaid Maid — the Saga Continues

If you recall, Adelade had established and lived for many years in a world of poverty, hard work, and misery. Then, one day she came to a point of saying, "I don't want to live like this anymore." This became her turning point. She had stated what she did not want.

Meanwhile, she had read enough about positive affirmations and their results to be willing to try them. After all, she had nothing to lose, and maybe it would work for her. So she began writing new goals on her goal cards, along with the steps needed for success.

> *Create in me a clean new heart, oh God, and renew a right spirit within me.*
> *— Psalms 51:10*

Mystical Magical You ⌣·

Next she stopped and prayed about it, asking for guidance and help in creating her new world. As so often happens, when one prays a sincere prayer she began to receive insights about her situation. The first one was to clean up her attitudes.

She was also led to clean up her old habits of faultfinding, criticism, and feeling victimized. She had to forgive herself and all those involved in her past unhappiness. Then she was to create a whole new inner world, one of peace and love. In order for her to have a peaceful, supportive world around her, it was necessary to have a loving, peaceful space within. (Now, this one took a while.) She also began to meditate on a regular basis.

Finally, she had to find some new, supportive friends to help her on her journey into the unknown. Therefore, she joined the local Unity Church, where she learned to clothe herself safely with infinite love and wisdom as a way of creating her safe new world.

Meanwhile, her goal cards went everywhere she went. At her job, she used them regularly, repeating the affirmations faithfully at every opportunity. With nothing to lose and everything to gain, she stuck with her new routine. Within two months she was promoted and given a substantial raise, filed for a divorce, moved to a new home, and changed her whole lifestyle. The next few months brought her another raise and a gentle, loving companion. Things were getting better and better. By the end of that year she was happily married and had moved to a much nicer home with better schools for her children. What's more, she even had her own healthy bank account. In less than a year she had moved from misery and poverty to middle class wealth, comfort, and happiness. That was a major change.

Now, if you are wondering why I refer to Adelade as "she" (I wondered about that myself) it is because I no longer relate to her as a part of me. She is no longer in my world.

Keeping Your Word

Speak the word only and it shall be done unto you.
—Matthew 9:29

The Bible is full of such promises, yet the average person's mind-chatter is a mixture of positive and negative thoughts and actions which, left unchecked, will negate creative decrees. Therefore, one of the most important steps to accomplishing your goal is to "walk your talk." Avoid speaking of your problems and upsetting experiences. Stay in a positive, loving place as much as possible, being mindful of the words you speak.

Since this is a thought-created universe, you would be wise to confirm your wisdom, ability, and power to succeed, if only to yourself. In this way, you actually draw to you the necessary universal energy (part of the co-creative process) to attract all that you need to fulfill your intentions. In this way you can feed and nurture your creation just as you would feed a child.

Co-creation is not only choosing a goal and launching it into the universe, but also the act of aligning your goals, thoughts, words, and actions with the Laws of the Universe — especially with the Law of Love. You reap what you sow as a way of understanding the affects of your thoughts and words.

Discipline

Discipline is deliberately training your mind to work in more self-sustaining directions, a practice which actually sharpens your mental acuity, feeds your mental body, and strengthens your willpower.

Reaching a desired goal can mean giving up one thing in order to obtain something of greater value. Your intentions and priorities must be held clearly in mind. Discipline can be sacrificing your immediate comfort for a long-term benefit. It can also be refraining from doing anything that would keep you from your goal.

Discipline is working with your goal cards several times a day. (This is crucial to your success.) For the quickest results faithfully work and play with them, including your visualization process and affirmation statements. Without this nurturing, success could either be a long time coming or elude you altogether.

Further discipline is needed to faithfully write in your journal every night, recording the ongoing events in your life and your feelings about them. Take particular notice of your successes and compliment yourself for each one. The failures also need to be noted along with the probable reasons, so errors and limiting beliefs can be corrected. (Dreams can help you here if you take time to understand them.) Allow no more than a moment on failures; keep your focus on successes both past and present. From time to time, ask yourself what you can be doing to help bring your ideal closer to completion.

Start Your Day with Clear Intent

Work with your things-to-do list with special emphasis on your expected results. (Keep those index cards handy.) Be clear about what you want, focus on the moment, think lovingly, and it will come to you.

- **Intentions:** As you hold your intentions in mind, you are actively creating your desires. Be consciously aware of what you are thinking and feeling and allow nothing to sidetrack you from your purpose. Know it will happen.
- **Empower Yourself:** Call up your latent power to be true to yourself, your dreams, and your visions. Be prepared to withstand doubts and taunts from others. Until you have the courage of your convictions, you cannot stand for anything.

  Remember to reinforce your creations on a daily basis. Doing your energizing exercises with your goal cards three to four times a day will facilitate this.

  Let go of struggle. Make positive, supportive statements like "I feel really good about this." Send out thoughts of love and appreciation for having your goal manifest. Picture yourself receiving your request, feel the joy and delight of having your treasure. Give thanks in advance for what you know you'll receive. Knowing is a positive energy linking you to your desire.
- **Enthusiasm:** Your enthusiasm is a great power, sparking action from within you as well as from others. It draws the right people and events to you quickly.
- **Safe Universe:** Bear in mind that the universe is a safe, supportive, and loving place. Earth is our school of trial and error; it is a special place to grow and play. In fact, we are encouraged to experiment and learn new things. (You don't stay in first grade forever; learning is an ongoing process year after year and lifetime after lifetime.)

Earth is especially designed as a mirror to reflect our thoughts, emotions, words, and deeds in physical form. In this way, we can see the results of our thoughts and words, and hopefully accept responsibility for creating and learn from these experiences.

Once we realize that we are doing it to ourselves instead of being done unto, we will stop blaming luck or other people. We will have a whole new understanding of the way our universe works and will graduate to higher standards of thinking and behaving. Our objective is eventually to master thoughts, emotions, and ourselves. As we do, we will create only that which is loving, peaceful, and harmonious. We are taking an active part in a grand and wonderful experiment.

- **Journal:** Every night, record ongoing events in your journal, and your gut reactions to them. Be sure to express your true feelings about the things you do not want, especially those which bring strong reactions. Now you are ready to change the old and create something new and better. This is a significant part of your growth and development process.

    Remember to take special notice of your successes and compliment yourself for each one. Allow only a moment to note your failures and the possible reasons behind them so errors can be corrected; recognize them, and move on. Keep your focus on successes, past and present. Your goal is to stay positive at least fifty-one percent of the time. When you reach that point you are definitely moving into receiving more good than bad. Keep raising your standards, working your way up to ninety-nine percent good. Then you can have it all!

Meanwhile, hold the thought that you will achieve your goal. Allow nothing to deter you. Think and act as if you have already attained your desire, as opposed to not having it yet. Dwell on what you want to accomplish.

Your soul always knows, so pay attention to those inner feelings. Whenever you are uneasy about your desire, know that you are working against yourself. Ask your inner self, "Why am I uneasy? Can't I accept what I am asking for?" If you still fell unsure, realize you are not accepting your creatiion. Put it aside for now, and come back to it when you can absolutely believe. Otherwise you are wasting your energy and are running in circles.

The ancestor to every action is a thought.
—Ralph Waldo Emerson

Maintaining a Joyful Stance

In nurturing your desires, your overall attitude about yourself is of major importance. Grumpy thinking can be an old habit that not only attracts critical people and unhappy events but creates a negative attitude which repels your desires. Start your day with as much happy thinking as you can muster. If you need a little cheer in the morning, try listening to some joyful music instead of the Dismal Daily News.

Start your day by finding something to appreciate. Look around for things to enjoy, like a beautiful sunrise, a bird's song, a smiling face. Bask in the spirit of good health and well-being. Let your dominant thought be one of joy. Expect to have a good day. Don't forget to sing, whistle, or hum your happy affirmation song. Make a list of things that make you feel good and refer to it often, especially when feeling a bit "out of sorts." Make it a point to include more pleasure-filled events into your daily schedule. Determine to have more joy, knowing your happy mood creates happy events and hastens your desires to you.

Join the Joy Team

Add happier, uplifting people to your list of friends. Remember the path of joy is in loving and valuing yourself. Don't wait for someone else to do it for you; do it for yourself. Deliberately plan to do something nice for yourself every day. Doing little helpful deeds for others also makes you feel good and boosts your self-worth. Learn to congratulate yourself often for even the tiniest of successes. Stop saving your best clothes for later (they will just go out of style). Wear them now and enjoy them. Good self-worth is knowing you are choosing the best in each and every moment. Determine to walk in your own, self-created world of love, peace, and harmony.

Putting It All Together

1. Prioritize goals and chores by importance.
2. Pick one project coming up in the next day or so.
3. Think of what you would like to see happen.
4. Plan in terms of win-win situations where everyone feels good. Think in terms of good will and harmony. Decide in terms of "Highest good for all concerned" or "All things come together in peace and harmony." Energize this with love and joy. Hold that attitude.
5. Write your scenario. Check it over. Rewrite if necessary. Fine-tune it. Place on your Goal Card where you can review it. Accept this as your game plan and pronounce it good. Remember you have the power to bless or to curse.
6. Review your cards daily, preferably a week in advance — minimum time, two days ahead.

Seeing Is Believing

Picture yourself in a special place you love to be. Enjoy the scenery around you, the sounds, scents, and the feelings. With eyes still closed, begin to picture your desire coming into manifestation. Feel how good it is to have your goal or dream coming true. Bask in the happy feelings of having your desire at last. Now that you have it, act out what you will do with it. Where will you go with it? what will you do with it? Who will you share the news of this wonderful event with first? Imagine what others will say and do. Act it out. Go through the motions of telling or showing others. See yourself overjoyed. Feel the great love and joy surrounding you. Add as many details as possible to make it even more real, more wonderful. See yourself dressing the part for this. This is your show—anything goes. Have a ball. Giggle. Laugh. Dance. Celebrate with your friends.

Spend at least five minutes several times a day replaying this dream come true, making it better and better with each showing. Part of what you are doing here is building a consciousness of having and enjoying that which you most desire, so don't neglect this step. Enjoy the ride.

Remember your creative energies are flowing as you are visualizing.[1] The *kind* of energies will affect the outcome. In other words, whatever emotional influence is dominant will override. So focus on love, joy, and good will for all, and happiness is what you will get. Pronounce it good, claim it as yours, and give thanks with great enthusiasm.

Repeat this several times a day for one week or more as desired. This is good to do on waking in the morning and just before sleep.

- **Daydreams:** Daydreams are also an excellent use of your imagination and you can easily put this to use in odd places at odd times in your day. Remember that your imagination feeds your thought forms with clear pictures to follow and fill. It is a powerful tool. Use it often.
- **A Song to Sing:** Another enhancement is to select an appropriate theme song to represent your desire and hum, play, or sing it often. You could even make up a suitable song or write a poem set to a familiar tune.
- **Prayer:** While working on your goals you could pray for guidance. You might ask someone to work with you, pray for or with you, or even start a group for nurturing one another with goals and affirmations.
- **Meditate:** Meditation keeps the floodgates open for answers to questions, insights, and guidance.
- **Goal Cards:** Radiate loving, joyful energies toward your goals as you practice feeling good about achieving your desires. Work faithfully on them several times a day, but limit their number. It is far better to have one or two come true quickly than to have a dozen or more still cooking on the back burner weeks later. Don't set yourself up for failure by overloading the circuits.

Mystical Magical You

- **Exercise:** A friend of mine likes to ride her exercise bike for ten or fifteen minutes each morning before going to work. She makes this time do double duty by chanting her goals and affirmations at the same time. This sets her day's intentions in place before her arrival. According to her, this has made a big difference. Things have gone unusually well since she started this practice.

  If you don't want to chant, you can speak, sing, whisper, or whatever works for you. You could also adapt this to taking a shower, washing dishes, driving to work, and so forth.
- **Sleep on It:** Another version is to write your goal, place it under your pillow and literally sleep on it. Often this results in a dream giving you some helpful insights on your situation.
- **Wear It:** Centuries ago, people would write down something that was important to them and place this in a special little box or pocket to be worn on their forehead (third-eye area). This was to impress the thought deeply into the mind. This old custom has been modified somewhat in other cultures to be worn under a headband or placed in a hatband. Another version of this would be to place your note inside a locket or in a pocket close to your heart. You may want to try some variation of this.
- **Reminder:** If you need a reminder of your newest intention, try wearing an unusual piece of jewelry, like a ring, chain, jangling bracelet, or an antique watch. Wear a special jacket, tie, hat, scarf, or whatever will catch your attention and be a good reminder.

The main idea is to do whatever works best for you. Since one of your goals is to live a happier, more fulfilling life, do whatever it takes to please yourself.

13

Rediscovering Your God-Self

What lies behind us and what lies before us are tiny matters compared to what lies within us.

— Ralph Waldo Emerson

From early childhood we, as a planetary people, have been taught to belittle our achievements and ourselves because we are "only human." Our unquestioning acceptance of these erroneous beliefs is one of the many ways in which we have unwittingly given our power away to others. The truth is that we each have strong, unbreakable connections to our God-self and through this link, we can know all things. God did not create us and leave us here to struggle alone and unaided. We have built-in help. In Psalms 91:11 we are told, "He gave His angels charge over thee, to keep thee in all thy ways...lest thou dash thy foot against a stone."

Guardian Angels

Our Guardian Angels are not only our God-given protectors but also our guides and messengers. They bring us inspirations, insights, intuitive hunches, and understanding. In addition, angels act as connecting links between us and our God-selves until we have firmly reestablished our own links, our own absolute knowing of our God-connectedness.

Their guidance is always to lead us back to our own sense of God's Presence. They are always waiting in the wings, so to speak. Yet all too often, we ignore their help, looking instead to someone outside of ourselves to solve our problems. We often take the advice of strangers rather than trusting our own inner knowing. This sad state of affairs can lead to our own undoing.

Meanwhile, we need to understand that we must ask angels for help, otherwise they are not allowed to render aid. If an angel gives help without our request, it is considered interference. So don't forget to ask for help when in need.

Recognizing Your God-Self

Should all this sound a bit confusing, let me explain that God, Christ, and Holy Spirit are all different labels for the same Being. Other commonly used names for Holy Spirit are High-self, God-self, Christ Consciousness, God Spark, Super Consciousness, and Super Being.

Being one with our God-self is simply living in the light of God's Presence, walking in the knowingness that we live, move, and have our being in God, conscious of our God-connection at all times. To walk "in the Spirit" is to be in awareness of God and of your God-self being "One." (Jesus often said, "The Father and I are One.") It is knowing ourselves to be children of God, gods in the making, and living in that consciousness every day. It is living within the Law of Love.

Meanwhile, until we make that connection, our Guardian Angel holds this link for us, guiding, aiding, and protecting us until we have grown into our full God-being. The ability to understand how we create our reality is an important step in the process of rediscovering and reconnecting with the God-self part of us. This enables us to work consciously with our God-self and to take full control of our lives.

Since God is love, a loving, caring attitude provides the perfect conditions for feeding and nurturing our thought forms and speeds the process of moving them into the fullness of materialization.

Understanding Ourselves

- **High-Self:** We each have a High-self or God-self that has its own carefully chosen ideals for this life and is committed to achieving them. But sometimes the personality gets in the way.
- **Low-Self:** Our low-self or ego is our personality. This is who we think we are. This self is closely associated with the physical body, material things, and knee-jerk reactions. It seems to be totally separate from the spiritual self or soul. The ego works mainly out of the intellect or conscious mind and is deeply infused with societal programming. It is often enmeshed in physical things and wanders off on its own selfishly motivated path.

These two selves, often working against each other, were meant to perform together. We are now working toward the union or reunion of these bodies. It is part of the "New Age" process.

The Soul Is Who We Really Are

Until we recognize our soul as being more valuable than our body, true happiness will elude us. The soul is the real, undying, everlasting part of us; the ego is merely a projection of the soul-mind, a temporary, expendable tool for gathering knowledge and experience. Each low-self is only a tiny speck in the skein of time as compared to all the many ego selves we have been. This personality self is easily sidetracked from its soul purpose unless we as individuals take time to center ourselves, meditate, and keep in touch with our God-self.

As we pray, meditate, and hold high ideals for ourselves we put our soul in control. Without these the low-self becomes a spoiled brat and runs about wreaking havoc everywhere it goes, eventually reaping a pigsty reward by the misuse of free will.

Which Side Are You On?

The most important need of the soul is to be at peace with itself and its Maker. When we are at peace with ourselves, we are relaxed, at ease, and feeling good about ourselves and about those around us. This is living in soul consciousness. At this level, we feel happy and loving. Our minds are at peace, we are in a state of compassion, understanding, and genuine caring about others. We are radiating love and harmony into our world.

The challenge is to find ways to live in peace and harmony more consistently. We could practice pretending we are spiritual beings acting lovingly. Then, as we act the part, we become the gods or goddesses that we really are.

You Are Unique

It is important to realize we are very special, unique, and beautiful beings, unlike any others ever born. We have a definite purpose for coming to earth at this time. Therefore, whenever we are feeling lost, separated, unhappy, or unfulfilled it is not because we are not "good enough," but rather we are feeling a sense of having failed to live up to our half-forgotten soul purpose. This is largely because we have been given so much false information about our true selves that we hardly know what to believe. Yet, in spite of all this, we are constantly being guided to our chosen purpose, our highest good, our greatest potential, and our fondest dreams.

Our God-self guides us by way of our secret desires and feelings, those familiar little heart tugs that urge us in the right direction. God speaks to us in this gentle way at the time of each decision and at every turning point in our lives. But all too often, no one is listening.

Finding Your Soul Purpose

When I was seventeen and about to graduate, a roving school reporter asked me what I wanted to do with my life. Without stopping to think about it, I answered, "I want to do something to help people." True, it wasn't very specific, but looking back, I can see this has always been my motivating desire. It was only recently that I began to fine tune my goals into becoming an author and teacher. Actually, it came as a sort of surprise. I did not know where I was headed until I arrived, and it felt good.

Perhaps you too can think back to younger days and remember your child-like dream of what you wanted to do with your life. If not, take this idea into your next meditation and get an answer or ask your God-self for a dream to remind you. Once you find your dream, write it down in your journal where you can find it again.

- **Things You Like to Do:** One way to discover or confirm your soul purpose is to make a list of all the things you like to do most, regardless of how silly they may seem. You may surprise yourself.
- **Things You Enjoyed as a Child:** On another sheet of paper, list the kinds of activities you most enjoyed as a child or teen.
- **Talents:** List all the things you can do well, especially those things you already knew how to do the first time you tried or could do better than others. (You brought these past-life talents in with you.)
- **Friends:** List a dozen of your best friends and their talents. As you go down the list you may suddenly realize the majority of your friends are teacher and leader types or highly creative. Generally, the talents and qualities predominating in your friends are your talents as well.

From here it is easy to determine what some of your talents and purposes are. Usually we plan to use our gifts as a means to uplift humanity or to make the world a better place. Some plan to further our own growth and that of humanity by taking our inherent abilities beyond all previous records. There are always new horizons to seek. Once we find and pursue these, we feel a sense of excitement, exhilaration, and joy. Conversely, when we fail to find and fulfill our predetermined soul purpose we feel unhappy, unrealized, and incomplete.

Feeding the Soul

Your feelings can enrich or defile your soul. Thoughts and feelings of harmony, peace, and love are nourishing foods for the soul, while smoldering anger, resentment, and negative feelings are damaging. Knowing this, you may want to make the effort to provide yourself with moments of tranquility and meditation on a regular basis. Find things that are pleasurable for you like flowers, music, or touches of beauty and make a deliberate effort to add these into your everyday life.

Working with Your God-Self

Good instincts usually tell you what to do long before your head has figured it out.
— Michael Burke

One of the rewards of working closely with your soul is the steady stream of guidance that comes to you, especially when you take time to ask. Writing your questions or challenges is a good way to start. You could do this in your journal. When you ask your question at night, you may find your answer in your dreams. (Much information comes to you in dreams and meditation once you begin to connect and work with your God-self.)

Your God-self helps you define your soul purpose, guides you in making choices, and gives you insights into situations that concern you. Your God-self assists you through difficult situations and helps plan a better future. Your senses will guide you to the right decision. All you need to do is to check your feelings to know where you stand in relation to your God-self connection.

Answers from Your God-Self

Answers from your God-self may come in a variety of ways, such as a picture in your mind, a feeling, a distinct impression, or a single, and potent, descriptive word. Occasionally there will be a sentence heard in your head, but mostly the answers are very brief and to the point. When I say brief, I mean one or two word answers.

For example, one day I was feeling kind of "stuffy" and had a desire to take a walk in a park. The nearest one I knew of was about seven miles away. So I got in my car and began to drive. At the corner where I usually turn right, a voice said, "Turn left." "There's no park that way," I argued. I paused, but I obeyed. At the next intersection the voice said, "Turn right." No clue. No explanation. Nothing. Then, less than a half-mile down that street there was a sign, PARK. As you have probably guessed, it was just what I wanted, a park with marked trails, mileage markers, and various exercise equipment spaced along the way. All this less than a mile from my home. How's that for instant answer?

As I continue to open up to this wonderful source of information, guidance comes with greater ease, as a continuing flow of energy, awareness, and knowingness. Often there are little reminders, bits of encouragement, a warning, or a helpful hint. Sometimes there are bits of advice or insights for greater clarity and understanding. Best of all is the bubble of joy or a little giggle of gladness in my heart as a confirmation that I have made the right decision.

One day, while stopped at a busy intersection, I watched the light turn green. My usual response is to hit the gas and go, but something made me hesitate. As I sat there wondering at myself for just sitting there, a huge, heavily loaded coal truck went flying through the intersection, red light and all! Had I pulled out a few seconds earlier I could not possibly have survived. I still get chills just thinking about that one.

The point I am trying to make is that anyone can do this. Children and animals do it naturally, but grown-ups who have been taught to stop daydreaming, be practical, and "get real" often have lost the ability to listen to that still, small voice. Those who do not seem to "hear" may feel, see, or sense their answers in some other way. We are not limited to any one type of receiving information. Just as we have five physical senses, we also have five spiritual (nonphysical) senses. All are at our disposal, although one is usually more dominant than the others. This one usually comes through first, but eventually, we develop all of them as we practice meditation.

Guidance

In the moment a new situation arises, there is within you a feeling from your God-self to guide you. Guidance comes as a simple, gut-level reaction, an instant feeling of attraction or repulsion, joy or dread, a "go for it" or "run from it" nudge. This guidance is always there. It never fails. You can count on it every time. It is one of your greatest gifts.

The old problem of not knowing what to do lies in your habit of not listening. Because you have been so carefully taught to distrust yourself, you tend to override and ignore your inner signals and your gut feelings. So you wind up saying "I don't know what to do" or go to someone else for advice. Please be aware that the advisor is rarely ever attuned enough to his or her own God-self to know what is best for you. Chances are that person doesn't even know what is best for him- or herself. Think about that.

Practice Awareness

For best results, for your greatest good, make a firm intention right now to be aware of your instant reactions to any new event, problem, or question that comes up in the moment of the incident. The key word here is "instant." If your answer takes a minute or longer to arrive, you have good reason to suspect that you are figuring it out by using your conscious mind. That is your old habit of using your intellect rather than allowing your intuition to speak to you. A very good test for intuitive input is the element of surprise. Whenever the answer is unexpected, you can bet it is intuitive, that is, straight from your God-self.

One evening, as a busy mother of five, I was hurriedly setting the table so I could hurriedly serve supper, so I could hurriedly get through the dishes, so I could hurriedly get the kids off to bed, so I could step off of my spinning merry-go-round of duties and have a bit of rest. Armed with a load of plates and silverware, I was slapping plates on the table like a drummer on drums: "ka-bang," "ka-bang," "ka-bang." Suddenly a voice spoke loud and clear, "Do all things lovingly." I spun around, eyes desperately searching for the speaker. I saw nothing. There was total silence and a Presence, still, serene, and gentle, yet powerful. I was stunned. I don't know how long I stood there clutching my dishes, but I do know I never forgot those words I heard thirty years ago.

Getting back in touch with your God-self and learning to listen is a simple matter of slowing down long enough to hear that wee small voice, to feel the gentle heart tug. It may be necessary for you to retrain your mind to pay greater attention to your gut reactions and innermost feelings, especially in the precise moment that a new situation arises.

Be aware that your intuitive answer is so swift in response to a new situation that you could easily miss it entirely. Quite frequently you will find information beginning to pour in before another person is finished speaking. This is your instant answer, your on-the-spot report that works every time. The challenge is to be alert enough to catch it.

These messages may come to you in one of several ways; words, a feeling, an urge, or an absolute knowing that a person is telling a falsehood along with the knowledge of what is the actual truth. You may smell the scent of flowers (or whatever) to symbolize a certain person or situation. You may hear a significant song or sentence inside your head (clairaudience) or see a descriptive picture flash into in your mind (clairvoyance). These pictures may be symbolic or can be an explicit scene that grants you an instant understanding of a situation. (These clairvoyant scenes can be from the past, present, or even the future.)

Occasionally, you may ponder a question such as "What is going on here?" or "What should I do about this?" then forget all about it. An hour or day may pass. Then, while you are driving down the street not thinking about anything in particular, you suddenly have the answer to the question you had forgotten about. This is intuition at its best.

When an answer pops into your mind from nowhere, it is your God-self answering you at a time when your intellect is not in the way.

Intellect Always Argues with Intuition

All too often, unless you discipline your mind, your intellect will immediately begin to argue with your intuition. It will bring up all kinds of doubts and objections. Expect it. It happens to all of us, especially at the beginning of learning to accept and use our intuitive abilities. Just remember through it all what the original message was. Then watch to see if it was right. You may doubt and test a number of times before you learn that you can trust your God-self every time.

Although each person will find one method more prevalent than another, it is not unusual to have your answers come in a variety of ways or in a combination of two or more. If this sounds surprising, let me assure you that everyone has these wonderful talents and abilities lying dormant within. It is up to you to activate them. Since you can't ask for better guidance, your part is to stop listening to your limited beliefs and learn to follow the subtle guidance of your own inner knowing, and that takes some practice. You may want to conscientiously devote more attention to your intuition and your feelings, especially when a problem, a situation or a question first presents itself. Then, if it feels good, joyous, loving, or desirable and will harm no one, go for it.

Body Signals

When you try something new, exciting, or different and find that it feels both good and right to do it, you can consider this as part of your guidance. Many a new career has been found in this manner, for your God-self is always guiding you into greater fulfillment and joy.

Conversely, if your body gives you signals of strain or fatigue, or should you find your muscles growing tense or your solar plexus area growing tight, realize that this too is a signal from your God-self giving you a warning that all is not well. Perhaps you are moving in an unwise direction, pushing yourself too hard, going against your better judgment, or ignoring your inner guidance. Whenever you have discomfort or "dis-ease" in your body, know that this is your God-self at work, striving to get your attention.

Your Soul Knows

When in doubt, instead of saying "I don't know," which is a negative statement, try saying, "my soul knows." All you have to do is listen and feel. Learn to claim, "I always know what to do." At some level of your being, you do know. It is just a matter of getting in touch with your inner wisdom.

As you learn to work with your inner guidance you will find you can ask questions such as "What is going on here?" "What do I do now?" or "How can I fix this?" and expect to get an instant answer. As you start your day you might want to ask, "What do I need to do today?" or "What does my body need today?" When you go shopping, ask to be guided to the kind of food you need, the best clothes for you, the best bargains, the best sporting goods. Whatever is needed, remember to ask for guidance. Remember to remain observant and consistently follow the pull of your heartstrings.

If your answer does not seem to be immediate, wait and see what happens. Look for your answer, watch for symbolic events, be ready receive new ideas and to move into new experiences. Sometimes your answer comes in the form of a friend, a book, a movie, or a chance encounter, but for the most part you have instant answers as needed.

Impulses

Your impulses, particularly the joyous ones, are yet another way that your God-self guides you into your right place. These spontaneous urges to take action often spring from the heart of your God-self. Learn to trust these communications with your inner being and let them lead you to be in just the right place at the right time. Trust them to show you the next step, your next joyous adventure.

Keep holding the thought of who you really are—a spiritual being and a god in the making, moving into oneness with your God-self. Meanwhile, remember that your loving Guardian Angel watches over you until the connection is complete. You are connected to your angel and your angel is connected to God. You are much loved, and you are never alone. All you have to do is ask for help (most of us forget to ask) and it comes immediately. All you need to do is listen. Trust that you are always being guided to your right place.

Your loving Father God gave us all free will and no one, not even an angel, may override this. For that reason, remember that your angel may not render any assistance unless you request it. Intuition, psychic impressions, and the "wee, small voice" inside your head come from your God-self as your constant guidance. However, you have been taught to ignore this and listen to the voice of authority, such as parents, teachers, books, and newspapers. The choice is always yours.

Never forget that you are a child of God, and children inherit the qualities of their parents. This means you are God in the making, capable of doing and creating many wonderful things. Most importantly, remember that

Life is meant to be a wonderful adventure, so dare to be the best you can be.

14

Meditation: Getting in Touch with Your God-Self

Meditation is the art of paying attention, of listening to your heart.
— Dean Ornish

One of the most valuable methods of gaining our desired creations is through our consistent empowerment. Power comes from our individual connection to God, by the way of our soul, often called the God-self. The path we take for this bonding is called meditation, or "going into the silence." It is extremely helpful for us to develop the ability to move easily into that peaceful place on a daily basis. Here we find the loving stance, sense of balance, and centered feeling that we need to create what we want.

In her book *Meditation—Gateway to Light*, author Elsie Sechrist tells us, "We know from the history of religion that the great prophets, the reformers, and founders of new faith, the men and women who walked with God, had all mastered this the art of silence, of meditation. Even Jesus retired from the crowds to seek periods of aloneness with God. It is by this means we are all renewed, through an overflowing of the Holy Spirit in our lives."[1]

Dean Ornish, author of *Dr. Dean Ornish's Program for Reducing Heart Disease*[2] says, "Meditation is the process of quieting your mind. When your mind is quiet, you feel peaceful. You lose your sense of separateness and isolation."

In general, meditation keeps the floodgates open to receive the flow of guidance, ideas, and insights from God. Our prayers can be as simple as saying, "God, I have this problem. Please help me make the right decision. Thank you God, for taking care of this for me." Then wait for your answer.

Prayer As a Prelude to Meditation

Whenever prayer is done with deep sincerity, concentration, and clear intent, a distinct thought form begins to build in the air above the person praying. Not surprisingly, the form takes the shape of a graceful, long stemmed glass, chalice, or Holy Grail. As the prayer thought is held, the chalice becomes the receptacle into which the manna of divine creative energy is poured to fulfill the request. The manifestation comes through this open channel. Often this comes about in the quiet time after the praying is done, in the silence following intense, heart-felt prayer. The formation of the instant answer comes into manifestation in exact accordance with the belief of the person who prays. This occurs providing that there is no doubting, negating thought, or statement made to cancel the request.

Meditation Is Prayer Without Words

For those who are unfamiliar with the practice of meditation, let me say that it is a natural continuation of prayer. When we talk to God, we tend first to pour out our troubles, then make our requests. Finally, having emptied our hearts, we rest and become reverently silent.

It is in this silence that we first begin to have a sense of God's Presence in and around us. As we linger in the stillness, in this Holy Temple within ourselves, we are able to hear our answers and receive guidance or healing. It is indeed, a Holy place, a Holy Moment which is readily available to all. However, the average person who looks for answers outside himself instead of within the "Holy of Holies" seldom visits this place.

Jesus taught, "The kingdom of heaven is within you." So is the "Holy of Holies." Meditation is the act of making that connection, of becoming attuned to God directly. Those who feel separated from God can connect by way of their Guardian Angel. Angels help us find our way back home to God when we feel we have strayed. (In truth, we are never separated, but through our own actions we can feel estranged.) Those who meditate regularly soon rediscover their God-connection and no longer need a winged go-between.

The Call to Worship

As you probably know, many cultures have set aside a special time or times every day for prayer, meditation, and entering the Presence of God. In many cities church bells still toll at the most holy times of the day—sunrise, noon, and sunset. (Many modern churches, having lost the ancient knowledge of sacred times, have switched to six a.m., twelve noon, and six p.m.)

The greatest value of meditation is in making the connection between the low-self (personality) and the God-self (soul).

Over time, this practice weaves a thread that becomes a bridge between the two selves, allowing the free flow of guidance from the God-self. As this develops, we become more attuned, more intuitive, and are guided into ever-higher levels of growth and awareness.

Those who faithfully make this connection over time become serene and centered. They always seem to know what to do in any situation and are seldom thrown off balance. They tend to have infinitely more patience than the average person does. In addition, these people appear to be highly sensitive to their surroundings, more aware of current situations and upcoming events. Often, they are also aware of the thoughts, feelings, and needs of those around them. For all these reasons, I strongly recommend meditation as a daily practice for all those who desire to improve their lives and grow spiritually.

My God-Self Contact

To give an example of what can happen from meditation and contact with one's God-self, let me share with you one of my most enlightening experiences.

I was attending a workshop with a group of men and women gathered in a classroom. Our teacher led us into meditation with some soft, soothing music. After a few moments of silence, she instructed us to blend into and become one with our God-selves. As I moved into this feeling of oneness with my God-self, I was immediately flooded with great radiance. This essence seemed to pour into my whole body, filling it with light, love, and joy. Then it seemed to overflow, filling my aura and spreading all around the room. I gasped in awe, totally mesmerized and spellbound.

After a moment or so of feeling greatly uplifted and inspired, I pondered, "What would I do if I really was fully connected to my God-self?" Instantly I had a strong urge to send love, healing, and blessings to my fellow students. Without a moment's hesitation I saw myself as my God-self in loose, white robes, standing up with arms outstretched in blessing, sending out this wonderful love and healing light. I could see these energies shimmering in soft, rainbow colors radiating to everyone in the room. The experience was astounding and wonderful, both joyous and highly uplifting. I was ecstatic, exhilarated, and in awe!

I sat in stunned silence until, our exercise finished. We each opened our eyes and looked at one another. Suddenly, the woman beside me turned, looked straight at me, and said, "Hey! I felt that." Surprised and quite certain that no one could possibly know what I had done, I countered, "Felt what?" The woman then proceeded to describe the outpouring of light and love that I had sent to the group. I listened in absolute astonishment while others in the group chimed in to say that they had also felt this radiance. Although a few were unaware of the source, everyone had felt the light and love. I was amazed to find that this visualization done inside my head could have such an astounding effect on so many people. Obviously, when we connect with our God-self we have far greater power than we have ever imagined possible.

Since that time and that fantastic connection I have been able to ask questions such as what to do? What is going on? Where is that misplaced article? And most of the time I get instant answers.

Comments on Meditation

"When a person learns to be still long enough to actually feel or be conscious of the Presence of God, a new understanding begins to develop in his consciousness."[3]

"Prayer is direct supplication to God, meditation is the attuning of ourselves mentally, physically and spiritually to the spirit with and without so that God may speak to us. It is stilling ourselves in order to listen, to become aware, to feel His presence and receive His guidance and His strength."[4]

Through meditation, you will enhance your spiritual growth and evolvement, bringing many new ideas and opportunities your way. You have nothing to lose but a little time and everything to gain from this practice.

Making a God-Self Connection

There has been frequent mention of your Guardian Angel as your guide and helper, but little about the details of making contact and getting "tuned in" to your God-self wisdom and power. I have included a special meditation exercise for contacting your God-self. You will greatly expand your ability to manifest your desires quickly and easily as you realign with your God-self and become more keenly aware of your guidance. You will also enhance your spiritual growth and evolvement, bringing many new ideas and opportunities your way.

Preparation for Meditation

Set a regular time each day for your meditation and keep that appointment as though it were very important, because it is. Your body and mind fall easily into the habit of being quiet at the appointed time, aiding the process immensely.

Meditation: Getting in Touch with Your God-Self

When beginning, meditate only four or five minutes, preferably twice a day. Later you can extend it to fifteen minutes or more. Plan to meditate twice a day, if possible, as this will speed your learning processes and increase spiritual progress.

1. Choose a time and place where you will not be disturbed.
2. Disconnect your phone or ringer.
3. If you wish to pray for others, have your prayer list ready.
4. Have pen and paper ready.
5. You may like some soft, soothing, non-verbal musical background.
6. Pick a spot where you can comfortably sit or lie down keeping your spine straight. (This is to allow spiritual energies [kundalini] to flow freely up your spinal column.) Once you find your "right place," use it regularly.
7. Loosen tight clothing.
8. If you feel a bit tense, do a few neck rolls. (Starting with your chin on your chest, slowly roll your head around over your shoulder, back as far as possible over your backbone, over the other shoulder, and back to the chin. Do three times to the right and three times to the left. This will ease neck and back tensions effectively.
9. Say, "I clothe myself safely 'round with infinite love and wisdom."
10. Relax, breathing slowly and deeply. As you exhale, let go of all worries and tensions. As you inhale, breathe in God's love and peace. Continue to do this until you feel totally relaxed and at ease.
11. Begin with a sincere prayer about how you feel and what you need. Take some time to review your present situation. Look at the conditions in your life that you would like to change. Ask for help in honestly evaluating these. You may want to ask how you are attracting the things not wanted, what is going on, what is the lesson, and which way to go.
12. Once you have poured out your problems, talk to God or your angel about your special needs, voicing the desires of your heart and asking for guidance. You are not asking God to do things for you, but are asking for help, insight, and understanding in order to create wisely for yourself.

Meditation

1. Move out of the physical, "only human" self.
2. Move out of the emotional, reactionary, "prone to upset" self.
3. Move out of your mental, "should/shouldn't" self.
4. Open yourself to receive God's love and wisdom.
5. In the stillness of your being, talk to God, inviting Him to come closer, to make His presence known to you. Feel yourself moving into oneness with your God-self.
6. Cease all mind-chatter. Listen quietly and intently for your answers and insights. Understand this may come as a thought, a feeling, a voice, or a picture within you. Take your time. Let it happen. Give yourself some time to develop these skills.
7. Move into your God-self, who sees the overview and knows the wisdom of your soul, your purpose, your lessons to be learned, your wisdom to be gained, and the understanding you need.
8. Feel the peace and love of God gently pouring into you, washing over you, filling you with love, joy, wisdom, understanding, healing, beauty, or whatever you feel you need.
9. See a beautiful, protective white light surrounding you, pouring into you, starting above your head and moving down into your body. Let the light fill your toes, your feet, ankles, legs, hips, chest, shoulders, and down into your arms and hands. Feel your hands tingling with light.
10. Feel God's light filling your neck and your head, then overflowing into your emotional body, your mental body, and into the wholeness of your being.
11. Allow yourself to be filled with overflowing love, light, and joy.
12. Feel yourself surrounded with God's loving presence and allow yourself to bask in that love light for a few moments.
13. Hold this loving state of God-connection, God Presence as long as possible without straining. If your mind wanders, bring it gently back to the stillness. You may feel yourself lifting or floating upward, then gradually coming back down. This is normal but does not necessarily happen all the time. At this returning point, you can end your meditation with a prayer.
14. Because you are in a very high state of vibration with good healing energies you may wish to close by sending love, light, healing, or blessings to your family members, friends, co-workers, or even your enemies. Send healing to yourself or others for any condition you feel needs it, such as peace or healing to Mother Earth.

15. When you feel complete, you may wish to state your intentions for a certain situation and ask your God-self to assist you in bringing this to a co-creative conclusion. Invite your God-self to be your companion and helper in this. See your present problems from the viewpoint of your God-self and reevaluate your position. Rethink your chosen paths and viewpoints in the light of your greater understanding and knowingness. Then end with a prayer of thanks.
16. Return to waking consciousness and quietly write down your insights, feelings, impressions, and/or answers. Also, write whatever else comes to you at this time. Do not stop to judge or question what comes until you are finished. Remember, your soul knows, but your intellect tends to argue.
17. Know that having once made this contact, you can return to this loving space again and again.
18. Should you feel your answer is not clear or complete, you may ask more questions another time, until you feel you have a good understanding or feel a sense of completion. If nothing else comes, then let it go. Be content that you have asked the question and it will be answered. Understand this may take some time. You may have asked for more than you can be given or understand at this moment. Be willing to wait. Keep a stance of alertness, watching and listening for your answers that can come to you in many ways in the next few days.

At first, you may see, hear, and feel absolutely nothing. Be at peace with this; it is normal for beginners. Record any insights or feelings, however brief or unbelievable. Later, as you learn to trust yourself more, you will receive stronger pictures, impressions, and insights. Experiences may vary greatly from one person to another. Don't judge yourself as having failed because your experience was "different" from someone else's. In fact, it is better not to make comparisons at all, at least not at first. Give yourself time to establish your own unique style. Remember there is no wrong way. Whatever happens is just right for you.

You may find you work best doing your meditation first and then asking questions, remaining "in the silence" for a while. Feel free to experiment with several variations of this suggested outline until you find the one that feels right for you. Also be aware that in the passing weeks, months, and years your way of meditation will gradually change. Be open to any change that feels good to you.

To help you get started, you may want to make a tape recording of the steps going into meditation to use for awhile. You might even do this with some special meditative music in the background.

Recording Meditations in a Journal

For myself, I like to keep a meditation and dream notebook beside me whenever I meditate. Ideas and insights often come rushing into my mind even before I have finished meditation. These messages are often highly personal, inspirational, informational, and instructional on many levels. The insights and advice that have flowed into my being have been excellent, reliable, and sometimes quite surprising.

I'll tell you a little secret: many of the insights and information I use in this and other books have come directly after meditation. Frankly, this is how I know I am ready to write another book. When the information comes through on a regular basis, it is time to go to the computer and write. I call this my "divine dictation," as it is not the same thing as "automatic writing."

Let me add a word of caution. One needs to be careful to write only what flows freely and naturally. You cannot force your intuitive flow. If you try to push for more you are likely to receive misleading information colored by your intellect or wishful thinking. Often this will cut off your flow altogether, so be careful.

There may be times when you are under pressure or there is too much on your mind and nothing seems to flow. On those days, it is best to just give your thanks, lay down your pen, and walk away. Never try to force anything — it will only delay things.

If you are a beginner, follow the above meditation exercise to start, later add your own personal variations. Read a book or two on meditation.

Some Meditation Seed Thoughts

For variety in your meditations, you may want to hold the following ideas.

- My God-self is filling me with love, wisdom, and understanding.
- My God-self is guiding me to my highest good.
- My God-self is guiding me to perfection through my life's experiences.
- My God-self is filling me with _____.
- I am always in the right place at the right time.
- I am always in God's Presence.

Meditation: Getting in Touch with Your God-Self

Additional Ideas for Meditation
Ask for a dream to help you discover your hang-ups or find the cause of some problem, or ask for insights into the best ways to resolve an unhappy situation.

Picture yourself basking in a beam of love, beauty, or whatever God-like quality you need. For added visual effect, add color.

Pink = Love, Joy, Trust
Gold = Wisdom, Divine Inspiration
Yellow = Intelligence, Success
Red = Life, Energy, Courage
Green = Healing, Abundance, Growth
Purple = Spirituality, Intuition
Blue = Truth, Strength
Lavender = Peace
Light Blue = Serenity, Faith, Forgiveness
White = Purity, Light
Rainbow = Harmony
Orange = Creativity, Positiveness

Mini Meditations
Overall, the regular practice of meditation is one of your greatest tools for mental, emotional, and spiritual growth. In addition, this is your way to feel empowered, enlightened, and connected to your Source. From this stance, you are at your creative best. Everything seems to fall in place for you. Your creations manifest quickly and all is well in your world.

Walk in love, wisdom, and joy.

15

Body Talk

The body is the servant of the mind.
—James Allen

Coming in As a Soul

In Genesis 1:26, God created man in "His image and likeness." In other words, God created us as spiritual beings, as souls. (Physical bodies came later, Genesis 2:7.)

As souls living in heavenly planes, we know ourselves to be eternal beings. We are born as babies in body only. The soul, which activates the body, is the real essence of who we are. We are born with far more wisdom and understanding than is currently acknowledged. We come in knowing who we are.

We also have a definite plan for what is to be accomplished in our lifetime and a time for when, where, and how we will exit our human body. Once decided, this blueprint is firmly imbedded in the soul-mind, showing up at birth in our astrology chart, fingerprints, and palms. In fact, our whole body is imprinted with our soul purpose.

As we grow from infancy through childhood and are able to give voice to what we know or see, the accepted beliefs of our family and society are quickly imposed upon us. At every new event we are firmly taught to conform to the norm and to look, think, and act like those around us. Anything we say or do outside the local belief system is promptly squelched. Under this kind of condemnation we quietly shut down our inborn psychic abilities one by one. The soul-knowing we had as children is usually lost by the age of seven.

Because of this societal training, most children beyond age seven have limited their ability to see nonphysical entities to peripheral vision only. A good example is seeing something "out of the corner of your eye" but when you look straight at it, you can't see it any more. This is a learned limitation. So it goes: incident by incident we are trained to doubt ourselves and shut down our natural, soul-given gifts. Society denies us until we learn to deny ourselves.

For this reason, psychic abilities seem to be inherited. Actually, all of us are born as spiritual beings with multiple soul gifts, but only those born in families where these abilities are accepted rather than denied can develop to their fullest potential. The rest of us are deprogrammed and unempowered quickly and firmly. Fortunately, our spiritual talents can be reawakened once we recognize the false programming and begin to accept and use our special gifts.

Becoming Disenfranchised

Disenfranchise: To deprive one of a right or privilege.
—Funk & Wagnall

To disenfranchise people is to subtract them from their heritage. Then they don't know who they are and can be made to do whatever someone else wants them to do.
—Robert Ghost Wolf

This is essentially what has been done to us. Because of society's "conform or else" policy, we begin to develop a growing sense of separation from knowing who we are, a soul living in a physical body. To bridge this gap, we begin building an artificial self to fit the mold our family and social circle demands. We begin to associate more closely with our false self. By the age of seven, we have taken on most of the local beliefs and social programming of limitation and fear. We have learned to hate the people and religions our relatives hate. We think, judge, and act out these teachings by way of our artificial, personality self. Our real selves, our souls, are shoved into oblivion. The process is complete. We have forgotten our heritage. We don't know who we are.

One of the most important things we need to regain as grownups is the ability to believe in ourselves once more. We need to trust our built-in power to know what is right for us, a power we should never have given away in the first place.

Development of the Personality Self

Personality development is a learned survival mechanism built to cope with the laws and beliefs of the society in which you chose to be born. Fear of ridicule, rejection, or punishment keeps you in line. You adjust and act out the role your family and their fear-based society have imposed.

As this separation increases, your energy and power flow into the false self. You engage in thoughts and acts that go against your basic soul purpose. Further separation occurs. You begin to feel divided. You may catch yourself saying, "Part of me wants ___ but the other part of me wants ___." (This is how you recognize that you are splintered.)

Meanwhile, deep inside, your soul remembers the plan. Eventually the ego self goes its own way. Later, as you stray further and further from your true purpose, your soul begins to give you important warning signals.

Your Soul Speaks

Your physical body is the product of the soul-mind and records everything you have ever heard into your cellular memory. Meanwhile, your physical body is also the vehicle your soul uses to work, play, and gather experiences while living on the earth plane. Therefore, the body is the bearer of messages from the soul, the real you, as opposed to the personality or false self. The body's discomforts, aches, and pains give warning. Its rashes, swellings, weight gain, tensions, heavy-heartedness, "dis-ease," and so-called "accidents" are all speaking a symbolic language to tell you where and how you are out of balance.

Your God-self often speaks to you through your body by way of your feelings, especially in the area of your solar plexus. The gut feeling area responds instantly to the words, actions, and emotional output of others, as well as to the situations occurring around you. A feel-good reaction is an instant sign of approval but negative reactions may warn of impending problems. These gut feelings are an excellent indicator of when you are "in the flow" (of your soul purpose), as opposed to struggling against the current, indicating that you are going against your own inner knowing.

Soul Talk

Your soul-mind has wisdom gained from many lifetimes and has unlimited access to all the knowledge of the universe. It is never at a loss for wisdom. Only the ego (personality) has to look things up in a book.

Out of this great wisdom, your soul speaks to you in many subtle ways that are easily ignored until you learn to understand and respect its valuable information.

Examples:

- **Intuition:** A sudden "knowing," a small voice speaking inside your head, a hunch, or gut feeling.

- **Insights:** Flashes of inside-your-head sights such as meaningful pictures or symbols giving you instant understanding.
- **Feelings:** Sudden body chills (usually confirms what has just been said). Sudden fear may be a repulsion, a gut feeling, a warning, or a hunch. You may also have good, happy feelings.
- **Dreams:** Daydreams are a natural way of visualizing the desires of your heart or can show you what you really want. Nightmares are warnings, usually spurring you to face your fears and overcome them. Symbolic dreams are usually problem solving. ESP or precognitive dreams can give glimpses of the future.[1]
- **Advice:** Helpful ideas, insights, or comments from friends, even strangers.
- **Synchronicity:** Meeting key people, finding a significant book, magazine article, radio commentary, or TV program that gives you the needed answer for the question or problem in mind.

When these simple devices are ignored, stronger messages become necessary in the form of body aches and pains, minor injuries, short-term illnesses like colds or minor accidents that force you to spend some time in bed. Should these fail to grab your attention, more drastic measures may be used, such as losing your job, home, mate, close family member, or serious injury or illness. (A few days or weeks spent in a hospital will give you plenty of time to think.)

How Your Body Talks to You

Scientists now agree that emotions not only define the size and shape of your body but also create chemical changes as you swing from mood to mood. You can literally make yourself sick from negative emotions as well as from spoken words such as "He gives me a pain in the neck." (Had any neck or throat problems lately?)

All problems found in your body come from a mental or emotional problem in your relationship with your soul, yourself, or other people. For instance, when you get "out of sorts" with your neighbor because of something said or done, who do you think gets the chemical spill from that?

Almost all of us have unresolved issues with our parents which need healing. In fact, any person at whom you are angry needs your forgiveness. Anger, grudges, and resentments held onto give rise to illness, usually in the form of cancer. Yet peace can be made, even when the person no longer resides among the living.

I worked on forgiving my parents for several years before and after they died. It took a very long time to realize I had chosen critical parents to help me forgive myself and work through my own self-criticism carried over from many centuries.

Body Talk

Difficulties with the right side of your body represent unresolved matters with a male or the masculine part of yourself. Issues on the left side indicate problems with a woman or your feminine side. Repeated incidents on the same side of the body indicate a real need to do some mental/emotional work on mending that relationship before it manifests as a serious disease.

The one exception to this left/right rule is the brain. Because of the crossover of the nerves, the left brain is male and the right brain is female.[2] (Intend to find a balance between these halves for optimum mental efficiency rather than using one or the other exclusively as many do.)

Look closely at synchronous events and the symbolic meanings in your life. Question what the message may be. Evaluate carefully to see where you need to change your thinking. Your guidance is all around you, everywhere you go. All you see and hear has a message for you to get your attention back to your spiritual roots. You are given whatever it takes to awaken and return you to your soul-knowing.

A good point to consider is that God's Life Force always flows through you, but your fears, false beliefs and doubts can stifle the flow to the point of illness and even death.

How Illness Speaks to You

> *I want to awaken that still, small, wise intuitive voice in all of us, that voice of our own body that we have been forced to ignore through our culture's illness, misinformation and dysfunction.*
> —Christiane Northrup, M.D.[3]

In today's society, you have learned to ignore or override your body messages. You take a pill for pain, coffee or a soft drink to keep going, alcohol or pills to speed you up or slow you down, and more pills to go to sleep. Somehow, it never occurs to you to listen to what your body is trying to say—as if it weren't the only body you have.

Your body was designed to last indefinitely. Therefore, the purpose of all body discomfort, however mild, is a message from your soul. When the body feels tired, it is time for a break, perhaps a nap. Fatigue is a warning that you are stressing yourself in a way that can eventually cause illness. A good example is how you feel when someone hurts your feelings and you retaliate by withholding your love, blocking its natural flow and thereby causing yourself to stagnate. Restricting the magnificent flow of energy from your God-self not only causes heart problems but is the basic reason for all illness.

Good health is a natural state of being. "Dis-ease" is a signal that you are out of alignment with your God-self. Ignore your body signals and your body will speak to you by means of minor pains, injuries, or "dis-ease." Keep ignoring the message and you can have major pain, accidents, or serious illnesses.

Anxiety and tensions are a physical sign of subtle fears. Left unresolved, they cause emotional resistance to whatever you are thinking, feeling, or doing. Most stress in the workplace is due to being in a job unsuitable for your talents. But if you are afraid of changing careers, you may elect to stay where you are, although you are uncomfortable. The result is stress-caused fatigue.

Many fears are totally unfounded or based on old programming, such as "not good enough." (Many of us have that one.) You should pause long enough to take a good look at your fears. Sometimes it is only a minor thing like, "What will people think?" Look at the things to which you are attached. Behind each of these is a fear that can lead to poor health.

Name your fear. Face it honestly, then think about what you would really like to be doing with your life. Play with the idea that every time you go against your soul's purpose, there is inner, fear-based resistance that acts as friction inside your body. It is as if the personality is stepping on the gas while the soul is riding the brakes. As you persist in going against the soul flow, the resistance produced is actually wearing down your body from the inside out. (Fear-based worriers tend to age early and die young.)

On the other hand, when you are feeling good about yourself and what you are doing, your body works in perfect harmony. Like a child at play, you are almost tireless. That's when you know that you're in the flow.

Are you happy with your job? Are you happy with your life? Or are you dissatisfied? "Dis-eased?" What do you need to add or remove to be happy and at ease?

Stress Is the Main Cause of Illness

Disease comes to those whose minds and bodies are receptive to it.
— James Allen[4]

Did you know that irritation is as destructive as toxic waste to your body? Negative, fear-based emotions are the main cause of physical strain and disease. People who feel they must be in control, must work hard, and must fight to win are usually overly defensive, pushing and stressing themselves in a process that soon becomes a destructive mental habit. Many problems are triggered by mental/emotional imbalances that gradually become habitual patterns of negative thinking. The cure is to face and deal with the basic fear. You may be surprised to find it only a trivial childhood trauma, no longer applicable in your life today. Whatever it turns out to be, once healed it is a simple matter to change your negative mind-sets to positive ones.

Some Typical Body-Mind Related "Dis-eases"

- **Arthritis:** Inflexible attitudes, such as resentment, lack of forgiveness, and unexpressed anger may become crystallized in the joints. In my case, I was being overwhelmed, overloaded, and stressed. I took on more than I could handle and the result was instant arthritis. I literally could not "stand" this, so my feet mirrored my fear and stress and the pain was so great I was hardly able to walk. When I realized this, I let go of the extra load and had instant remission. P.S. I got the message.
- **Arthritic Hands or Fingers Curled Tight:** Unable to give, receive, let go, or forgive.
- **Arthritic Feet:** Unable to "stand" the situation.
- **Asthma, Hay Fever:** Inner weeping, acute need for love, affection, and nurturing.
- **Backache:** Unsupported mentally, emotionally, or financially. In what way do you feel unsupported? In what area of your life?
- **Blisters, Burns:** Slow inner burn (anger), irritation, and hot spots. This includes sunburn and poison ivy.
- **Cancer:** Unexpressed anger, grief, pain, resentment, and unforgivingness. (Often starts with deep grief or pain and can take two to seven years to develop fully.)

- **Choking, Coughing:** Something you said, choking on your own words, thoughts, or attitudes; a needed soul message.
- **Cold:** Confusion, mixed feelings not sorted out. Take time to re-evaluate your situation.
- **Constipation:** Holding on, an outer manifestation of inner inability to let go of old stuff; mental, emotional, or physical.
- **Depression:** Suppressed anger that depletes the body. Once started, may be worsened by indulgence in self-pity.
- **Diarrhea:** Upsetting, emotional situation. Wanting to get it out of your system. Urgent need to let go, forgive, heal the hurt, or depart in peace.
- **Headache:** Mental battle between you and an authority-type figure.
- **Heart:** High blood pressure, pressuring, pushing, and stressing yourself. A high resistance to what you are doing or how you are doing it. Beware of doing things when your heart isn't in it. Can be inner rebellion toward your boss. Feeling that you must be in control, struggle, or fight to win. Attitude of defensiveness. Can't let down your guard. Unable to trust your soul or the universe. Withholding expressions of love.
- **Poor Circulation:** Restricting or withholding your love flow.
- **Hemorrhoids:** Mad bumps.
- **Indigestion:** Mental/emotional inability to digest or handle a situation. It is not what you ate — it is what is eating you. Who is the matter with you? Who or what is it you can't stomach?
- **Acid Stomach:** Suppressed anger, tension, irritation, and lack of peace, something "eating you," soured outlook. A call for love and attention to your needs. What will make you happy?
- **Heartburn:** Mini version of indigestion. Can be fear-based stress or uneasiness. Soul message that you are out of balance.
- **Butterflies, Knots-in-the-Stomach:** Tension, usually fear based. Fear of failure, judgment. Name and face your fear. Make needed changes in attitude or job, because it won't go away; it will just become an ulcer. (See Acid Stomach.)
- **Overeating:** Feeling unfulfilled. Life is not satisfactory; the soul wants something more, but food is not the answer. May be feeling defenseless.
- **Overweight:** Extra weight can be a protective coat of armor, especially for abused persons. Or one may need to throw his or her weight around, be a "big wheel" to be in control and to feel safe.
- **Rash:** Outer manifestations of inner irritation, aggravation, and anger.
- **Shoulder Pain:** A feeling of being overwhelmed, an overload of responsibilities, pain, or guilt.

- **Sinus Drainage:** Inner need to cry, release pain and sorrow, and deal with hurt feelings. Chronic sinus problems: go back to when this began to find and make peace with the pain.
- **Sore Throat:** Guilt and pain for failing to speak or for speaking or revealing too much.
- **Sweet Tooth:** Craving for the "sweet things in life," trying to fill a void, need for love, fulfillment, or soul satisfaction.
- **Ulcers:** Gnawing fears eating away inside. May be failure to make a needed change in job or lifestyle or a soul need ignored.
- **Underweight:** Feeling helpless, vulnerable, and powerless. Not big or strong enough, can't pull your weight. Can be a "pity party" or need for love and attention. Ask, "What am I denying myself?" Why?

Just a few of the more common physical manifestations of our inner thoughts, feelings and attitudes are listed to give you an idea of how illness works for you. Further information can be found in a list of recommended books at the back of this book.

All disease is a result of an inhibited soul life.
—Alice Bailey[5]

"Dis-ease" is a lack of ease and harmony between soul and personality. Any number of things can trigger the accident or illness but the basic, underlying cause is always the same—lack of forgiveness. When you dig deep enough to get to the bottom of the problem, the final answer will be not forgiving yourself. (Usually for overriding your soul-knowing and doing something unloving.)

You are accountable for the quality of your life and health. You are also accountable for your life and your body health. Regardless of what you have been taught in any lifetime, the soul *knows* and never forgets that the basic Law of the Universe is *love*. Your soul holds the goal of love as its standard. Therefore, any unloving acts go against the soul goal and contribute to disharmony and stress, which eventually affects the physical body. Anything out of alignment with love must be made right before the soul can return home to its Father God.

Since the human body is a direct result of the soul's condition it is vital to pay attention to the messages your soul is giving you. Take a look at what is bringing you discomfort or pain and make an effort to set things right. Not long ago there was a popular saying, "If Mama ain't happy, ain't nobody happy." Think of your soul as "Mama" to your personality self and get happy.

A good point to consider is just what is your soul purpose? What is your spiritual ideal? Look at the things you have always longed for or wanted. This will help you describe your soul goal. Even though you may not be really clear as to what that may be, if you are reading this book you are probably following a soul-directed path anyway. For greater clarity, try daily meditation at least ten minutes a day. (Meditation is the Internet of information for the soul.)

Love Is the Only Law We Need

Earth life is a battle of what the soul knows versus what the personality thinks it knows. Love is the only law you need. When you practice gentle, loving kindness to all, no other law is needed. Eventually, you will recognize yourself as a soul with a body, rather than a body with a soul, and allow your God-self to be in charge of your life.

Meanwhile, if you fail to listen to your own inner knowing, do not express your own original soul-born ideas, or follow your intended soul path, you will have betrayed yourself. You can literally become soul sick: sick at heart, sick in mind, and sick in body. Talk about being depressed! In addition, no pill and no treatment ever devised will cure soul sickness.

The Message of Tension

Whenever your mind is anxious or frustrated and your body is becoming tense, realize that you are out of tune and into struggle. Why are you struggling? What are you struggling against? Do you love your job? Are you in your right place? If tensions build up at work, it may be your time to move on to something better. Look at your fears about change. Look at what you would really love to do.

Solar Plexus — Your Radar Screen

Deep stress starts as a tiny wave of anxiety running through your solar plexus. That quiver is an important message bearer. When it is disregarded you begin to experience pressure that gradually becomes full-fledged stress that can quickly destroy your body like termites eating your home.

Your solar plexus is your message center. Your feelings are the message bearers of guidance from your soul. The feel-good feelings are encouragement and the queasy feelings are warnings that you are moving in the wrong direction.

Think of your solar plexus as a radar center, constantly scanning your world and sending you messages about what is going on out there. It keeps you informed, warning you of impending problems or dangers. It is your faithful servant, giving insights through your feelings by day, guidance through dreams by night. Yet what do you do with those signals? Ignore them, of course. At the first sign of queasiness, you reach for an aspirin or antacid. If that doesn't work you go to a doctor and get something stronger. Yet all you are really doing is covering up your telltale symptoms. You have not treated the cause. All this fuss just to cover up your signals and ignore the message. Time to rethink.

Ignorance Is Not Always Bliss

Lack of understanding can get you in deep trouble. Rethink that habit of overriding your information system. If you were in a war-like situation you would watch your radar carefully, recognizing it as an early-warning system for your protection and knowing your safety would depend on heeding those messages. Now apply that thought to your solar plexus. Pay attention when a signal, however faint, quivers through your mid-section. Learn to quickly ascertain where it is coming from, who is sending or triggering it, and what is the message. (At times, you may also need to ask when to get the time frame.)

Often it is just a simple message such as, "Boss is coming ... he is upset ... be prepared." It may be someone sending a message: "Call me." Or, you could be "picking up" someone's anger at you. Justified or not, they are "mad at" you and there will be an angry confrontation unless you act to defuse the situation beforehand. These are little things, easily handled one by one but difficult to sort out when they are allowed to pile up.

Bigger gut-level tensions often denote many little messages piling up, pressing for attention. Ongoing, unrelenting tensions are often urgent needs too long ignored, that now press down like a weight on your shoulders. These can lead to serious illness. It could be a long-overdue soul need for a job change gnawing at your insides like an ulcer or cancer. In this case, your soul is actually threatening your personal, physical life if you don't change.

Understand that your initial message is only the tip of the iceberg. You can reach deeper into your feeling box and dig up much more information about a situation, especially as you learn to trust your senses, feelings, and inclinations. Your mind is not as limited as you have been led to believe. Your intuitive body/mind can pick up information anywhere on the planet and beyond once you learn to ask and listen.

Beginning with tension (often evidenced as butterflies), recognize this as your first signal of being out of tune with your soul. Instead of your usual response — ignoring the symptoms and pushing yourself even harder — stop a moment and ask yourself why you do this. Remember, working with high tension is wearing your body down from the inside out.

Who, What, When

Notice what part of your body is uptight. Note when it starts. Exactly who or what triggers your anxiety? Ask yourself why you are tense. (Anxiety is usually fear based.) What are you afraid of? Why? Is the job worth it? Or is the job okay, but your attitude is out of line? Do you dislike what you are doing? What needs to change? Ask who or what is bothering you. Try to pin down the basic fear or cause of the tension and work on the problem.

Continue with "What is the worst that can happen here? What are my options? What feels good?" Pray about it. Ask for guidance on what to do. Ask for help in accomplishing this. Remember, your soul prompts you with these little feeling signals. Its guidance is always gentle. You always have free will to say "no" or to ask for another option. Whatever it is, consider the message, do what needs to be done, and keep those signals from piling up into a major breakdown. For example, you have an every-day on-the-job tension headache that goes away at night and on weekends when you are not working. Hmmmm. Guess what that is telling you?

One of the most common causes of mid-life crisis is a buildup of all those signals and road signs you have avoided. When ignored too long, needed changes come suddenly in one big catastrophe that forces the change — like "You're fired."

Understand that when your soul shows you a problem area it always has a better, happier plan for you. So to quit (or graduate from) an uncomfortable position or relationship is to move on to a much better place. When you are in soul flow, peace of mind, good health, and prosperity just naturally come along with it. Trust yourself and go for the gold.

Once you learn the language of the soul, it is like having a Guardian Angel guiding and protecting you at all times.

Once Illness Strikes

Disease is caused by friction or stress between two of our selves, between the body and the soul. The soul knows the

purpose for which it came, and when it realizes that the human part of us is not cooperating, it becomes sick.
— Alice Steadman[6]

When illness strikes there are several things to consider. First, realize that "dis-ease" is always a mental/emotional/soul malfunction. More simply stated, it is a lack of harmony between the personality and your God-self. Second, bear in mind that most modern doctors only treat the symptoms, leaving the basic soul cause to recur repeatedly, often in a variety of other forms. Losing this battle can be dangerous to your health. Third, avoid claiming the "dis-ease" by saying "my migraine," "my arthritis," "my heart condition." The word *my* is claiming the condition as yours, so you get to keep it.

Finally, look for the source of the difficulty by asking yourself:

- What soul message(s) have I been ignoring?
- What have I secretly yearned to do, but have not done?
- Who have I failed to forgive? (Could be yourself)
- What do I need to release?
- What would it take to make me happy?

If this brings no answers, follow up with:

- What is the symbolic or literal meaning of the affected body part?
- What meaning is implied?
- On which symbolic side is the problem located, masculine or feminine?
- What person of that gender am I reacting to or against?
- What is the real reason for that reaction?
- What action does it signify?
- What is the result of the "dis-ease" and how does it change my life?
- What does it cause me to do?
- What does it keep me from doing?
- What are the immediate results?
- Name your fears about this. (Fears and victimhood go together.)

If that doesn't help, ask:

- What am I not seeing, hearing, or giving attention to?
- What have I been judging, condemning, or criticizing?

Once you get to the core of the whole chain reaction:

- Name it for what it is.
- Ask yourself what you need to forgive and release.
- Make a definite decision about it.
- List some positive changes you need to make.
- Write out your intents for dealing with the basic problem.

A Little Touch of Healing

All healing is self-healing.
— Albert Schweitzer

If you can get to the basic mental/emotional cause of the "dis-ease" and work out the soul/personality problem, your body will heal itself. So think twice before going to a doctor and getting some chemicals, especially if it is only a minor illness.

Deal with the body/mind/soul causes and you will have healed yourself at the point of origin. Treat the physical symptoms and you may get temporary relief, but the underlying cause is still at work and will reappear repeatedly, possibly in different forms, until the original cause is healed. This often calls for some serious soul searching, using your journal to find the reason behind the message (illness), and doing some forgiving. Your only cost will be some quality time spent with your soul, but the cure will be priceless. This is truly understanding the message of your soul.

An additional touch is to go into meditation, especially when you are feeling out of sorts. Lovingly command your body to adjust all parts back into perfect alignment and keep them that way. Affirm "My heart is in perfect harmony with the heart of God, and I am at peace."

Be Kind to Yourself

There are words that wound and words that heal. Most of us have been thoroughly taught to beat ourselves up over every little mistake. Remember that your body is a direct result of your thoughts, feelings, and beliefs. Knowing that your words and emotions are highly creative, stop criticizing yourself right now. You are actually doing damage to your body temple. Make yourself a promise to exchange the habit of harsh judgment for one of complimenting yourself for every good thing you do. Practice saying something nice about yourself every day. Learn to love and appreciate yourself just as you are. Regard yourself as a wise, kind, beautiful soul, which you are.

When making plans for your leisure time, avoid people who are quarrelsome, faultfinders, complainers, and negative, especially when they are family. Negative people drain your energy. Stay away from those who manipulate you into feeling guilty if you don't do something for them. Never let anyone talk you into doing something you really do not want to do. If your feelings say "no" it is a clear signal the other person is trespassing on your boundaries. Realize the person who is asking does not want to do his or her job and is asking you to do it for them.

Be aware of the damaging effects of forcing yourself to do something you don't want to do. What it amounts to is going against your own (soul) grain. This often stresses your muscles, because deep inside you are resisting. For example, my friend Ted loves to play tennis, but his friend Greg prefers other sports. One very hot day Ted persuaded Greg to play tennis in spite of the heat. Obligingly, Greg overrode his own feelings and played well, but guess who wound up with a tennis elbow? Was that a coincidence? Or a message?

It is more important to heal the heart than to heal the body. Be quick to forgive yourself and others when you have a problem. Get it solved as soon as possible rather than letting it fester until it becomes an illness.

Spend more time with happy friends. Laughter is healing for body and soul. Cultivate more loving, supporting, positive-thinking friends. Make a list of things you love and keep it handy for times when you are feeling a bit blue.

When tired, soak yourself in a hot, fragrant, relaxing bath; add candles or even bubbles. Pamper yourself. Take a long walk in the woods and commune with nature. Find a fairy or a rainbow. Look for happy people and events. Indulge in warm, loving, and appreciative thoughts that bring more joy into your life. Remember, what you think is what you get. Think goodwill, love, joy, and laughter. Keep on the sunny side of everything. It is good for your health.

Practice the fine art of meditation on a daily basis for the ultimate peace of body, mind, and soul. Close with something like "I now give myself permission to be kind, gentle, and serene with myself and others. I allow myself to go with the flow like a beautiful swan on peaceful waters."

Mystical Magical You

> Our birth is but a sleep
> And a forgetting;
> The Soul that rises with us,
> Our life's Star,
> Hath elsewhere had its setting
> And cometh from afar;
> Not in entire forgetfulness,
> And not in utter nakedness,
> But trailing clouds of glory
> Do we come
> From God, who is our home.
> —William Wordsworth[7]

16

Mirror, Mirror on the Wall

O would some power the Giftee give us to see ourselves as others see us.[1]
— Robert Burns

If you have ever visited an amusement park, you have probably walked down the Hall of Mirrors at least once. Think about those tricky mirrors and how they exaggerated your features. Do you remember how one made you look extremely tall and skinny and another made you appear ridiculously short and fat? Or what about those that mixed the areas of width and length to give your face or body comic proportions? It was great fun to look at yourself and laugh, a harmless little joke, all in a day's adventures.

Life itself is very much like a Hall of Mirrors. As creators of our worlds, we are constantly running into people and circumstances that not only reflect but often exaggerate our faults in a way that allows us to look at ourselves and laugh. All too often though, we fail to see the humor.

People as Our Mirrors

All of our person-to-person relationships are interactive in nature. Friends, coworkers, and especially family members are constantly acting as mirrors, reflecting our mannerisms, attitudes, and habits. This constant interplay, when seen in its proper perspective, enables us to adjust our behavior patterns into greater harmony with those around us. Consequently, we learn flexibility and keep ourselves aligned with whatever is expected of us. This continuous interchange is so subtle that we often are totally unaware of the ongoing process. However, when we fail to "get the message" or worse, refuse to heed it, the dynamics become more aggressive and the reflections are more exaggerated, just like those crazy amusement park mirrors. At this point some of us become annoyed, even angry. Like the proverbial pot calling the kettle black, we may blame the mirror for the faults we see reflected there, not realizing the defects we find are our own.

Seasons and Cycles

He who lives by the sword must die by the sword.
—Matthew 26:52

Everything moves in cycles and seasons and people come and go. Even the thought forms we send out cycle back to us. We set things in motion by our thoughts, words, and deeds, so in time we reap the results—good or bad. When we are kind and loving to those around us, we enjoy the cyclic return. When we dwell in anger, resentment, or vengeance, the results are somewhere between uncomfortable and downright horrible. We have no one to blame but ourselves. Moreover, we have to deal with it. Our lesson is to experience the pain of being on the receiving end of what we have thoughtlessly done to others; to understand the heartbreak, learn from the experience, and hopefully, to change our attitude to something more loving. If not, the lesson comes back repeatedly until we recognize and clean up the negative thoughts and deeds we so carelessly committed.

Parents

Any close relationship is, in effect, a teaching/learning experience. This is especially true in our family life. Remember, we deliberately chose our parents and siblings as part of our classroom structure for this life's lessons. Both the good and the bad things are a portion of our curriculum for graduation from the School of Earth. Former errors in attitude or behavior must be balanced and brought back into loving relationships.

As babies and toddlers, we learn first by observation. We take in the feelings, emotions, and actions of those we see around us. We are strongly imprinted by those closest to us. Our first model for male qualities comes from the image of our fathers, and our female impressions come from our mothers, or the most prevalent caregiver. This early programming can last a lifetime, strongly affecting our male/female belief systems, our boy/girl behavior patterns, and our choice of mates in later years.

Early in life we begin to mimic the actions and mannerisms we have observed around us, carefully watching to see the expressions of our parents, always seeking their smiles of approval and adjusting our behavior accordingly. Needing their love, we repeat patterns that bring approval and strive to avoid parental anger. Notice how quickly toddlers learn to go to the most permissive parent or grandparent to get their wishes met.

→ Mirror, Mirror On the Wall

As we grow older, our parents teach us their philosophy of life by word, deed, and thought, including religious beliefs, political views, prejudices, and opinions, as well as their preferred methods of doing things. We learn their house rules and their way of playing the game of life — impressions we may hold forever. Sometimes the guidelines are good, but often they show us the lack of wisdom and the unfairness of some of society's rules. This leads us to realizing just how harmful some teachings are so that we will make the needed changes in our beliefs and perhaps do something to improve the ideologies of those around us.

Parents not only mold our character, but label us. The "baby" of a family is often thought of and treated as a baby, even after the age of forty. The family clown remains the clown and so forth. Both parents and siblings tend to hold us mentally in old patterns and labels that no longer apply. Consequently, we may be goaded into standing up for our rights before we can "graduate" from these unpleasant situations. It is good to realize these are all necessary parts of our growing up process.

Karmic Lessons and Family
Learning to take full responsibility for all your thoughts, words, decisions, and actions

People having difficult relationships with others are people who have lessons to learn and debts to pay. Generally, if difficulties started in childhood, the basic problems were carried over from previous lives. For example, a man lives a life of raping, pillaging, burning, and mistreating others from the standpoint of believing it was "his privilege" or with the excuse that he was "under orders."

How can this be balanced? Think what that person would need to experience in a subsequent life in order to learn how painful it can be to the recipient of those acts. What would have to happen for him or her to learn the pain and shame of rape? Having his or her home burned? Children taken away? How could this person learn except by personal experience? The lesson is usually called cause and effect, or karma. Again, the scales of justice must be balanced before that person can move on.

Even before birth, we draw to us those who will mirror our worst faults. Often this is in an exaggerated manner in order to be sure we will be offended enough to master that unwanted trait. This is how we choose to teach ourselves. Along with the obvious parental teachings there may be some difficult, built-in lessons, sometimes referred to as karma (soul lessons), which other members of the family do not have to endure. As a rule, the soul has chosen these carefully selected personal experiences as a high-priority learning for this life (prebirth agreements). Meanwhile, our parents and family members are, at soul level, aware of these special plans and have agreed to serve as both teachers and catalysts. At times, the lessons can be extremely painful. Learning may come through illness, accident, abuses, or whatever was needed for us to develop the life quality or virtue our souls desired. This may include all kinds of pleasant or unpleasant situations designed and agreed upon by our souls to help us develop certain qualities or to lead us in a special direction.

For example, vision or hearing impairments may force people to go deep inside themselves and develop traits and skills that would never have been gained living a so-called normal life. While living with these difficulties and enduring painful events it is all too easy to feel angry, resentful, and perhaps cheated out of all that could have been. In such cases, many children, having been denied the knowledge of reincarnation and not understanding the process of reaping and sowing, will become bitter, reeking with rage and resentment and feeling victimized. They may waste much time in blaming those around them for their apparent misfortune, greatly prolonging and possibly preventing the growth and understanding their soul is seeking. Yet we can avoid all this if we understand that there are no accidents and that "All things work together for good" (Romans 8:28).

Yes, each of us has agreed upon a plan. All we need to do now is stop complaining about our bad luck and *get on with the program.*

In cases where family members show little or no love and encouragement the child may soon quit trying to please and feel deeply wounded, rejected and unworthy. (This lays the emotional groundwork for becoming victims.) Eventually the child may rebel, feeling strongly that life is not fair. Yet, most often this is a karmic situation from a former life when the child was cold and unloving to others. Experiencing a lack of love can be a painful but very effective way of learning and understanding the immense value of loving and nurturing others. We always get what we deserve and reap what we have sown, not as punishment, but as lessons to teach us the immense value of creating loving relationships with all beings, not just a chosen few.

Inherited Family Beliefs and Misconceptions

A friend of mine confided that her mother often told her, "You are no good without me." This statement, heard in her early childhood has become part of her basic belief system and is still causing deep pain even today, some thirty years later. Although she has now moved far from her mother's influence, she still has difficulty making decisions without mom and allowing herself to enjoy life, because she still feels that she is no good. What can be done?

So far, counseling hasn't helped much. In cases like this, when a false belief has been deeply implanted, it often requires hypnotherapy to go back to the original cause of the problem. This usually reveals past-life actions when the client has done something similar to someone else and is now learning how easily, how deeply words can wound. When one comes to this understanding, there is a need to step back and take a good look at the so-called problem. It is important for the "victim" to see this as a needed lesson and to evaluate carefully what was learned from it, rather than spend the rest of his or her life being angry and resentful. This only brings more lessons to learn.

> *Love one another, even as I have loved you.*
> —John 15:12

Once we understand the great wisdom and beauty behind the concept of reincarnation we can let go of our anger and get on with our lives by learning the Law of Love. From there, we must make the effort to set new and better patterns.

We need to allow ample time to understand the lesson and realize our co-creative roles in the Law of Cause and Effect. Take full responsibility. Then, to graduate from victim to victor, we must recognize the value of the wisdom gained. This paves the way for the most important step: the act of forgiveness for all persons, including ourselves. We must pause long enough to recognize the value of what has been learned and to acknowledge it with thanks. Only then are we ready for the final act that is to mentally replace the unhappy scenes by making a new scenario with more loving episodes and visualizing this in detail.

Lacking a therapist, this can easily be done through your own guided imagery. All you need is a quiet place where you can relax deeply. Then, in an imaginative reverie, you can reframe the painful memories and replace them with more pleasant ones, bringing relief from both past and present.

This exercise is just like reprogramming your computer or recording a new movie/message over an old one, for the subconscious mind cannot tell the difference between the real happening and an imagined one. The process of substituting a pleasant story to replace a painful one can be used on all kinds of abuses as long as we do not allow our minds to go back and revive the old memories.

You need to remember that the painful act happened long ago and that the memory is only one of millions you hold. What is keeping the wound alive and active now? You are! Only you can hold or release the emotional pain held in your mind. In essence, if you have not forgiven the transgression or the transgressor you cannot release the pain. Unforgivingness is what holds the wound in your auric field. The only real way to remove it is to forgive and let go. You need to pardon the words, actions, and all the people involved, then absolve yourself for being a part of the lesson. The final act is to give thanks for the gift of the lesson, appreciate the wisdom gained, and see this as a big step forward in your spiritual growth.

You must begin to trust yourself and to know that your problems, regardless of how unfair they may appear from a purely physical viewpoint, were very carefully chosen with a specific purpose in mind. In other words, there are no accidents. All of this is a part of a well-made plan for your greatest growth and achievement in this life. Realizing this, there is no need to feel hurt or angry with your family members. When you remember this is a prebirth agreement with your family for the sole/soul purpose of your personal growth, you can treasure the lesson and be truly grateful for the knowledge you have gained from it.

A Note to Parents — Present and Future

One of the most important skills to be mastered by everyone is the ability to communicate well. The primary foundation for this is respect for others. Almost all religions are based on love, honor, and respect for one another. Parents should not assume they have the right to beat and belittle their children. Yet many parents tend to rule the nest by force through screaming, shouting, and making threats of violence. This iron-fisted tyranny can do far more harm than good and could cause irreparable damage. The result is often rebellion. Children learn to live with resentment, anger, and hatred. They then grow up and pass this on to their children, who pass it on and on.

Children learn self-respect by being respected. A child learns respect for parents, authority, and other people from their parents. Family failure to respect a child's feelings, opinions, and needs can cause the child to feel unworthy. Without this vital love and honoring of one another in the family, they have no respect for themselves or for others. With this basic belief they can then be easily swayed to join gangs and/or commit criminal acts of all kinds for they feel they have nothing to lose. Lack of self-respect is at the bottom of almost all crime.

- **Family Discussion:** All family members need to respect one another. Since children learn their speaking skills early in life as it is practiced within the family circle, it is highly important for parents to teach respect by setting a good example. Telling a child, even in jest, that he is dumb, stupid, or not as good or as smart as someone else is extremely damaging and has a long lasting, negative effect on the child. Those who desire respect from their children must follow their own rules by honoring the rights and feelings of their children. This means that instead of giving orders without explanation or regard to their offspring, they should learn to talk things over calmly and patiently with all family members, perhaps explaining why things must be done in a certain way. Letting them feel they are an important part of the family unit not only brings greater cooperation and understanding but also helps them to develop loyalty and pride in their family values.

    Children have a right to question authority. Whenever something new needs to be done, there should be a discussion, stating what needs to be done and why. Encourage young children to speak up and ask questions. Allow them to ask what or why, for when they can get reasonable answers to their queries, they will cooperate willingly. More importantly, this promotes quick, clear thinking and teaches them to be open-minded. It also helps them learn the fine art of thinking things through for themselves rather than blindly accepting orders without understanding. Practice explaining things in terms they can grasp. A good explanation promotes cooperation and respect, instead of resentment.
- **Differences of Opinion:** Listen to both sides of the matter. Discuss the differences, the options, and the non-options. Help the little ones to understand the need for cooperation. Explain the reason or logic behind the rules, because understanding automatically brings peace and harmony.

    All opinions should be heard, including those of the very young, even though they may be unreasonable. Hear them out and thank them for their contribution. Answer their questions with patience and dignity. Explain where they went wrong or why their idea won't work well. Honor their right to share in family discussions. This brings the whole family closer together.

- **Teach Peaceful Solutions:** Carefully lead discussions into peaceful settlements by insisting on respect to all and by all. Take time to check each person's vote, opinion, or feelings along the way. Teach and practice the art of cooperation and of concluding things harmoniously in win-win situations. Let everyone contribute to the family decisions in a fair and wholesome manner. In this open and honest environment, everyone benefits and parents can learn much from their children. This is as it should be.

Siblings

Constant interaction with brothers and sisters speeds up your learning processes, especially when acquiring new skills. Lively discussions and arguments are necessary counterbalances to new ideas, helping us develop our own individual ways of thinking and believing within the family framework. Siblings' quick reactions to our ideas and daily behavior patterns give us instant feedback on what is or is not acceptable. They also furnish clear insights as to how easily people can be wounded by "mere words."

Siblings often play the role of antagonist, being very quick to let us know when we have stepped out of line, hurt their feelings or made a mistake of any kind. They "tell it like it is," in no uncertain terms. Their teasing, criticism and occasional tattling can be extremely annoying; yet they also serve the purpose of developing greater understanding and sympathy for others. Overall, our siblings both challenge and support us in ways no others can.

Friends

Our friends serve as excellent mirrors as we begin to grow up and leave the safety of home. Because their family training and experiences are different from ours, they provide a wider range of mental and emotional feedback to aid us in judging our thoughts, words, and deeds. They can be great catalysts for our growth. Close friends teach us easily, and oftentimes better than family members, as we laugh, play, or fight together. We can joke about our mistakes, become aware of our faults and failures through being teased about our shortcomings and misbehaviors. We even learn through our disagreements. All these interactions help us learn when and how to stand up for ourselves. We also learn the art of giving, taking, and cooperating happily with one another.

Even our serious arguments can serve to bring home an important point in relationships. If we become a bit too bossy and our friends walk away, our personal pain in being left alone is an excellent teacher. We learn the hard way that courtesy and cooperation are necessary for having good friends. We quickly discover how to forgive and forget, to be on our best behavior, to win new friends, and best of all, to keep our old ones.

When things go wrong, especially within our family unit, we turn to our dearest friends for understanding, self-assurance, and support. In receiving loving kindness from others, we also learn how to give love in our relationships — and loving others is the most important lesson of all.

Authority Figures

Authority figures who are outside of the family unit include teachers, preachers, doctors, and so on — in short, anyone who has the power of authority over us. These leaders help set the rules and boundaries for living within the expected societal framework and provide the needed background for perfecting our skills. From them, we learn when to obey orders and when to stand up for our principles. They often open our minds to wide new vistas and act as catalysts to send us on our way.

Bosses in general can try our patience and stamina as well as our sense of integrity. They both teach and challenge us to do our very best in the work place, demanding both responsibility and loyalty; they often push us to develop new skills and improve old ones. Cooperation and obedience are highly important, as is punctuality. They act as slave drivers, who seem to disregard our needs and feelings, and demand respect, deserved or not. Although this treatment seems unfair, we need to see these people as teachers and testers helping us to hone our skills. When the work load gets to be unbearable, we need to pause and consider the whole scenario, carefully evaluating whether or not we have learned all we need to know in that situation before deciding if it is time to leave. When matters come to a crucial point, there is often a very fine line between quitting and graduating. Before deciding, remember that escape is running away, usually in anger, without having mastered the problems presented in that situation. In that case, no matter where we go we take our problems with us. Eventually we will have to undergo similar problems and circumstances again and again, until that lesson is finally learned. Graduation, on the other hand, is when we know we have completed our education in that arena and are ready to move on to better things.

Most authority people are well meaning, working for the good of the whole, but some are prone to take advantage of their position to do more harm than good. There is a lesson to listen to our own gut feelings in determining which is which, for even at a very young age, we have a natural, soul level instinct that guides us when someone is trying to deceive us.

Mates and Partnerships

- **Law of Attraction:** We attract who and what we are. For example, a woman who has a lesson to learn with males will choose a father who will play the teacher/villain/mirror role. (Males with female issues will do the same with their choice of a mother.) As the child matures and begins to date, he or she will attract mates with similar teacher/villain traits and eventually marry one of them. Unless the problem has been worked out with the parent, the new partner will then take on the role of teacher until the lesson has been learned and parent or mate has been forgiven for any misdeeds (real or imagined). Only then can the person attract a more compatible partner. The purpose for this is to work out our differences, balance our debts, and learn the infinite value of loving relationships.
- **Mates:** More than any other relationship, the mates we attract are our biggest, and sometimes hardest, lesson givers. Once we are grown and beginning to date, our sweetheart of the moment will almost instantly begin the learning, mirroring process with us. Our chosen mate becomes both teacher and catalyst, and conversely, we become a teacher/mirror for our companion. We fall madly in love with someone who reflects our worst fault(s), and since love is blind, we don't recognize it until it is too late. First, we are mildly annoyed with the reflected trait, then frustrated, then angry. We do not like what we see, so we try to change the other person. (It never works, but we try anyway.) Soon, each is angry with the other. Tempers fly. Both want the other to change. Not realizing they are mirroring each other's faults, nor understanding the significance of the reflections, they continue the blame game until one or the other changes or both agree to part—sometimes in bitter divorce.

  The number of mates we can go through in a lifetime depends on how soon we recognize and correct our fault. It can, and has, taken lifetimes, but with the New Age coming in we are running out of time. Graduation day is near.

  One of two things needs to happen. We can learn to look at our partner's accusations, see and understand the mirroring effect, and decide to change that behavior, or we can refuse to learn our lesson and allow the relationship to disintegrate. However, keep in mind our next romantic partner will reflect the same faults, possibly even more, for these are lessons we cannot escape. They will follow us forever, because these are our errors to correct.

All difficulties occur for our growth and understanding. We seem to learn best when we are challenged. Problem situations occur in all kinds of partnerships, whether it is a love relationship or a working, moneymaking agreement. In either case, there are ample opportunities for learning our life lessons. One of the tests of partnerships is learning the fine art of cooperation, harmony, and respect for those who do not think or believe the way we do. Another test is learning to be honest in all things, which includes working or playing by the rules. Earth is a school that our souls use on as many occasions as possible for the learning experience. Our partners, like siblings, provide plenty of mirrors for us to see our faults. So we might as well make up our minds to laugh as we learn because they won't go away. They will simply repeat and repeat and repeat.

Coworkers

The people in our lives, especially those we work with, are constantly acting as our mirrors, reflecting (usually in an exaggerated manner) our own faulty attitudes, beliefs, and habits. Here we are most likely to meet the "Control Freaks," the "Wanna-be's," and the "Users and the Climbers." If we have any of these traits, they will most likely show up as the "users" look for people pleasers to lean on and the "controllers" hunt for weak-willed "worker-bees." (Opposites also attract when learning balance between extremes.) Lessons here are often about boundaries: when, where, and how to set them—learning exactly when to stand up for our rights, how to refuse extra work dumped in our laps, and making sure others do not get credit for our work.

Because this occurs in the workplace, the emphasis here is usually upon our ability to cooperate with our fellow employees. There is a need here for people to be friendly and respectful of one another and to work in harmony. When this fails, bosses, friends, and coworkers reflect our worst faults, moods, and actions for us to see and reflect upon, not react against. Of course, none of this is done on a conscious level of awareness. It is more like the face we see when we look at ourselves in the mirror. It is neither good nor bad, nor is it meant to provoke. It is merely a reflection for us to see and perhaps to change.

Problem People

Most of us have heard it said that the faults we find most offensive in others are those which we have within ourselves. Not only is this true, but we faultfinders tend to project those flaws onto other people, seeing those defects as theirs, not ours. Perhaps you have noticed that people who are most flagrantly deceptive are the ones most often heard accusing others of deception, and those with a strong tendency to tell falsehoods are the first to call others liars. Pay close attention to the names and accusations people use to label others. The faults they project the loudest are their own.

I knew a man who loved to protest about all the pushy people in his life. It seemed everyone he met, with few exceptions, was pushy. His mother was pushy, his boss, most of his friends, and especially his girlfriends. He grumbled constantly about these problem people and claimed to be unable to understand them. Whenever he grumbled, his friends just shook their heads and smiled. They knew there was no point in arguing. He simply could not see and would not believe that he was the pushy one. But we knew it all along.

The problem people in our lives are the most difficult to understand and work with; at the same time, they are our greatest teachers. Their lessons seem most strenuous for we can literally bring out the worst in each other. But once we recognize them as mirrors for our enlightenment and rise to the challenge of changing our attitudes, the lesson is learned and the difficulties disappear.

However, it doesn't take long for another teacher to emerge, for each has a different lesson to teach us. We might as well be prepared to grin and bear it. Since like attracts like, we can understand that we draw to ourselves the people and situations we need for a predetermined reason. No use fighting or complaining, for we are all teaching and mirroring one another. And we are all learning together. If we learn well, there will be only one teacher per lesson.

How It Works

Each habit pattern we hold, such as attitudes, beliefs, or emotions, emits a vibratory wave that automatically attracts to us people with the same pattern. This is not a conscious action, but a soul-guided attempt to teach us what we most need to learn. The purpose is for each of us to mirror that fault or virtue to the other so both will recognize this in themselves and make the needed changes. However, most of us simply grumble about the flaws we see in the other person and quickly move out of range.

Consequently, we will attract, via the same vibration, someone with an even greater imperfection to challenge us. In failing to understand the purpose of the unwanted reflections, we usually see the problem, complain about the other person's faults, and again move away, avoiding both the mirror and the message. Therefore, we keep attracting mirrors that are more difficult. The universe is trying to teach us something about ourselves and we keep saying, "Yes, I see what they are doing. That's their problem. Not mine." Meanwhile, the Universal Law of Attraction keeps drawing ever larger mirrors to us until at last we finally stop to question "Why me?"

The question automatically evokes the answer if we are willing to listen. It is possible for us to go for years without "getting the message." In ages past, we could take years, even lifetimes to learn our lessons.

That time is gone. Now that the Aquarian Age is upon us, we are all feeling the pressure to "clean up our act" and "get on with our lives," preparing ourselves for something we vaguely know is approaching. Now more than ever, we need to understand the reason for the problem people in our lives and the principle behind our "funny mirrors." We are all working toward our perfection, whether we are aware of this or not.

The Faults You See in Others Are Your Own

The way you treat your fellow man
Can set your fate far from your plan,
For what you think, say, and do
Will always come right back to you.
— Author

We all have our share of imperfections. Ordinarily we accept and overlook one another's shortcomings, at least most of the time. The faults we see that disturb us most are the undesirable traits that we know, at soul level awareness, we have within ourselves. These we see with great clarity, seldom realizing our frustration and resentment is actually our disgust with ourselves that we are projecting onto others. Our anger toward someone else's behavior is much like pointing a finger at them, not realizing there are three fingers pointing back at us—thus, highlighting an area of our lives that we need to clean up.

Let us take a good look at our repeated problems as "stop" signs, warning us to stop, look, question, and correct. Recurring difficulties are lessons that we must master before moving to our next level of advancement. We cannot run from them, for they or something like them will follow us wherever we go until we have eliminated those faults.

Life is a reflection of your everyday thoughts and feelings. You really can't afford to hold hate, anger, or depression, nor can you afford to be critical. The universe is more than a reflector, it is more like a magnifying glass, and your thoughts return magnified.

Usually, we pay no attention to the signals we see until someone, by word or deed, steps on our mental/emotional toes. Then, not recognizing the universal message being given, we tend to react in instant anger. We are furious. Our blood pressure shoots up. How dare they do this to us? We love to indulge ourselves in our hurt, anger, and sense of betrayal. We may complain bitterly about the other person's nasty behavior. We can't sleep or even think straight. We want to strike back and get even. However, the solution is to heed the message rather than blaming the messenger.

At this point of recognizing our anger, we need to step back and look at the behavior, not the person who is so annoying, and realize that all our experiences are lessons in disguise.

The Saga of Broken Promises

Once upon a time, I had a friend whom I shall call Ms. Bragalot. She was a very good talker and would have made a great salesperson. She could talk people into almost anything, always painting glorious pictures of what she had done and what she was going to do. Ms. Bragalot easily persuaded friends and even strangers to assist in her wonderful causes. To be quite honest, she smoothly manipulated many people into doing her work for her—free, of course. After all, she was on her way to being a millionaire and she was gracious enough to allow you join her. Like Tom Sawyer, she would promise you anything. The trouble was she never kept her promises.

Like many others before me, I happily joined her team of unpaid workers and allowed her to "honey-do" me for a long time before I realized the insincerity of her numerous promises. Ms. Bragalot was consistently inconsistent. Finally, she broke one promise too many and I was furious. I shouted at the universe, "I don't do things like that. I certainly don't treat my friends like that. I am very careful about keeping my promises (to others). How could this happen to me?" Grrrrrrr! No answer, of course.

Looking back into the mirror of broken promises, it became apparent that this had not happened overnight. There had been many, many hints and clues from others in months, even years gone by—all blithely ignored. There were little incidents, which I first brushed off. Then gradually the problem became bigger, more intense, and increasingly frustrating. Yet, because I did not fully understand the principle of "nothing happens by accident" I still didn't comprehend the situation. So naturally, it kept getting worse and worse before it finally caught my full attention. At that time, I felt betrayed, then angry. Nasty little thoughts of revenge slithered through my mind. It was so devilishly tempting, but I knew in my heart that wasn't the right answer. I had to pay attention to the message instead of venting my anger at the messenger. Only then did I stop to question, finally asking myself, "Why am I attracting people who consistently fail to keep their promises? Do I fail to keep mine? Of course not."

Later, in meditation, the subject came to mind and I heard the words, "You promised yourself you would wash windows last week, but someone called and you allowed yourself to be distracted. You promised yourself to write those letters, but something happened and you were distracted. How often have you promised to spend the day writing then allowed yourself to be distracted? You are always breaking promises to yourself." Oh, I didn't think about that.

After pondering this awhile, I had to admit that because of my low self-worth, I did not realize that what I did to me mattered. My basic belief was to always put myself last. And this erroneous belief attracted my teacher, Ms. Bragalot. What an amazing discovery that was. I would never have recognized or understood this lesson if I hadn't stopped, looked, and questioned what was happening.

Another key issue was my habit of allowing myself to be distracted from my chosen purpose. This too is a repeating pattern with me, especially when I am unsure of my ability to be successful. The more uncertain I feel about my ability to perform well, the more I allow distractions. I have learned to be much more aware of distractions and procrastination and their underlying causes. Obviously both these issues are repeating lessons I should have learned long ago.

Most importantly, I learned to walk away from anger as soon as it hits me. I now know this is the first sign that something is badly wrong which needs my full and immediate attention. It also needs a little soul-searching, a little praying, and a bit of writing in my journal until I finally get the message.

The message had to do with breaking promises to myself because of my low self-esteem. This, in turn allowed me to be sidetracked from what I really wanted to do in my life and led to people-pleasing thoughts.

When I sacrificed my own needs for happiness and fulfillment in order to please others, I became a resentful, grumpy "do-gooder."

Looking back at how I attracted Ms. Bragalot into my life and the lesson she taught me (broken promises), I began thinking about her life and the kind of people she attracted. Her former husband and a long line of boyfriends (plus some female friends) were all described as being devious, manipulative, and irresponsible. Every male she dated had turned out to be evasive, deceptive, and generally unreliable. At that time, neither of us understood the symbolic meaning of this, but now it seems a perfect example of how like attracts like and eventually teaches us the lessons we need most.

Reprogramming Ourselves

To thine own self be true.
—William Shakespeare[2]

Having learned from mistakes or problem people, the next step is to reprogram ourselves in a positive way. We can add to our list of intents some simple statements such as:

- I attract people who empower me, for my greater awareness.
- I am more aware of the mirrors in my life and "get the message" quickly—loud and clear.
- I do only what feels good to me.
- I always stand up for my rights, hopes, and dreams in a loving and positive way.
- I now have an abundance of love, joy, and laughter in my life.
- I am the very best person I can be.
- I keep getting better and better.
- I am now a channel of inspiration and blessings to others.
- I now live in perfect health and vitality up to the very moment I decide to leave.

These are just a few affirmations you could use to realign your life. Or, better yet, make up some of your own to suit your individual needs.

Minimizing Problems and Avoiding Nasty Repeats

One of the best ways to stay out of trouble with repeating lessons is to journal daily. It doesn't matter whether this is done in the early morning, noon, or late in the evening. The important thing is to set aside a definite time at least once a day to write about your feelings, especially when you are stressed or frustrated.

You may want to start with a list of those who disempower you, as well as the people and/or situations where you tend to give up your power, just to get things clear. Then you will be more alert and less vulnerable. Keep your list handy.

On a daily basis, jot down whatever annoys, pleases, or puzzles you. Just jot down a brief note about your life and how you feel about the people and events of the day. This will help you see any repeating patterns or problems as they begin to develop. Once recognized, you can deal with the situation quickly, before it can overwhelm you. It won't stop the lessons, but it will help you handle them much more quickly, easily, and efficiently.

Putting It All Together

Most of us have difficulty realizing that on our soul level of knowing, both the offender and the offended have co-created each incident for the purpose of enlightenment. All too often, we fail to realize that the person and circumstances are actually one of life's "funny mirrors" to help us to see our faults, laugh at our mistakes, and hopefully correct them.

Some pesky, irritable people are kind of like the grit in an oyster, which creates a pearl. They help us develop patience, strength, and endurance. In the end, they have stimulated our growth toward perfection and qualities we might not have developed without their irritating presence.

The good news is that when we fully comprehend this unique process, we also begin to see the real purpose behind everything that "happens" to us as being one great, grand and joyful learning process. We no longer need to be angry and resentful at life's events. Instead, we can appreciate the careful planning, the loving purpose, and the delightful humor in which our world was originally created. We were created to live life joyously.

Now, with this expanded perception of how our universe really works, we can quickly recognize and work through our faulty patterns of behavior—never to have to repeat them again. We will just keep getting better and better as we clean up our mistakes and misunderstandings.

It's not what happens to you—it's what you do with it.

17

Surroundings as Symbols

*Mind is the master power that molds and makes,
And we are Mind, and take,
The tool of thought, and shaping what we will,
Bring forth a thousand joys, a thousand ills.
We think in secret, and it comes to pass—
Environment is but our looking glass.*
—James Allen

Planet Earth is like a school in which your immediate surroundings become your personal classroom. You will see friends, family, and coworkers as your teachers and catalysts. With this in mind, you are now ready to evaluate your surroundings as additional mirrors, giving you a three-dimensional picture of your mental/emotional thought patterns.

As you survey your surroundings, you will discover exactly what you are creating and attracting. The people, things, and circumstances around you are reflecting, with great accuracy, your thoughts, expectations, and beliefs about yourself.

Home Sweet Home

*Whatever enters your life is the material expression
Of some belief in your own mind.
The kind of body you have,
The kind of home you have,
The kind of work you do,
The kind of people you meet..
Are all conditioned by the mental concepts you are holding.*
—Emmet Fox[1]

The place you call home is symbolic of your overall state of consciousness. It is an immediate reflection of your overall thoughts and feelings over a period of time.

As you walk toward your door, look at your home as though you were seeing it for the first time. Take a new look at what you see and feel.

Does your house look inviting? Does it feel safe and sound? Do you love where you live? Is it attractive? Is it in good repair? Are there touches of beauty? What statement does your home make about you?

As you step inside, what is your immediate impression? Is your home neat, clean, and attractive? Warm and inviting? Are there beautiful things surrounding you? Does it feel like a safe and peaceful haven? Are you glad to be home? If you can honestly answer yes to all of these, you can rate it a one hundred percent. Anything less says that you need to improve your mental outlook.

If you are unhappy with your home, you may need to pay more attention to your thoughts and attitudes. (To attract a lovely home you need to construct a loving state of consciousness.) Look for anger buried beneath your thoughts. Try searching within to find what is causing your anger or distress and work on changing it.

Extreme hate and anger (being "all burned up") will often manifest physically as fires in your home.

Living Room

The condition of your living room describes where you live mentally and emotionally. Your living room is an expression of your attitudes, your lifestyle, and the way you look at life in general. It may also symbolize your self-esteem as well as the way you present yourself to the world.

If your living room is disorganized, so is your way of dealing with life. If you postpone cleaning as long as possible you may also have a habit of procrastination that indicates difficulty in making and executing decisions. This extends to taking care of your daily affairs, such as setting priorities, keeping your agreements, living within your income, and paying bills on time.

Kitchen

Your kitchen is the heart of your home. Looking at your kitchen, how does it appeal to you? Is it warm, cozy, and inviting? Light, open, and spacious? Do you have plenty of room for friends and family? If so, your heart is open to those you care about. You are in control of your life and feel good about yourself. Your heart is in the right place and your attitude is generally positive.

On the other hand, if you have a cluttered and dirty kitchen, it may indicate that you don't have the heart to go on living the way things are. It may say you are heartsick and really need some change of

→ Surroundings as Symbols

direction. It may also show that you really don't want friends to visit. This is especially true if you have filled your chairs with stuff. No seating room for guests infers no room in your heart for others. This boldly states that you don't love yourself.

You may feel so hurt, miserable, and discouraged you no longer want to face the world, or so angry, defensive, and fearful your heart may be closing down. Something needs to change.

If most of the time your kitchen, or any other room, is clean and pleasant, rate it by the way it usually looks. Then, when it gets out of control, let it be a signal to stop and consider what is going on mentally and emotionally to cause the chaos. Use chaos as a warning to stop, think, and deal with what is bothering you, rather than letting it drag on without making a decision.

Your kitchen also represents food, health, and the way in which you nurture others and yourself. If your diet is mostly junk food, it is a reflection of junk level thinking and poor self-esteem, meaning you do not take the time and effort to nurture yourself properly. Ask yourself, "What kind of thoughts and feelings about myself would produce this?"

Bedroom

Your bedroom is your private, personal world, a place for your most secret thoughts and feelings. It is your place for rest, sleep, dreams, and healing. If you have a partner, it may also represent love, sex, and your closest, personal relationships.

This room should promote rest and relaxation. If you really love yourself, there will be touches of beauty to add to the feeling of peace and harmony. Its colors and accessories should contribute to a serene atmosphere. Evaluate this room for beauty, harmony, and peace as well as neatness versus clutter.

Bathroom

The bathroom is symbolic of cleansing, relaxing, and letting go of old, negative emotions. It is also for refreshing and renewing body, mind, and spirit. (A shower helps cleanse your aura, in addition to your physical body.) Your bathroom is for pampering your body or ego, applying products that help you look, smell, and feel better. It should be a rejuvenating place for you.

A neat, clean bathroom is a sign of a person who values personal cleanliness. It doesn't matter who cleans the room, just whether it is bright and inviting. With this in mind, how does your bathroom look and feel? Does it smell fresh and inviting? Can you find what you need easily, or do you need a search warrant? How well does it serve your needs? In other words, how well do you care for yourself? Give this room an honest rating, then use that evaluation as a measure of your self-esteem.

Basement

Basements represent the subconscious mind that is a storage place for the memories of all you have ever experienced in your past and present lives. Here, if anywhere, you will find clutter and disorder. The amount of no-longer-used stuff you have stored here or in other storage areas can symbolize how much mental/emotional baggage you are carrying around with you.

Carefully observe your basement. Is it neat and clean? Are your things clearly labeled and placed where they can easily be found? (This indicates an orderly, disciplined mind.) Huge collections of out-dated things may signify many old disappointments and grievances that need to be forgiven and released. Make it soon, for as you clear your basement of old "stuff," you will also clear your mind. You may actually feel lighter and less burdened when you are finished.

Closets and Cover-ups

What are you hiding from yourself? Closets are convenient places to put things away for "later." Like everything else, you should keep them well organized. How do your closets look? Storage places packed with clothes and things you no longer use show a surplus of problems and situations not yet handled. Unlike basements, which represent buried, subconscious issues, your closets represent more current dynamics you are mentally "stuffing" away, keeping them out of sight, even from yourself. The indication is that you are unwilling to deal with the issues those items represent. For instance, some sporting clothes and equipment you haven't used in years. Why are they stored away? What happened the last time that you used them? Were your feelings hurt? Did you ever discuss this? Or was it buried?

Take a good look at the things you may be hiding from yourself. You may need to do some mental closet cleaning and get some of those things "out in the open." What is it that you fear? What is the worst thing that can happen if you bring these issues up for healing? Do some soul-searching and write in your journal before discussing your real feelings with other people, especially with those who have hurt you, whether deliberately or not. As you clean your mental closet, you clear your mind of that unfinished business.

Confrontation Is Cleansing

A vital point in the art of nurturing and caring for yourself is using your ability to state, gently but firmly, how you really feel about something painful. Get clear about the desired results before discussion begins when it concerns another's words or actions. Quietly speaking your concerns opens the way for peaceful clarifications of problems and misunderstandings. This allows those involved to explain, apologize, or reconsider the role they have played. When one person is unhappy, everyone nearby feels the discord, but few are willing to deal with it openly. When you gently bring up a problem for discussion, you give everyone a chance to improve their communication skills and clear the air, relieving all the tensions gathered there. You may also be teaching others the art of confronting kindly instead of the usual heated accusations and denials.

As if you have taken a refreshing shower, you will feel much better about yourself afterward. You will know you have built a needed bridge of communication for solving future problems, preventing similar difficulties in the future. This is a very valuable skill and you can be truly proud of yourself for your contribution.

Message of My "House from Hell": What It Taught Me

I grew up with constant criticism and became an expert in faultfinding, quite capable of expressing my criticism freely and frequently. This has been an ongoing, undesirable trait, overdue for correction. Let me tell you my story.

Not long ago I was living deep in the country and decided there were too many problems with living that far out, so I began complaining. Obviously, it was time for me to "return to civilization." It took several months of searching before finding a house I really liked. Naturally I bought it and moved in as soon as possible, only to find that once the other person's furniture was removed there were many glaring problems. I groaned and asked, "Why? Why me?" (With my overall mental focus based on finding faults, naturally I was strongly attracted to a house with many faults. Like attracts like, right?)

At first, I was dismayed but determined to fix it, one thing at a time. However, the more I fixed, the more faults I discovered. The more I fussed and complained, the worse things became. Now these were not loud, spoken complaints but more like a constant mumble, grumble, cuss, and fuss muttering in my mind. The more faults I found the angrier I became and the angrier I became the more faults I found. It was a rapidly repeating cycle of unhappy events. I couldn't believe what was happening. Again, I had to stop and consider what was really going on. (You are probably way ahead of me here.) Finally, I realized that my focus on fault-finding was manifesting as more and more faults being found. How clear can it get?

All this was going on as I was struggling to finish this book. (Be warned that struggle is not a good way to accomplish anything.) It seemed as though each time I mentally asked a question about how something would work — *zap*. Lesson number six thousand, four hundred and ninety-three came bounding into my life. (I had to ask!)

To break the vicious cycle I had to sell my "house from hell" and find a more suitable home. Having learned my lesson, I worked to clean up my critical attitudes then closely watched my thoughts and words. Programming my new home with great care, I chose my intentions with meticulous forethought. There were no vague descriptions. No more guesswork, I was precise. Finally, I found a home that I could love and appreciate.

Message of Your Home: What It Tells You About Yourself

Take a good look at your house as a whole, the individual rooms, and the messages they are giving you. Using the criteria below, see what you find out about yourself.

Positive Qualities

- **Attractive:** As a whole, if your home is neat, clean, and attractive, it says that you have good self-esteem and present yourself well.
- **Open, Light-Filled Rooms:** These reveal an openness of mind, a positive outlook, sunny disposition, and a good spiritual foundation.
- **Neat and Clean:** Shows positive thinking, discipline, good habits, and a well-balanced lifestyle, which adds to your overall feeling of joy and well-being.
- **Touches of Beauty:** Symbols of love, peace, harmony, and beauty reveal a person of gentle-loving kindness and a well-ordered mind. This infers lofty ideals and spiritual tendencies. Having beauty in the home is a way of loving yourself.

- **Rooms and Furnishings in Good Condition:** Reveal a sense of order, discipline, pride, and well-being.

Negative Qualities

- **Doors Shut Tight:** Doors and windows closed and kept locked can show a sense of fear, insecurity, or even depression. This may indicate a desire to withdraw from life.
- **Darkness:** House shut tight, drapes drawn, and blinds closed; clear evidence of negative thinking, depression, and lack of a spiritual foundation. This may indicate a fearful attitude, withdrawal, and avoidance of life's issues.
- **Shabby Furnishings:** Worn-out furnishings can imply withdrawal, depression, despair, lack of self-love, and beginning of illness.
- **Dirt, Disorder:** Product of negative thinking, procrastination, lack of decision making, lack of goals, and lack of discipline.
- **Neglect:** A pileup of things not done and many areas of clutter show a lack of order, lack of goals, and lack of discipline. If the area needs cleaning, painting, or repairing there is lack of confidence and low self-esteem, which often leads to depression and mental illness.
- **Stacks of Outdated Items:** Symbolizes things that you should have decided, released, forgiven, and forgotten long ago. There may be painful memories or unresolved issues that you need to cleanse from your life or there could be things undone and promises made but never kept. Overload leads to a feeling of being overwhelmed, fatigue, and eventual depression. Time for spring cleaning, no matter what day it is.

Final Analysis of Your Home

Inner peace creates outer harmony. Does your home say your life is in order and running smoothly? Or does it express stress, negative thinking, and perhaps some anger? If so, what changes do you need to make?

Rate each room by the way it appears most of the time. This gives you something by which to measure. Outer chaos is often a clue to inner upset, confusion, or fear. Learn to look at the mental/emotional causes behind it and deal with them quickly and you will have far greater control over your thinking and feeling nature. You will also become more effective in your creations.

On days when one or more rooms become disaster areas, let this be a warning signal that your mental/emotional problems are piling up.

Stop to consider the cause and take time to write about your feelings in your journal. Consider which room(s) are affected and what area of your life it represents. Ask yourself what triggered this upset. Get to the bottom of the problem and deal with it promptly. Remember you need to have inner peace and tranquility to create outer peace and serenity.

A quick physical cleanup of the house may sound good, but it is not the whole answer. Like the "House from Hell," the first thing to change is the mental habits such as faultfinding, which keeps you in a state of negative mind-chatter.

Workplace: Your Home Away from Home

Everything you see or feel on the material plane, whether it is your body, your home, your business or your city, is the expression of a mental equivalent held by you.[2]

Your workplace, whether it is a small cubicle, a room, or a whole building, represents your chosen profession and how you go about your job, whatever it is. Its condition reflects your work habits, goals, and expectations. It also reveals your integrity, ethics, and attitudes about yourself and your career. The same criteria mentioned in rooms of your home also apply here. The general condition of order or disorder indicates your general mental and emotional state of mind concerning your work as well as your basic beliefs about yourself.

A disorderly area can indicate mental chaos or could suggest that you hate your job. Definitely it would say you are disorganized, perhaps careless, and would much rather be elsewhere. If you dread going to work each day this would positively affirm your inner desire to be doing something else. Consider a major change in both your job and attitude.

Consider what have you learned about yourself. What kinds of thoughts have you contributed? What needs most to be changed? Do some serious writing in your journal about your feelings concerning your career. Decide whether it is the job, your boss, the people, the location, or yourself which needs to change.

Procrastination Is the Name of the Game

Procrastination is another word for failing to make choices and invariably leads to feeling overwhelmed. For example, when you tell yourself, "I'll just put this over here for the time being," it really means, "I won't make a decision about where it should go now." Which also means, "I choose not to decide." The backlog of your "unfinished stuff" keeps you

↪ Surroundings as Symbols

constantly in a should/shouldn't decision battle that drains your energy every time it comes to your attention.

Additional problems occur if you have a habit of starting more things than you can reasonably expect to finish, which throws your mind into an overwhelmed state. The ensuing pileup of things undecided and undone then manifests as clutter, confusion, and chaos in your home, life, and affairs. This adds to your frustration, irritation, and sense of being overwhelmed. Your energy is spread throughout your list of things left undone causing a major drain on your energies. Could this be the real cause of chronic fatigue? Yes. Could it be the cause of depression? Yes.

Disorder: Failure to Make Decisions

Disorder in the home or workplace is the result of unwillingness to face and cope with life's challenges and opportunities as they enter your life. Recall once more your gut-feeling guidance, which comes along with each new event. Remember you are always guided, so why the indecision?

Often it is merely a bad habit based on some old fear of having made a poor decision in the past. You may have been punished or ridiculed for your "mistake" and never forgot it. It could also be a fear of taking responsibility for similar reasons. Whatever the problem, it is in your best interest to talk with a trusted friend or use your journal to work through this. The bottom line is to get to the cause of your reluctance to make decisions. Once you understand why you are ready to make the needed changes, you can easily build a new way of handling your problems as they arrive.

Instant decision making may be a big step to begin with, but you can make a firm commitment to goal card all new events by the end of that day, if not in the moment.

Begin by remembering the many little decisions you have successfully made. Dwell on your successes rather than the mistakes. Then start by making small but deliberate decisions on a daily basis. Keep score of your successes and congratulate yourself for each good decision.

Make prompt decisions. The longer you hesitate, the more you vacillate back and forth between soul-knowing (gut feeling) and the people-pleasing personality.

Making choices and taking appropriate action is a learned skill that, together with clear goal setting, keeps you on track. Procrastination and avoidance of life's problems leads to chaos and depression.

Your Automobile: An Extension of Yourself

The condition of your automobile sends a message about your life and your health.[3] When it is running smoothly, all is well. If engine trouble develops, it can be a symbolic warning of a possible breakdown in your health. It may even signal a need to see your doctor.

Besides representing your lifestyle, your car shows the status of your self-esteem and the way you want the world to see you. (Sport car, luxury car, truck, etc.)

Consider how you treat your automobile. Do you drive with care, avoiding potholes and situations that could damage it? Or do you drive it hard and fast, with little regard for your car, yourself, or others? The way you drive your vehicle can indicate the way you drive yourself. Rough treatment and frequent accidents (no matter how small) often show repressed anger manifesting as hate or devil-may-care attitudes.

Research done at Findhorn, Scotland has shown that physical items treated with love and respect actually last longer and need less repair than those which are cursed or treated with anger and neglect. Also, a loving attitude attracts a better product and keeps it in good condition for a greater period of time.[4]

Do you keep your car clean? Check on its needs? Keep it well maintained? How you treat your car describes the way you take care of yourself.

- **Dirty and Dented:** Automobiles obviously in need of repair often denote poor self-esteem, a poverty mentality, and/or rebellious attitudes. You may be lacking in goals, ambition, or self-esteem. If your auto is loaded with all kinds of stuff it may be saying you don't "have room" for anyone else in your life. You may secretly prefer to be left alone. If so, ask yourself why. Has someone hurt you badly? Are you punishing yourself? Get to the cause and you will find the cure.

The Polka-Dot Car

A friend who once taught me the power of the spoken word wanted to buy herself a nice, new luxury car, but didn't have the money for a brand-new one. After much thought, she decided to look for a demonstrator model. Within a week, she found just the kind of car she wanted at a price she could afford. The only drawback was the color. She hated the color, but bought the car anyway.

A few weeks later, she noticed several spots where chips of paint were missing. Still later she found more bare spots. The pace seemed to

↪ Surroundings as Symbols

be picking up. A ding here, a little scratch there and slowly but surely the unwanted color was coming off. She quickly realized that "thoughts are things" and that her repeated remarks about the ugly color were actually manifesting as disappearing chips of paint.

You might say she should have known better; however, knowing what to do and living what you know can be two very different things. Folks don't always practice what they teach. But seeing the effects of your thinking is the best way to learn. As we like to say, seeing is believing.

Your Neighborhood: Another Reflection of Your Thoughts

Most people assume that the thoughts and emotions inside their heads are harmless. This is not so. Your thinking and feeling vibrations radiate into your aura first, affecting your "own little world." This in turn flows into the room you occupy, affecting those around you. This is especially true of those of like minds and vibrations. They pick up those thought forms and add their own energies, multiplying them, creating a group-consciousness field of energy. Then off they go throughout the building, into the streets and neighborhoods, spreading their influence. Each neighborhood reflects the accumulated effect of the mental/emotional (race consciousness) energy field of the people who live and work there.

As you can imagine, it is vitally important to create an area of peace and goodwill within you in order to have harmony around you.

As you come home from work, look around you and begin a serious, in-depth observation of your local neighborhood. See it as a revealing reflection of your most dominant mental/emotional activities. Pay close attention to what you see and feel as you approach your home. Consider the correlation between the tenor of your thoughts, beliefs, and attitudes and their physical manifestations such as the streets, lawns, houses, neighbors, and parked cars. Notice the overall look and feel of the area. When viewed in this manner, these reflections can help you realize exactly what you have mentally attracted or brought into being. Upon arriving home, grab pen and paper and write your impressions for further consideration.

What You Think Is What You Get

Everything in your city is the embodiment of a mental equivalent held by you.

—Emmet Fox [5]

If you do not like what you see around you, look at your attitude. Knowing how this works, you may want to change those thoughts to more loving ones, confident that your surroundings will change as you change. If your thoughts tend to be angry, despondent, or critical, you will see the corresponding effects as old, run-down houses, yards, and streets littered with trash and broken-down cars. Your neighbors may appear depressed, shabby, or unsavory. Their language may be crude and the area unpleasantly dirty and noisy.

- **Ugly, Run-Down Sections:** Sign of negative thinking, critical attitudes, lack of self-respect, and ambition.
- **Drug-Ridden Areas:** Drugs represent a desire to escape life's duties and responsibilities, signifying unwillingness or inability to cope with life itself. This indicates you are living mentally or emotionally in the "neighborhood" of irresponsibility.
- **Crime-Laden Vicinity:** This shows poverty thinking, lack of discipline, lack of responsibility, and lack of respect for self and others. It represents an absence of pride, ambition, and honesty.

Have you ever taken advantage of another or stolen anything (no matter how small)? Remember your neighborhood is reflecting who and what you are. Crime is a lack of honor and respect for yourself. You could be unconsciously living in poverty thinking or a neighborhood lacking in respect.

On the other hand, if your thoughts are generally light hearted, caring, and kindly, you should find yourself in a pleasant neighborhood of attractive, well-kept homes and yards. There may be an abundance of stately trees, beautiful flowers, and attractive shrubs. The ideal neighborhood would be quiet, peaceful, and pleasantly inviting.

The above descriptions represent two extremes of possibilities in your overall thought processes, moods and attitudes. No doubt, your neighborhood will be somewhere in between. See how well this system works in describing your overall mood and thought. You may be surprised.

Guidelines for Choosy Creators

The Rule of Attraction faithfully brings you the fruits of your thoughts and feelings. Be aware that you are creating all the time. Whatever you see before you is your creation. When you fully realize you have created it, you also know you have the power to change it. When

Surroundings as Symbols

something turns out to be less than you had expected, just see it as a lesson showing you what not to do.

1. What kind of thoughts, feelings, or beliefs would manifest that result?
2. Write out what you need to change to be able to create exactly what is wanted (goal card).
3. Describe how will you initiate that change and list the steps needed. Post these steps where you will see them often.
4. Exercise your steps for twenty-one days.
5. Record your day to day progress in your journal. After twenty-one days, evaluate, and record your results.

For best results in your life, you must deliberately choose to be the best you can be every time. Then nothing but good can come to you and surround you, for Like Attracts Like, always, always, always!

Choices
This is what I choose to be,
The best, the highest I can see.
This is how I choose to live,
The best, the finest I can give.
— Author

18

Circumstances as Symbols

*Whatever you impress on your subconscious mind
is expressed on the screen of space as condition, experience and event.*
— Dr. Joseph Murphy

Dr. Joseph Murphy, author of *The Power of Your Subconscious Mind*, says, "Every thought is a cause, and every condition is an effect." He adds, "Remember, it is the world within, namely, your thoughts, feelings, and imagery, that makes your world without. It is therefore, the only creative power, and everything which you find in your world of expression has been created by you in the inner world of your mind consciously or unconsciously. In order to change external conditions, you must change the cause."[1]

Change your thoughts and you change your destiny.

The circumstances we find ourselves involved in add more information to the picture of our current thoughts, beliefs, and feelings. Too often, we are unaware of how and why we are manifesting, especially when we are engulfed in something distasteful. All these situations are giving us vital, necessary feedback on just what we are bringing forth with our thoughts, conscious or not.

A good example of this came to me as I was shopping for a new home, after the horrible "House from Hell." Unaware that my thinking was focused on what was not wanted (dark and gloomy) rather than on what was wanted (open, bright and sun filled), my real estate dealer and I went house hunting. Every single house we went to was unsuitable and incredibly dark and gloomy. I was amazed to find so many dark and dingy houses in one day's shopping. Yet it took another day of seeing dark, cave-like houses before I finally "got it." Although I was very clear about what I wanted, my creative mental energies were obviously focused on what was not wanted. The Universe, always responsive to human thought, was showing me my error.

An undesirable circumstance, yes, but with a powerful purpose. It was my wake-up call to really see what I was attracting and finally connect it to my train of thought. This was a real eye-opener and the first time I truly connected the circumstances as being a message from the universe. From that, I learned that anytime I am unhappy with what I see in my world, I am playing the wrong record, singing the wrong song, and definitely need to change my tune.

Discomfort Is Your First Signal for Change

We can see how the circumstances in our lives act as lessons from the universe. Like a gift, they inspire us to learn the truth and move up to a higher level of enlightenment. However, the "gift of awakening" most frequently comes to us as a problem that requires solving. When something goes wrong, we become upset. Our first inclination is to react in anger and, out of old habit, look for someone to blame. However, before we go off on a personality-based temper tantrum, we need to stop and remember this is our wake-up call. Like stop lights along the road, the universe is reminding us, as creators, to make new assessments and decisions for something better. Anger, too, is a message that something in your thinking world is in need of reevaluation and correction.

Because most of us dislike change, we tend to resist the "gift" in the lesson. We would rather stay in an uncomfortable, but familiar, rut than change our attitudes or our old way of life. Consequently, we often have to face not one, but a series of challenges which make us so miserable we are forced to rethink our stance and make the changes. Sometimes the universe literally has to pull the rug from under us before we are willing to change. Life will be much easier when we learn to look for the message and the lessons imbedded in our so-called problems.

Patterns of Change

As I was pushing myself to finish this book I found myself repeatedly bogged down with phone calls, visitors, small crises with grandchildren, and other family members. The more pushed and hurried I got the more delays and sidetracks occurred. As the crunch of too many things to do and no time to do them kept building I found myself saying, "I don't have time for that." "Times seems to be moving so fast." "I don't have time." "Not enough time."

The pressure kept building. The harder I tried, the worse it got. "Hurry, hurry, push, push, gotta get it done." On and on it went until finally exhausted, I asked myself, "How am I creating this? It must be something I am attracting. What? How?" Of course, the answer popped into mind immediately. "I don't have time." "Not enough time." The answer was obvious. My pattern of thought was repeating "not enough time," so of course I manifested not enough time.

When we learn to watch for and identify the patterns of coming events in the early stages we can move quickly and gracefully into making the needed changes, avoiding unnecessary hardships in our learning process.

Cycles

In school, we stay in one grade for a while, then "graduate" to the next level. Our life's events also move in cyclic rhythms graduating to the next level. Careers start small, grow, and change. Discontent and uneasiness mark the cosmic push to move on to bigger and better. Learn to recognize the signals, complete that cycle, and move on.

The same idea works in relationships. As we learn, grow, and change, our friends and family members also change. Some go and some stay. We grow and move on, leaving others behind. It is all part of our growth cycles. There is no need for guilt or shame. We advance to higher levels of thinking and behaving unless we are stuck in fear or stubbornness. Even then, the universe will give us a push. It is the natural flow of things. Let us accept change gracefully and move upward, going with the flow as we do.

Repeated Signals

Problems which repeat themselves in various guises are like the universe knocking on our doors, bringing us lessons to be learned, or incentives for us to step up to something better. Life often pushes us to make needed changes in our thinking/believing patterns in order to eliminate old habits that no longer serve us. Consider them as personal upgrades from the universe.

In a way, we are detectives, working on the mystery of life. We search for clues among our friends, surroundings, and circumstances. We often do not realize that whatever is happening in our lives is giving us a big clue as to what we need to work on. We can be sloppy detectives or master sleuths.

Our first big clue is the feeling of dissatisfaction and discomfort. Things that once made us happy now become boring and tiresome. We feel restless and vaguely uncomfortable. It's time for a change. We can feel it coming. Yet, we resist. We may stall, but things just get worse. Unhappy circumstances begin to pile up, pressure increases. More things go awry.

Pressure continues to build, muscles tighten, tempers flare. Left brain logic may try to dodge the issue or bluff its way through but nothing works. Finally we can't stand it any longer and we are forced to make a decision. We must move out or work our way through.

Dealing with Problems Constructively

When a situation is less than loving or comfortable, we can start by acknowledging that we have attracted or created this for a reason. Ask yourself what kind of thoughts, beliefs, attitudes, or emotions in me would create this circumstance?

- **Sneak Previews:** These are physical manifestations of a negative focus. Generally, these are only mildly uncomfortable situations like my house-hunting adventure; they give us a quick glimpse of what we are creating with our present mindset. Our dreams may also be pointing out what we are actually creating as compared to what we intended to create. For further verification, these would only occur with a current, in-process situation.
- **False Teachings:** These are all the erroneous teachings our personality has taken on in place of the truth. They come up, one at a time, for us to replace them with information that is more accurate. These are issues to be cleansed and may need to be done in steps rather than in one big leap. In general, anything out of line with loving attitudes and actions is considered to be of major importance. As always, the bottom line is gentle-loving kindness.

The cleansing process is similar to deleting old, outdated software with a new, improved model. You eliminate a negative attitude/belief and replace it with a more positive one, then practice it until it becomes part of the new you.

Those who are already on a spiritual path tend to recognize and work with these "challenges" far more readily than those immersed in personality do. The better we understand these "setbacks" as a spiritual growth exercise, the easier it is to work through them, for we are no longer defensive or resentful.

We are always being led to graduate to the next step. We can go willingly or wait for signs that are more drastic. Pay attention to your feelings and "wake-up" circumstances. At the first sign of discomfort or negative thoughts, stop to analyze the source. Ask, what is causing this? What have I been focusing my attention upon most? What is the universe reflecting to me? Where do I need to upgrade my thinking?"

Once you have answered the questions, decide on a happy resolution and make the appropriate mental changes before things get out of hand. Of course, we can always wait and let the pressure build, knowing that as things become more unpleasant we will become more willing to change.

Boundaries

Your Personal Safety Zone

Boundaries are important to our self-respect. Like a house with no doors, anyone, desirable or not, can walk right into your space. Boundaries are like fences, keeping the uninvited at a respectful distance, saying, "You can go only so far, and no further without my permission." We all need fences and doors to keep out would-be intruders.

A small child knows his sacred spaces and guards them well. A good, hearty yell can get instant results. Once these have been trampled, the child loses his sense of self and then becomes a victim. He then remains there for a long time unless, at some point, he learns to set new boundaries and regain his self-respect.

Children whose boundaries have been violated have real problems setting up the much-needed protective limits that give them time to evaluate the person or situation. They need the freedom to declare just how much space or time is needed before allowing others into their "sacred space" or personal safety zone.

My Lesson in Boundaries

Being raised with no bedroom, no bed (I slept on the living room couch), no dresser, or even a drawer I could call my own, I definitely did not learn about boundaries. I had none.

Consequently, I have often allowed those in need to share my home until they "got on their feet." Having no boundaries to go by, these episodes always ended unhappily, but that was long ago, before I learned all this. Once again, I invited a needy friend to share my home for a little while. Even before she had settled in, I became aware this was going to be a lesson in boundaries. "Oh, well," I thought, "I guess I need that. Might as well learn it now." That shows how little I knew at the time.

My friend moved into her allotted space. In less than two days her "space" grew and continued to grow and expand on a daily basis. She was all over my space. She took full advantage of my generosity and intruded heavily upon my privacy. I felt invaded, victimized, and extremely unhappy.

To cope with this, I sat down and carefully composed a note listing some very simple boundaries. We discussed it. She agreed. Then she went right on bursting through my boundaries. When I quietly mentioned her transgressions she took immediate offense, agreed not to do it again, and then conveniently "forgot." This happened over and over.

Once more, I took time out to sit down, get centered, and ask.

Q. What is the problem?
A. No respect for my boundaries. But of course, I knew that.

Q. So what am I supposed to learn here?
A. How to stand your ground with love.

Q. What am I feeling?
A. Frustration. But of course, I knew that too.

Q. Exactly what bothers me most?
A. No respect for my things. She takes things out but doesn't put them back.

Q. Is there any of this in me? Oooh yeah. (One of my worst faults.)
A. That one really hit home.

Other answers popped quickly into my mind as though they had been waiting for the question. First thought up was "No respect for me and my possessions." That concept had been growing in the back of my mind for several days. "Not good enough" was another item going back to my childhood. I recognized both of these as old issues, but I hadn't tied them in with a lack of boundaries. Now, in seriously analyzing the situation, it all fit. I had the whole picture.

Clarity was another thing learned that day, along with my need to hold myself in greater honor and respect, in my own mind. (This is where it all starts.) I felt good once I understood the main principle involved and changed my attitudes. I had lovingly solved my problem. I was no longer feeling cramped and uncomfortable and I had a greater understanding of the idea of respect. I now realize I have to have respect for me if I want respect from others. Amazing stuff!

I followed through by acting on an impulse to rewrite and clarify my boundaries, typing them in a very simple mode. I made several copies and placed them in conspicuous places. The meaning was clear. I had set my boundaries. No further discussion was needed. I had completed my lesson, and I felt very good.

It took me about two weeks to face it, name it, and come to a decision. After that, it was a matter of minutes. In addition we are still friends, and it was a good lesson for me. Simple but effective, you might say. Half the battle was to realize what was happening and see it as a lesson. The other half was asking the right questions, listening for the answers, and then following through with decisive action.

Afterthoughts

I thought I was finished. Lesson learned. I had set my boundaries. But, that was only a part of the problem. So it came up again. Remember the part about no respect? I mentioned it several times but did not realize that this, too, was a major life-long lesson.

What I finally realized was that her total disrespect for me, my home, my time, and my personal needs was a reflection of my own lack of respect. Again, because of my "not good enough" home training, I had a strong tendency to sacrifice my needs to favor those I saw as being in greater need. Because I felt unnurtured, I overcompensated by trying to nurture others, trying to "fix" their problems while ignoring my own. Not only that, I had repeated this pattern of behavior many, many times but never understood it nor learned from it.

This "teacher," whom I had attracted to me, was actually showing me, by reflection, that I was not respecting myself. Respect was another key word. What I finally understood, with the help of a loving friend, was that I did not love myself enough to allow me to do what I really wanted to do—a pattern I have repeated all my life (I am a senior citizen). Talk about a slow learner.

Bottom Line: Not Loving Myself

I have been unconsciously vibrating "not good enough" for years and since we all attract what we vibrate, I've experienced endless disappointments in life. One of the by-products of "not good enough" is victimization in various degrees. What a major lesson this has been!

Funny thing, I have been working around the fringes of this problem for many years with no real resolution. Positive affirmations were unsuccessful. What it really took was getting to the root of the problem. Boundaries were only an offspring of my feeling and vibrating "not good enough." Lack of respect was another offspring. But, not loving myself was the real message.

An additional gift I have had is a painful, long-burning problem with my parents' inability to express love or nurturing to me. Finally, I now clearly understand it was because I needed to learn to love myself.

New Decisions

The whole point of this find-and-name-the-problem process was to come to a new, higher level of understanding and make new decisions about my life.

I see my mistake. I am "good enough." I now love myself enough to allow myself the pleasures I desire and deserve. You can bet I made a lot of cards and "stickies" of this and stuck them at eye level all around the house as reminders. After that, I dug up the courage to ask her to leave. She was miffed, but she left.

P.S. I wrote this out in detail because this "not good enough" stuff, along with feeling unworthy and victim-type vibrations are an all-too-common problem for many people.

Typical Problems We May Face

- **Unloving Actions, Attitudes:** These are based on erroneous teachings. We are upgrading our old state of consciousness, parts of which may be carry-overs from childhood or other lives. These may appear in the form of lack of self-love and respect; a strong faith in the worst that can happen; fear-based attitudes which may manifest as a need for absolute control; and manipulative behavior in order to feel safe. This over-defensive stance can be very pushy, bullish, and rebellious. Unloving attitudes about ourselves are often the most debilitating. If any of this sounds familiar, you would be wise to start working through this problem right now.
- **Anger:** An extension of unloving attitudes. We all have occasional bursts of anger that can be a very healthy outlet. But, frequent blow-ups, especially when over trivial matters are a sure sign of deeply buried pain and anger coming up to be released. This anger, when ignored, is stored deep in the muscle tissues of our bodies and often eats away at us, like cancer, from inside out. It is important to deal with the attitude problem

by forgiveness and love until all symptoms vanish, then get some good massage and bodywork done to release the poisons out of your system.
- **Unhappy Relationships:** Symptoms of unloving attitudes and feelings of unworthiness bring a lack of ability or desire to cooperate with others, a fear-based need to control, abusive behavior tendency, and lack of honor and respect for both self and others. The bottom line is often one of being unable to love ourselves because of childhood training.
- **Career Problems:** We often refuse to listen to soul guidance; consequently, we fail to rise to our highest potential. We tend to remain in an unsuitable career because we are afraid to take a chance or afraid of change. Rethink career options. Listening to our soul guidance and receiving messages from our dreams can be helpful.
- **Prosperity Challenges:** Old belief patterns, such as vows of poverty taken in other lives or our own lack of self-worth here and now can keep us poor. Another factor to consider is the "Crash of '29," which affected the USA up to the mid-forties. People who went through this were deeply imprinted with a strong feeling of lack, and by association passed on their beliefs in poverty. Remember that poverty is only a state of mind that needs changing. Jesus told us in Luke 12:32, "It is the Father's good pleasure to give you the kingdom." So we know it is available.
- **Fears:** Fear stunts our spiritual growth and is often described as a lack of love. It may be described as having more faith in the worst than in the best. (We all have faith — where is yours?)
- **Pet Peeves, Things We Hate, Defenses:** We usually fight against something we fear will happen. Then, as we give our strong emotional attention to what is not wanted it actually grows larger and is energized by our focus upon it. The same rule applies to all the things we dislike. Hate is a potent emotion that actively energizes the situation, making it more powerful than ever.

Whatever we are signaling or vibrating is what we are living. If we are feeling that others take advantage of us, then everywhere we go we will attract people who will take advantage of us. Some may even be people who never took advantage of anyone before. Why? Because the universe also brings about what we constantly fear as well.

Give some serious thought as to what kinds of circumstances you are attracting — and the kind of belief or vibration you have been holding. It should match up. If you are unsure, ask yourself, "What kind of thoughts would attract that kind of person, situation or circumstance?"

Changing Your Thinking: Finding a New Attitude

Since the universe always responds to whatever you are vibrating, whenever you find yourself in a bad mood make it a game to quickly catch yourself and turn your thinking to something happy. Think anything that brings you peace, joy, or contentment. This is a simple trick you can learn and is the first step in changing your mental and emotional outlook forever. However, it does take willpower and daily practice. Only you can make the change, but as you do, you will notice significant changes in your circumstances and surroundings.

The ability to shift your attention from gloom to gladness is a fine art gained only by deliberate practice in changing old mental habit patterns into new, healthy, happy ones. Once you master the shift from negative mind chatter to more joy and appreciation, your whole life will change.

The Universe Is a Safe and Loving Place

Our loving universe, filled with God-Mind, is especially designed to out-picture our thoughts and feelings in such a way that we can see and experience the results of thinking and fine-tune our abilities to the point of mastery. We are learning to create from soul level (love, perfection, and beauty) rather than from personality (possessiveness, selfishness, and greed). Therefore, when we have a problem or a bad habit that needs correcting we invariably attract to ourselves a situation that will highlight the issue and teach us whatever is needed at that time.

> *The bottom line is always love.*
> *Enjoy your lessons.*
> *See them as a postgraduate course.*
> *Earn your Ph.D. in life.*

19

When Things Go Wrong

This is a thought-created world; nothing happens by accident.

We have attracted/created everything we experience through our thoughts, emotions, beliefs, attitudes, hopes, and dreams. We, as young creator-gods in training, are creating and attracting it all. Earth is our Creator Training School.

When we work on a computer, the monitor shows us exactly what we are creating. Without the screen we could not see, let alone correct our errors. In the same way, earth is our holographic computer screen that brings 3D pictures, people, and events to show us exactly what we are mentally/emotionally creating. When we truly understand the "what you think is what you get" principle we will no longer be upset by unsatisfactory results. But, like the scientist, we will examine the evidence, figure out what we did wrong, make corrections, and try again. It is simple trial and error. What better way to learn?

When things go wrong in our lives, we are often hurt, frustrated, or angry. We may even feel that life is just not fair. Some folks will simply accept an uncomfortable situation, others will try to ignore it, some will try to escape it, some will blame others, and a few will elect to change it on a physical level. None of these tactics work. We need a better understanding about problems and uncomfortable situations.

The universe is always working for our good and all the pains and the problems come to us for a reason. They aren't going wrong, they are simply reflecting our creative mental/emotional output. They are three-dimensional copies of our vibrational flow. Like the writing on the blackboard, we can erase it and start over. We learn by our mistakes only when we stop to look at what we have created, own it, and change it accordingly.

Because this is an important part of our training, these incidents will either persist or keep recurring until we learn to face, acknowledge, and solve whatever is upsetting us. Our problems are turning points and triggers for transformation.

Repeating Patterns and Problems

Matters unresolved become recurring patterns of discomfort and "dis-ease." For example, I was looking forward to going to a group affair with some family members when I received a phone call saying there would not be room for me. I knew it was not a matter of room for me. I could easily have come and gone in my own car and the affair was to be outdoors — plenty of room there. It was clearly a matter of that person not wanting me to be there.

Of course, I was hurt. I felt rejected. As I thought about these feelings, I recognized this as an old repeating pattern. I didn't want to face it, but realized this has been going on far too long and it was time to fix it. But how?

One of the best methods of getting clear on anything is to sit down and reflect on what has just happened and how that made you feel. List all the emotions and insights that come with it, then record them in your journal. So, I began to write my feelings in detail to get a good grip on what was really bothering me.

As I wrote down my pain and frustration, with the intent to know, I suddenly understood that rejection was only the first layer. The second was betrayal (I had been invited), but the bottom line was my old, "not good enough" beliefs deeply imbedded in my psyche. Further soul-searching brought up the fact that I grew up expecting rejection and I carry this concept with me to this day. As I exude or vibrate this mental pattern, others reflect this back in many shades of rejection. (I hadn't realized that previously.) The only way I knew to stop rejection from others was to remove my old beliefs and replace them with new positive affirmations. I would have to repeat these until I had my subconscious mind thoroughly saturated with the new programming. With this clarity, I summarized my plight.

Whenever something occurs which leaves you feeling hurt, abused, or victimized, it is your notice from the universe that you have not yet cleared out all your "victim issues." Instead of bemoaning your fate, as I did, consider this latest upset as an urgent reminder to look at the underlying cause.

The Story of No Goals

When unfortunate things occur we often hear the claim, "I didn't do anything. It just happened." The key words here are "didn't do". The person did nothing, made no choices, took no responsibility, and created by default an unwanted "happening." But there are no accidents. All this is set into motion by thoughts, goals, choices and decisions—or the lack of them. When we make no plans—we deserve what we get.

Many people try to dodge responsibility by not deciding, believing that in this way, whatever happens won't be their fault. Let someone else take the blame. Often these people have been unjustly ridiculed, or blamed for their "mistakes."

When you have trouble deciding or find yourself procrastinating, you need to search within yourself to find the real reason for your delay. Remember that procrastination is often fear-based. Search to find the specific doubt or fear held in mind. Try talking things over with a trusted friend. Do whatever works to get to the cause of your indecision. Write it clearly in a journal to ponder over, then take appropriate action to release it. This is truly taking responsibility for all your creations, including the unplanned ones.

Write what you want and why you want it. When you truly want something and don't have it you are blocking it in some way, usually from a sense of not deserving. Writing what is wanted and why you want it helps you to work through your barriers.

Be aware you cannot create success while blaming other people for what is happening in your life. Understand that no one else can create events in your life. Every situation you find yourself in is the direct result of choices you have made or failed to make. Yet sometimes you have to find yourself in deep misery before you are ready to make the needed changes in your thinking.

Misery Is Not a Place to Live
It is the manure that makes us grow.

Misery is something like sitting on a tack. When it hurts enough you will get up and do something about it, but not before. Truth is, you will never know how strong you are until apparent adversity tests you. Often this becomes a great turn-around point in your life.

Every event that happens is a result of your thoughts and feelings over time. If you spend ten minutes of positive thinking and the rest of your day in fear, criticism, and mumble-grumbles, ninety percent of the day was negative. No one can get positive results from negative thinking. Worse, when you blame your unwanted results on someone else, your lesson goes unlearned and as a consequence, a new and more uncomfortable incident may be chosen by your soul. When you persist in avoiding responsibility, those lessons are repeated, ultimately becoming so severe you can no longer ignore them. You are forced to cope with the problem you created in the first place. Eventually, you will realize your lessons are always for your greatest good.

Knowing this, you would be wise to view each problem as one more step toward your perfection. For example, losing a job can seem to be a disaster, but usually turns out to be the best thing that could have happened.

Do a Review

Take a good look at the goals you have set, the plans you have made, if any, and the ideals you hold in mind. Consider whether you have honestly followed them.

Three main things are needed to create:

- **Plan:** A specific dream, desire, or intent clearly stated.
- **Decision:** Specific steps for attainment: lists, schedules, appointments, affirmations, goal cards.
- **Follow-Through:** Taking positive actions to make it happen.

Almost all of us do the first part, some of us take the second step, but very few follow through to completion. Do you follow through to the finish? If not, why not? Think about it.

Check Your Goals

Without a clear goal in mind, you are subject to manipulation and control by those who know what they want and are ready to go after it. The act of careful planning and setting clear goals quickly separates the winners from the losers.

If you really want to be a winner, remind yourself that it only takes a few moments to make plans and set intentions for the day or week. But it may take hours, even days, to clean up the messes that result from no planning at all. Of course, you can't plan for every contingency, but you can have a clear, overall plan for everything you expect to do each day. These can be as simple as:

- I intend to have a happy, fulfilling day.
- I am happy and peaceful so I naturally create a peaceful, harmonious world around me.
- I do all things in love and harmony and so my world is full of love and harmony.

- I refuse to let others' words and actions upset me. (No one can upset me unless I let it happen.)
- I send my love and blessings to those who are angry and disruptive, creating harmony where it is needed most.
- Everything is beautiful and running smoothly in my life.

This is a good plan that you can add to your daily, weekly and monthly intents. Intend to think, speak, and feel from a place of inner peace—better yet, from a loving, caring attitude. My favorite one is gentle-loving kindness.

A Day of Joy
Laughter is good for the soul.

The day I turned my manuscript in to my publisher was a day of relief mixed with great joy and excitement, for I had been working on this book for many years. (This event was a last-minute addition.) I was on a big "high." Afterward, as I went shopping I found many hard-to-find items I had been searching for not only available, but on sale. On top of that, it was Senior Citizen's Day, so I got a ten-percent discount. Everywhere I went people were friendly, pleasant, and smiling, even those who were usually gloomy. Sales people seemed to go out of their way to help me, give good advice, and even followed me around to other parts of the store. It was then that I first realized my joy was attracting, even extracting feelings of happiness from others. I could literally feel the difference in the air.

As I walked through the mall with a big, silly grin on my face, I could see others literally "lighting up" in smiles directed at me. Since I was so happy I could freely give friendly greetings to strangers with concerned faces and watch them break into smiles, their cares temporarily forgotten. I became acutely aware of radiating love and joy everywhere I went and could actually see the results all around me. It was a delightful, yet profound understanding of just how much we each influence others by our attitudes.

End of story? No, it is the beginning. The next day, I was determined to hold onto my high spirits as long as possible because it felt so good. A number of small, unexpected, and pleasant events occurred. These joyful happenings went on for several days. Things I wanted came my way with great ease. People still responded with happy faces, reflecting mine. It was a wonderful experience, which I stretched out as long as possible. I refused to give life's little irritations more than two seconds of consideration, and I was determined to hold onto that wonderful, joyous, and loving high.

When things go wrong, check your signals. If your life is not what you want it to be, the chances are you are not truly connected with what you want. Look at your life to see what you are creating or attracting. Check your body talk; what is it telling you? Look at your relationship mirrors. What are they reflecting? Recall that the things that irritate you most in others are an unfailing indicator of your own faults or weaknesses. These must be cleaned up if you are to create the things you really desire.

Remember your home, your circumstances, your surroundings, and the people around you are all giving you important messages about your life and beliefs, as well as your attitudes, expectations and faults. Again, even your auto is giving your messages about your life and your health.

Are you paying attention? It is wise to watch for the symbolic meanings in your life, for they help you see what you are attracting or have already brought into being. They can also warn of impending problems or pinpoint where you are out of balance. Look closely at the synchronous events and symbols to see what they are revealing and evaluate them carefully to see where you need to change your thinking.

As you begin taking responsibility for all your creations, you learn positive creating very quickly and your life will improve dramatically. You will also be able to put a stop to the things you do not want in your life before they can settle into place. Then you can create something much better. Constantly claim your power and ability to do this.

Check Your Focus

Another thing to examine is your overall focus of attention. For instance, if you have been worried about something or focused on not having something, then you are actually creating more of not having. When you focus on what you fear or what you do not want, you create more of it by your attention to it.

Trouble Shooting

Anything that annoys, frustrates, angers, or upsets you will be yours to do battle with for an undetermined length of time simply because you are giving your energy to it. You are feeding and nurturing it so that it grows larger, stronger, and harder to overcome.

Focusing on things not wanted causes inner tensions and resistance that manifests as frustration, stress, and impatience. To speak from a place of aggravation or anger is to create chaos. Voicing your irritation attracts even more annoying events.

Your body is a good indicator of "trouble in paradise." This often begins as a headache, warning you of an errant attitude needing to be addressed and changed before you unwittingly create an unwanted event. When you ignore or stifle the headache with aspirin, the next area is often the neck and shoulders. (For some, it is the stomach area.) Take careful note of your particular warning signal and learn to deal with the situation quickly and lovingly before it gets out of control, remembering you cannot find a solution while looking at the problem.

Stress-O-Meter

Recognizing the first, faint signals of oncoming stress is an art you need to cultivate. The sooner you realize tensions are building within you, the more quickly you can act to overcome the impending problem. Aspirin is not the answer; neither is anger. Our lesson is to learn to solve problems before they get out of control and to come to that all-important "point of peace within."

Your first step is learning to identify oncoming irritation at the earliest possible moment. Having some clear definitions will help you shorten your turn-around time. Check the following to find the point where you begin to recognize stress.

- **Mild Stress:** Feeling vaguely uncomfortable, slightly on edge, mildly annoyed or frustrated. Your neck and shoulder muscles may be starting to tighten.
- **Advancing Stress:** Feeling greater body discomfort, building annoyance, irritation, and impatience with yourself, others, or both. You may have a mild headache building.
- **Moderate Stress:** You body is definitely tense, you may be experiencing an oncoming headache. Slight annoyance has become frustration, irritation, and aggravation along with rising impatience.
- **Strong Stress:** Body tensions and frustration building rapidly; your headache has moved to full strength. Anger is about to boil over. You are losing control and on the verge of explosion.

Venting your anger and frustration may make you temporarily feel better, but it does not solve the problem. In fact, it only makes matters much worse and far more difficult to resolve later. You have failed your test, and must repeat the lesson again and again until you get it right.

Addressing Your Stress

At the moment of recognition, identify your stress level and pause to ask:

- When did it start?
- What, exactly, is annoying me? (Don't even bother to ask whom. Your answer lies in the event or acts which triggered a reaction in you.)
- What was said or done that triggered stress/resistance in me?
- What, exactly, am I resisting?
- Why?
- What does this relate to, or remind me of?

Your goal is to make quick identification and confrontation, usually with yourself. Once you can identify the cause, belief, attitude, or childhood memory which attracted the incident, you are on your way to permanently eradicating the problem. Overcome the errant belief in yourself and you will have learned your lesson. You can now graduate to the next level. Congratulations!

Check Your Basic Belief System

Stop trying to fix things on the physical level and focus on finding both the cause and the solution. Do whatever it takes to keep yourself at peace to prevent unwanted creations. Here again, paying attention to your body signals in the moment keeps you creating good things in your life. Your mood sets the tone or vibration and loving vibes are needed for perfect creating.

Anytime your creative efforts are disappointing there is a good probability that your overall thoughts, emotions, and focus were less than positive.

Laying the Groundwork for Success

Be aware that in the twenty-first century, all our painful, buried memories are coming up to our conscious minds to be cleansed. There will be no more hiding things from ourselves. All our mental and emotional garbage is rising to the surface of our minds, where we will have to admit it, deal with it, forgive it, and get over it before we go further. Why? Because painful childhood memories act as anchors holding us in our old fears and limitations, actively preventing us from breaking out of old patterns of fear and limitation. We must release the pain, anger and resentments that go with them because these wounds, held firmly in mind, keep us from obtaining our desires. Failure to cleanse leaves you fighting against your own basic belief system, where you can never win.

Positive Support for Your Beliefs

- **Thoughts:** What kind of thoughts, attitudes, and emotions have you been sending forth each day? Were they mostly pleasant and positive? Are you building those bridges of new, more prosperous states of consciousness? Are you sending out blessings or damnation? We each have this power to bless or damn, but most of us fail to recognize the power we wield. Think twice before damning anything, knowing it will surely return home to roost.
- **Mind Set:** Is it hard to stay in a positive mind set about your goals? Or do you get into negativity regularly? How often? Do you catch yourself and take counter measures? How does your mind-chatter run? When you slip up, do you quickly correct yourself?
- **Focus:** Are you centered on what you want, knowing you can have it? Or do you spend time thinking about not having it yet? To focus on "not having" creates more negative results.
- **Right Stance:** Are you standing/living in a state of benevolence? Of gentle-loving kindness? Are you in a good mood most of the time? What kind of movies do you watch? Do these support your happy stance? Do you keep yourself surrounded with beautiful things, flowers, favorite music, and other things to compliment your need to keep happy?
- **Goal Cards:** Are you supporting yourself by working regularly with these tools? Are you spending twenty-one days with each new intent? Are you working with monthly, weekly, and daily goals? What was your game plan for today? How well did you do?

Supportive Self-Talk

- **Conversation:** Watch your self-defeating comments about poverty, illness, or lack of any kind. Pay attention to these and immediately counteract them with two or more positive statements. This starts pulling you out of the deep hole of negativity you have been digging. Also watch any "I don't have it yet" remarks. The focus on "not having" effectively keeps you in the "not-having" state that defeats your whole purpose. Back up your intentions with positive words about their attainment. "Walk your talk" on a daily basis. Stay positive about your goals.

- **Supportive People:** Do you surround yourself with friendly, supportive and positive-minded people? People who encourage you, your hopes, and dreams? Stay far away from those (friends and family) who "rain on your parade" or dwell on problems—yours or theirs. Avoid those who love to "feel sorry" for you. You don't need commiseration; you need upliftment and support.
- **Social Events:** Do you attend only those which you enjoy and keep you in a pleasant mood? Or do you "should" yourself and people please?
- **Supportive Entertainment:** Everything you see, hear, and think becomes a part of your consciousness, your belief system, which affects all your decisions and creations.
- **TV, Movies And Videos:** Do you watch those programs that are uplifting and supportive of the healthy, wealthy, and happy lifestyle you desire? Or do you enjoy watching vengeance, violence, hate, crime, and other negative-type things? If they don't make you feel good, switch channels.

Improving Your Skills
You can alter your life by altering your attitude.

Concentrate on the areas where you feel less than good and consider the kind of changes you need to make. To be a better creator, write these on your goal card and put them into action.

Attitudes = Vibrations

Vibrations Obey The Law Of Attraction

Therefore, Attitude Is Everything.

Look at the areas of your greatest negativity and begin to make your life positive by making new choices about your attitude, mind-chatter, friends, habits, and surroundings. Make as many positive changes as possible starting with the worst areas first.

- **Friends and Relatives:** Realize that anytime you are around people who are predominantly negative in their attitudes and actions, these "vibes" rub off on you. Their "stuff" can pollute your aura and your world unless you are a strong, positive thinker. You may need to reassess the value of some of those friends and coworkers. You may need to avoid some of them and find a whole new group of friends.
- **Job and Coworkers:** You may need to consider a different job or find a way to create more harmony and loving relationships where you are.

Since this is a thought-created world, the only way to improve your world is to improve your thinking. Create a new, positive and loving attitude about yourself and your life. Stop focusing on what is wrong, stop singing the blues, and find some happy things to think about. Then back it up with clear, positive intentions.

How to Change

1. Change mind-chatter with positive affirmations and intents.
2. Exchange negative, pity-party friends for positive ones.
3. Find a new, positive song to sing and sing it.
4. Select some positive affirmations and sing them, too.
5. Remember this is a thought/feeling created world.
6. Keep yourself in a warm, loving, appreciative and happy place.

Understanding Your Mis-Creations
A Holographic View

Most of the people in our society are living in a very limited, three-dimensional consciousness, believing they are only human. They believe that there is only one life to live and that physical matter is all that is real. If it cannot be seen or felt, it simply does not exist for them. Therefore, when things go wrong, it is easy to conclude that if so-and-so had not said or done such-and-such, all this would not have happened. It is his or her fault. Although this over-simplified approach may seem quite logical when one is limited to 3D thinking, it is also a very effective roadblock to spiritual growth and understanding. Failing to see the whole (holographic) picture leads to faulty conclusions and multiple misunderstandings.

I am a Spiritual Being, living in a Spiritual Universe ruled by Spiritual Laws.
— Unity Church Statement

When you realize that you are a living, breathing hologram, a spiritual being composed of many layers with the physical body as a vehicle your soul uses to gain needed wisdom, the whole business of living comes into perspective. Problem solving from this vantage point is not only simpler, but also much more effective. The cure is permanent soul growth, never to be lost.

When Problems Occur

When things go wrong in your life, use your holographic soul consciousness to view your problem. Begin by making a list of the things that have gone wrong lately. Write these out in terms of the type of situations and how they made you feel.

Example:

Situation	Feeling
I was fired from my job without good reason.	Betrayed, victimized
Someone stole my wallet.	Felt victimized
I had a fight with my best friend.	Betrayed
People tell me one thing, but do another	Betrayed, angry, victimized

In looking through this list, it becomes obvious that victimization is the main issue in most of these events. Although the triggering event happened in childhood, you still feel like a helpless child. The trauma is stuck in time and in the belief system, drawing more victim incidents until the original trauma is forgiven, brought into balance (point of peace), and released.

If you are feeling powerless, to whom have you given your power? Teachers, preachers, parents, relatives, neighbors, friends, or doctors? List the names of all those you feel have power over you. Then, ask yourself how and why? Try to pin down the cause or reason. This will help you to overcome the powerlessness.

↪ When Things Go Wrong

Be determined to be victorious, rather than a victim. When fear strikes, instead of buckling under, take a deep breath and picture yourself standing in a pillar of love and light. When you are at peace with yourself, you are in touch with your God-self and you are standing in your god/goddess power. This is a powerful stance of knowing who you are and will automatically repel victimization. Love repels all evil. You can't lose.

As often as possible, practice standing in your god/goddess power, centered in love, wisdom, and joy. Frequently picture yourself connected to your God-self, sending love and blessings outward to all. Determine to stay in a positive, happy, god-like stance at all times. Overcome victimhood by consciously reclaiming your god/goddess power.

Problems Are Lessons in Disguise
Every problem is an opportunity to achieve mastery.

As long as we are perfectly content and happy, we tend to become complacent. We have no need to go searching for anything—so we can sit comfortably in first grade indefinitely. But there is no growth or expansion in this contented mode. We need something to stimulate our minds.

Enter problem number one. As soon as a difficulty enters our arena we begin asking questions. What went wrong? Why me? What should I do? How can I fix this? We begin to search for answers, ways to solve our dilemma, and in the process, we learn. We grow in knowledge and understanding and expand our horizons. We discover new ideas and things, and thus when we return to our comfortable first grade desks, we find they no longer fit. We have outgrown both the seats and the curriculum. We do not belong there anymore, and we have graduated to a higher level.

Problems Stimulate Our Growth

Let us learn to consider each problem solved as another graduation time. As this problem-learning process is repeated, we eventually earn our Ph.D. in Earthology. This is what Earth life is really all about. It is a training school for souls. Perhaps you recall the statement Jesus made, "Be ye therefore perfect, even as your Father in heaven is perfect" (Matthew 5:48). It takes many, many lifetimes to perfect ourselves. In general, if you are still living on earth, you are not perfect yet.

Dissatisfaction or desire can also bring new growth. Wanting to learn to drive an automobile is a great example. Your first step was probably learning to master the tricycle, then a bicycle. Possibly, your next step was a ride-around mower or some farm machinery. You may not have recognized those baby steps as learning skills leading up to driving your own auto, yet each step led to one more accomplishment, which eventually brought you to driving a car.

The main difference is the desire to learn, which feels easy, versus a problem situation that forced learning. It seemed much harder because of your resistance to the challenge. Yet you learned new skills from both. Your struggle was heightened by your attitude.

Problem Situations Made Easier

With your new understanding of problems as growth stimulators, make an effort to embrace each new situation, challenge, or problem, knowing it is for your greatest good. Stay out of reluctance, resistance, and why me? Instead of reacting negatively, accept each new challenge in the manner of one seeking to learn something new. Try to understand it. See it as another mirror and ask, "What is the lesson?" Absolutely know that you can handle it. Affirm your acceptance of this scenario with love and appreciation for all the good that it will bring. Look forward to your new adventure in life. As you do this, your new, wholesome attitude will let you work through each new situation with ease and grace. Remember problems are for growth and learning. Accept this as a gift, not a problem.

Most of us scatter our energies in many directions and then wonder why we get unwanted results. Looking for how you created things you did not want and pinning down the cause helps you to avoid mistakes later. Learn to analyze your results and take full responsibility for them, then you can change them more readily into exactly what is wanted. This is one way to fine-tune your skills.

- Describe what you think the problem/lesson may be.
- Ask for insights through prayer, dreams, and meditation.
- Watch for answers from everywhere.

- Check your surroundings, circumstances, and people/mirrors for additional information and understanding.
- Record your results and learn from them.
- Set new goals and affirmations to correct this.

Your close inspection of your thinking/feeling world gives you understanding, growth, and wisdom in the art of manifesting. The sooner you perceive the relation between what you think, feel, or focus upon (positively or negatively) and what happens in your life, the sooner you can be a master creator.

Dealing with Disappointments

Disappointments are often important turn-around points in learning how not to create. Seeing what you don't want actually brings clarity when you recognize the problem as a needed lesson. Turn your anger, disappointment, and pain into clarity. "This is what I do not want. I am very clear about what is not wanted." Follow up with; "This is what I want." State this clearly, concisely, and with happy, loving feelings.

Stay in this loving, appreciative place until you are wholly, totally there, being in that dream world, loving it, delighting in it, and at one with your desire. Be there, belong, be an integral part of the picture of having your desire and being delighted with it. Think of the wonderful things you will do with it. Appreciate it. Give thanks for it. Enjoy.

Problem Prevention

Intend to live within the Law of Love, starting with the little irritations such as rude drivers, selfish actions, and harsh words of others. Instead of reacting in kind, try to realize they must be hurting to act so crudely. Send a little prayer of love their way.

Learn to say, "God bless you," to the evildoers, even if you have to say it with gritted teeth. Just start a new habit of blessing others who are less knowledgeable.

Deliberately begin to establish new patterns of thinking and behaving. Tell yourself, "I can forgive ___ ." "I can understand how ___ feels." "I can see why ___ is upset."

The practice of compassion, good will, love, and appreciation keeps you in a state of gentle-loving kindness. These loving vibrations are needed to create prosperity, joy, good health, and all the wonderful things you want in your life.

Create a new habit of saying, "God bless this person, place, or situation." Send your love and blessings toward those in trouble, accidents, floods, fires, and tornadoes. Use every chance you get to send good thoughts, love, and blessings, knowing that all the love you send out comes back to you multiplied.

Greeting New Things with Loving Acceptance

Be careful not to prejudge a new situation or a change as bad or difficult. Remember, whatever you name it is what it will be for you. So be sure to pronounce it good. Tell yourself, "This will be an interesting and wonderful new experience." Make a habit of naming all new things as "good." Then add your intentions of what you want to have happen and how it will be happy and harmonious, even fun.

When making plans for something, tomorrow's work, a visit, shopping trip, whatever it may be, take a few moments to picture in your mind how you would like it to be. Remember that you are creating the events in your world. James Allen once said, "In all human affairs there are efforts and there are results and the strength of the effort is the measure of the result." So, put some strength into your efforts and literally create the experience of having a good day, every day.

Check Your Score

In the following quiz, give yourself positive points for anything that makes you feel uplifted, happy, and fulfilled. Give negative points for that which makes you feel ashamed, unworthy, depressed or generally unhappy.

Self Analysis Quiz

Question	Positive	Negative
What is your mood as you wake?	❏	❏
What is your attitude toward fellow travelers going to work?	❏	❏
How do you feel about your job?	❏	❏
What is your overall attitude towards your coworkers?	❏	❏
Your attitude toward your boss/bosses?	❏	❏
What is your mood on your way home from work?	❏	❏
What is your home atmosphere?	❏	❏
How do you feel about your family?	❏	❏
How do you feel about other relatives?	❏	❏

→ When Things Go Wrong

How do you feel about your parents?	❏	❏
How do you feel about your brothers and sisters?	❏	❏
How do you feel about your mate?	❏	❏
How do you feel about your mate's parents?	❏	❏
How do you feel about your children?	❏	❏
How do you feel about your friends?	❏	❏
How do you feel about social contacts?	❏	❏
How do you feel about your neighbors?	❏	❏
How do you feel about your church or religion?	❏	❏
How do you feel about your minister or leader?	❏	❏

This is your theme song. If your score is less than fifty-one percent positive, you have been singing the blues and reaping the results.

Analyze your results by examining the negative issues. Pick one or two of the most troublesome areas and design a way to change the worst one first. Goal card it, and work with it for the usual twenty-one days before tackling the next offender. Remember, you are working toward improving your thinking/feeling stance in order to become a master creator, the god in the making you are meant to become.

Negative emotions are from your God-self saying, "Pay attention. This is important—you are not in line with what you want." It is time to bring yourself to the point of pure loving vibrations, known as gentle-loving kindness.

Although all emotions energize your thought forms to some degree, love is one of the best and most important. Joy, laughter, and gratitude also help reinforce the good things in life, so dwell on these happy thoughts frequently.

On the other hand, fear of failure or of not getting your desires will act like the pull of a magnet slowly drawing your most dreaded events to you. Avoid dwelling in anger, self-pity, frustration, or outright rage, for these pack such a punch as to give instant birth to the words you speak.

The Purpose of Our Lives

Let us not forget the real purpose of our lives. We were not created to be puppets, subject to the whims of various dictators, or hapless pawns in the Game of Life. Nor were we designed to be slaves to other people's whims, being battered about by life's uncertainties. We are here to learn the Laws of the Universe and become co-creators with God. We were given free will and dominion over the earth. What we do with our gifts is entirely up to us.

Ten Talents

The Biblical story of the Ten Talents (Matthew 25:14–29) illustrates this well. The master gives his servants many talents (money) to keep while he is gone on a long journey. When he returns, he finds the first servant has wisely invested his share of money and doubled the original amount. The master is pleased and rewards him. The second servant, who was given less money, had also doubled the amount and was duly rewarded. The third servant, given only one talent, was "in fear" and buried his share in the ground. The master was displeased and took away the one talent and gave it to the servant who had ten.

We also have "talents" which we are to invest wisely, creating more. We are meant to become masters over our minds, bodies, and our emotions. We are to be careful managers of all we have been given and are to rule our kingdom with wisdom, honor, and love. Yet, many of us cannot even rule our own bodies. We often allow our appetites to rule us. Abuse, addictions, and selfishness run rampant in our country.

Look at Adam and Eve. They had it all—everything they could want, except for the fruit on one, lone tree. They, too, failed to exercise control over their appetites, and lost it all.

To become masters of our lives we must have plans, make decisions, and take full control of our affairs on a day to day basis. The ability to rule wisely comes from taking full responsibility for whatever we have created or attracted. We need to recognize our problems as challenges we have chosen to learn by and to keep learning, growing, and refining our skills. Through this we become masters of ourselves and our lives.

In Genesis, God gives us dominion over the earth, fowl, and beasts—not to pillage, pollute, and misuse. We are to manage wisely, with love and honor toward all beings, including the Earth and all its riches. As we learn to rule honorably over the little things, like the servants, we are given more while those who are careless and selfish lose what little they have. (King Solomon was wise first, then wealthy.) We need to learn wisdom and good stewardship first, and that starts with taking good care of the little things.

Whatever happens, always come back to a point of peace and love within you first, then with all beings and all things.

When Things Go Wrong

When things go wrong, as they sometimes do,
Just look at the clues surrounding you.
For all around, the signs abound
To show you what you've planned,
If you only understand
The tools at your command.

The people that you meet each day
Can halt or help you on your way;
Your home, your car, your neighborhood
All pointing toward your greatest good
To help you get a clearer view
Of how the things you think and do
Will always come back home to you.

So take a good look at your life —
The peace and joy or hate and strife —
And understand that all you view,
Comes from deep inside of you;
Your attitudes, your hopes and fears
Which manifest as Joy or Tears.

For you and you alone can change
The things you find within your range
By knowing that your thoughts create
The good, the bad, the love, the hate.

Yes, you and you alone create
Your world and all you have to date.

—Author

20

Your Life, Your World, Your Universe

Our thoughts are the threads weaving the garment which the world tomorrow will wear. You and I created a piece of tomorrow by our thoughts today.
— Frank Laubach[1]

You now have the tools you need to create the desires of your heart, providing you keep your heart in a loving place and your words in line with your desires. The realization that you can change your life — the mere acceptance of this concept brings change. If you believe in your own power and ability, no one can keep you from creating and manifesting what you want.

All you really need to do is to put yourself in a state of love and joy, focus your intentions clearly on your objective and say, "I intend to create _____ in my life" and in due time, it appears. That is, if you have no basic beliefs to contradict it.

Your Own Little World

Remember that you carry your own little world of beliefs and their related thought forms around with you everywhere you go. For example, when a man believes himself to be a failure he cannot be anything else, for he carries within him the mental picture (thought form) of failure, thus succeeding to fail regardless of his intentions. Jesus explained it this way: "According to your belief it is done unto you" (Matthew 8:13). What could be plainer?

Vibration

The Universe responds more to the totality of the vibrations of our thoughts and feelings than to the words that we speak. This brings a new perspective in the laws of creation. It seems that we, as humans, vibrate our beliefs, attitudes, and feelings at all times. The Universe supports us fully in creating a vibrational match to these, whether positive or not. The Universe does not judge, it simply fills the "order" based on our "vibes."

Like a pebble thrown into a pond, making ever-expanding ripples, everything we think, feel, or believe is sent out as a vibration to which the Universe responds. We know what we want mentally, but our vibrations often create the opposite. When we are ill and concerned about our health, we are more focused on our lack of wellness than on recovery. We may be more concerned with our lack of money than on our intent for prosperity, thereby producing poverty. This duality is often difficult to recognize and change since the time lag is long. Consequently, we may fail to see the connection between our thinking and feeling vibrations and the circumstances in which we later find ourselves.

Understanding the Nature of Vibrations for More Accurate Creating

- God is love and love vibrates in rounded waves.
- The Universe, created by God, vibrates in rounded waves.
- When you are in love you vibrate in rounded waves.
- When you are happy you vibrate in rounded waves.
- When you are in tune with the Universe, you vibrate in rounded waves.
- Negative thoughts have sharp, pointed edges.
- When you are angry, frustrated, and upset you vibrate in sharp, jagged edges.
- When in fear, worry, or struggle you vibrate in sharp edges.
- When out of tune with the universe you also vibrate in rough, jagged patterns.

Negative thinking/feeling vibrations repel the good and attract disease, accidents, and difficulties of all kinds. Therefore, when the undesirable manifests there has to be a corresponding vibrational belief in there somewhere. It is then necessary to find and erase the false beliefs and patterns. The best way to stay on track is to confront and deal with each situation as soon as possible. Don't go to bed until you have confronted the cause behind the effect. The main idea is to complete each day's lessons before going to sleep by writing in your journal and questioning the day's events. When unsure, ask for insights and understanding in your dreams. Get to the bottom of the problem quickly and efficiently. This provides a fresh start for each day.

Vibrational Harmony

Again, it is important to watch for the signals the Universe offers, knowing you can trust it to support you in all you think, believe, and vibrate. That which you focus upon becomes your vibrational point of attraction and whatever you see around you is evidence of what you are vibrating. Everything works according to Divine Law—the vibrational Law of Love.

Living More Consciously

Writing in your journal helps you to recognize your old patterns or upcoming problems quickly. For more accurate creating, it is necessary for you to be more aware of your choices—or lack of them—by questioning old assumptions.

Examples:

- Rethink old agreements.
- Question authority.
- Frequently look at life's mirrors for relationship problems.
- Check surroundings and circumstances often.
- Ask why old patterns seem hard to change.
- Find what is being held onto or held back. Why?
- When things don't work out as planned, question beliefs.
- Write problems, list possible answers, ask questions, seek until answers are found.

Continuously take full responsibility for everything you have created, especially when your expectations are not met. Stop to question why. In this way, you will quickly learn from your mistakes.

You have noticed that people who are always angry, defensive, and looking for a fight automatically attract other angry people so they can "go at it" until satisfied. Each one is teaching/reflecting the other and neither is understanding the role they keep playing over and over, often blaming the other one for their plight. It is easy to see what other people are doing: now you must watch carefully for your own role.

In Tune with the Universe

Making a joyful vibrational attunement with your inner being or God-self is an important prerequisite for creating your desires quickly and correctly. Since we are all extensions of God-energy, we have a natural ability to be in harmony with that energy.

As you move through the day, one of the best ways of attuning to your God-self is to appreciate as many things as possible on a moment-to-moment base. Thoughts of appreciation and gratitude are uplifting to the soul.

Chanting "om" can help soothe and uplift you. Prayers of thanksgiving and good will move you to a higher vibration as does relaxing to good music. The better you feel, the higher your vibrations become. Feeling really good is proof that you are connected to your God-self. Your most important task is to be happy.

Joyful Creating

The Rule of Attraction is always at work. Once you are centered in your blissful place of joy and feeling good, all you need to do is state your desire and radiate that happy, loving energy into thoughts and pictures of its fulfillment. Savor the joy of having it now. Revel in the feeling of having what you are wanting, get into the feeling of the excitement and pleasure of acquiring and enjoying the reception of the desires of your heart. Practice holding that excited, happy feeling of having and enjoying your heart's fancy. Launch your intents in a moment of joy and passion. Love it into being.

Embrace those joyful scenes and feelings as long as you can without wavering. Hold this energy at least two or three minutes nonstop. The longer and stronger, the better. Manifestations flow quickly on these happy, loving energies. (This is truly being in the flow rather than working hard.)

Follow Your Bliss

Once you have spoken your creative word and sent it out with love, all you have to do is follow your feelings. When you wonder which way to go, do what feels good and brings you the most joy. Always listen to your inner being and stay in touch with your feelings.

Staying in That Happy, Loving, Vibrational Place

Intend to be keenly aware of all those who "rain on your parade," making you feel used, wounded or diminished. These people are hazardous to your health. Learn to stay in a happy, loving place and love your desires into manifestation.

Now that you can enjoy creating the things you desire for yourself, what about those around you? How can you, using your god/goddess power, help to make the world a better place? One thing you can do alone, or with others, is to pray/intend for those who are in trouble, sick, poor, hungry, and war-torn. Another gift you can give is to radiate your thoughts of love and peace to all you contact while walking, driving, shopping, or working. The chances to give your love are endless.

It is especially helpful to send your blessings to those who are experiencing problems. This could be a crying child, a frustrated mother, a disabled car on the highway, or an angry crowd. You name it, there are endless opportunities to make your world a better place, just by expressing your god/goddess self through gentle-loving kindness.

Sharing Personal Upliftment

Think back to a person you have known who was overly critical of you, constantly finding fault, correcting your every move, and making you feel inept, useless, or inferior. Pause to remember how you felt. Were you uncomfortable? Perhaps you dreaded seeing them walk into the room because of the way that you felt when in their energy field. You may even recall that you made more mistakes than usual when under their critical gaze. It was as though their expectation of seeing you fumble actually drew that bungling behavior from you.

Now think about someone who loved you. How did you feel in their presence? Were you happy to see them or have them near you? Were you at your very best, your wittiest, and most efficient when in their loving, approving presence? Did they actually bring out the best in you?

As you go about your day, deliberately direct your love and approval toward others, knowing you can affect their attitudes, work habits, and behavior just by your own gentle-loving kindness. Like the god/goddess you are, you will actually bring out their very best qualities. You will inspire them to higher levels of thinking and living. You will make the world a better place. You have so much more influence than you ever imagined, so much more power to uplift or destroy. In addition, you are responsible for the way you use that power. Use it wisely.

Helping One Another in Positive Changes

The most powerful tool on the planet today is Tell-A-Vision. That is where I tell a vision to you, and you tell a vision to me. That way, if we don't like the programming we can change the channel.
—Swami Beyondandonda[2]

If you are looking for something helpful and uplifting for yourself, family, or friends, it is more advantageous to work with a group. Then, having agreed on suitable, personal goals, you can each share, advise, and support one another through the process of changing yourselves, your thinking, and your personal lives. You could join or create a self-improvement group, a study group, or a prayer and support group, all with the aim of improving yourselves, and eventually others. The ripple effect is always working.

Improving Family Affairs

And how to build a better world?
Well, not by chart or plan,
Unless we start to teach the boy
To be a better man.
For all our dreams of nobler things
Will meet the same old fate,
Unless we turn to fellowship,
And do away with hate.
—Edgar A. Guest

You and others may want to set some special goals for your families. Work together to set higher standards for your homes and children, intending to express more love to one another and looking out for one another's needs in loving ways.

You could make plans for adding more beauty in and around your house and yard, making your home environment a better place to live in and enjoy. As a few neighbors join in sprucing up their homes and yards, others will be inspired to do the same.

Neighborhood

Expand into your neighborhood, finding ways to aid one another in creating a cleaner, safer, and more beautiful area. Let each individual declare their chosen ideas and desires for improvement. Between meetings, support one another through work, prayer, meditation, visualization, and affirmations. Start with reasonably small goals and work up.

When together, each can share their triumphs, feelings, and experiences while group members give physical, mental, and emotional support until each one's goal is reached. New desires can be added as old ones are attained. This could become an uplifting experience for all concerned. Using your god/goddess power and imagination, you can make your fondest dreams come true.

Community

Extend these principles into your community. Your group can agree on common concerns and goals for the neighborhood, community, and city or further. Use your group power to create a positive, peaceful outcome with joy and good to all concerned.

You might pray and intend prosperity, bountiful crops, health, or better understanding and cooperation with minority groups. You could work on local problems, such as fair and just treatment for all in your community.

You could get involved in ecology, pollution, education, health care, creative arts, and safer playgrounds. Together you could intend and work for your area being a clean, safe, beautiful, prosperous, loving, and supportive place for all. You might even protect your area, through prayer and group intentions, from crime and drugs with your group circle of protection.

Take advantage of the power of a group effort concentrated on one specific goal. You could intend prosperity in your fund-raising ventures, or peace, harmony, and justice in some controversial issue. This could easily extend from small matters into local, city, country, or worldwide matters. Politics, pollution, and other issues can be addressed, especially as your group connects with other similar-minded groups around the planet who are also working for the good of mankind.

Bear in mind, you can be as a small boat tossed about by wind and wave, or you can do as Jesus did and say, "Be still." The waves obeyed, for Jesus knew he had the power to command the forces of nature, as do you and I. We are all one. Like a pebble tossed into a pond, what we think, say, and do affects us all for better or worse.

Weathering the Storm

In the area of weather, you can intend more or less rainfall, as needed. You can spread your protection over the area from threats of storm, flood, fire, and drought; calm a damaging wind or send a dangerous storm harmlessly out to sea. (Of course you can do that singly, but you may prefer to try it as a group project first, just to gain confidence.)

I had a delightful experience of this once as we heard radio warnings of a severe storm watch. My youngest son, then eight years old, was instantly concerned. "What about my pet pigeon?" he asked. Realizing the "pigeon house" he had built himself was no challenge for high winds, I replied, "Don't worry, son, I will put my circle of protection around it and both bird and birdhouse will be safe." (I had learned the protective circle idea at Unity Church.)

Several hours went by; there were dark clouds, but no storm. When the sun came out my son and I went for a walk. As we crossed the street to the next block, the sight of many fallen leaves, branches, and other debris immediately struck me. It was evident everywhere we walked. Coming back to our block, I realized there was no sign of a storm on our whole block. There was not a leaf out of place. My son was rather nonchalant about the whole episode, but I was really impressed. I had no idea I was so powerful.

Tornado Alert

On another occasion, I was working downtown when my son, Ken, was baby-sitting, and called to tell me there was a tornado alert for our area.* He was frightened and asked me what he should do. Again I opened my big mouth, "Don't worry, I'll put my protection around the house. Tell the kids to come home because our house is safe." Then I went on with my job.

When I arrived home, I was greeted with great excitement. "Mom! Mom! We watched the tornado come down and touch the house next door. We saw their shingles flying off. Then, as it moved to our yard it just went straight up in the air and moved off. A few minutes later the tornado went by the airport tower. We saw it on the news." Wow. This time, the whole family was impressed.

A few years later a friend told me an even better story about manipulating weather. It seemed he was out on the plains of Iowa when he looked up and saw a tornado coming down over a nearby town. He lifted his hand, pointed his finger just below the tornado (by line of sight), and pushed up. The tornado went back up into the clouds. A moment later, another twister came down, and again he pointed his finger just below the bottom and pushed up. The tornado went obediently back up and stayed there. The next day, when he traveled to the same town people were talking about the disappearing tornadoes. One person commented, "It was just like someone had taken a finger and pushed it back up."

If you recall, Jesus was well aware of his power. He knew who he was, and often said, "The Father and I are one" (John 10:30). He also taught his disciples, "The things I do, you can do also" (John 14:12).

* April 3, 1974, a major tornado event in the midwest

→ Your Life, Your World, Your Universe

When you know who you are, a child of God, a god in the making, then you do not need to grab power from others — because you have your own. Think of all the wonderful things you can do with all that power.

Each day you manage to dwell in a more joyful, loving place, you not only lift your own vibrations but significantly add to the upliftment of all those around you. You can literally make the whole world a better place by living your truth, following your heart, and radiating your joy. And, since love is far more powerful than hate and fear, your influence is like the tiny pebble thrown in a still pond, sending ripples of love and upliftment.

The Ripple Effect of Being Connected to Your God-Self

When you are feeling good, you are connected in a positive way to your highest good, to your God-self and the universe. The happier you feel, the stronger your connection. You become the god/goddess. Then, like a well-connected light bulb, you shine brightly, walking in your wisdom and joy, radiating enlightenment to others, making positive changes in your world. Realize you can create peace and harmony around you, in your home, your place of work, in a group, or anywhere at all, simply by joyfully intending it to be.

You Are Creating Your Future Now

According to the interpreters of the Mayan Calendar, August 17, 1987 was the end of an era. Some said it was the end of time as we know it. Most agree that between August, 1987 and December, 2012 there is a kind of "space of choice" where we, as the human race, are now creating our future, by our thoughts, our prayers, our fears, and our intentions.

Realize our daily thoughts are not only affecting our personal lives and the lives of our families and friends, but also the world in which we live. As TV news coverage expands, our world seems to be shrinking. News from the other side of the world becomes common knowledge in a matter of minutes. We can see more and more clearly how the thoughts and actions of one person can affect the many.

Expanding Into Planetary Consciousness

In our every deliberation, we must consider the impact of our decisions on the next seven generations.
—Great Laws of the Iroquois Confederacy

You can see how pollution is affecting not only land animals, but also sea creatures. Species are dying, the earth's poles are melting, and there is widespread hunger and chaos. The weather is changing. What next? What kind of world will your present day thoughts bring? Are you thinking, praying, working toward more loving acts, less cruelty, and less pollution? Are you recycling? Refusing to buy non-recyclable materials? Or are you standing back waiting for someone else to do something? Remember, "Ye are gods" (John 10:34).

What about wars? Are you praying, intending, and meditating for peace? Or are you going about business as usual, distracted, doing nothing, feeling powerless, and looking the other way? Those who do nothing are standing in the way of those who are seriously working for a better world. Decide whose side you are on, today.

Earth Changes

The thoughts of men can influence reality.
—Llama Ramposhki

How do you feel about the predicted earth changes? Are you in fear? Are you struggling, hoarding, and storing supplies to preserve your existence? Remember Job, "That which I have feared the most." Consider creating a happy, peaceful, and harmonious future for yourself, your family, and others. Those with the clearest goals always win.

What if the whole earth were a hologram, reflecting accurately your every thought, belief, or fear? (It is.) Race consciousness is the grand total of all the thoughts of all the people in any given area, your home, community, city, country, and planet. Our weather is a result of the collective thought forms in any given area.[3] What are you creating for your future?

Gaia

If we are to use our creative minds wisely in extending our thoughts and prayers out, into, and around our planet, we need to have a greater understanding of who Mother Earth really is.

Scientists now agree that our earth, Gaia, fulfills all the requirements for being a living, breathing entity, capable of making certain decisions on her own. Most indigenous people and many ancient traditions have considered "Mother Earth" as a great being and regarded her with respect and reverence. If this seems shocking, think of this being as a very old soul who was once like you and me, one who has lived numerous lives, has graduated from many of life's universities, and now has a rank similar to that of an Archangel. Later, Gaia will, as a soul, move to even higher levels of loving service to God and all beings, flora, and fauna included.

We, too, are forever learning and moving to higher and higher levels in God's Universes. We need to respect and honor the path of all souls equally.

Other planets in our solar system are also loving, angel-like beings embodying the planets and stars of the Universe. These highly developed and enlightened beings not only care for the various species inhabiting their planetary bodies but also send loving energies, rays, or vibrations to other planets, including our beloved earth. This is one of the reasons why Astrology works. For example, Mars, known in ancient wisdom (now called mythology) as the God of War, is the energy of courage, strength, and action. These energies are neither positive nor negative but can be used in making love, making war or any other activity.

Venus is known as the goddess of love and beauty and radiates those energies. Mercury's energies stimulate the mind, and so it goes.

It is time for us to understand the energies around us and start using our God-power for good in matters small and large, local and global. Take time to consider the kind of world you would like to create.

You must be the change you wish to see in the world.
— Ghandi

Our little acts of gentle-loving kindness can be powerful tools to uplift and transform. We are far more powerful than we know, so it is time to put on the robe of kindness, don the rose-colored glasses, and act like the god-beings we are. Create a more loving and beautiful home, neighborhood, community, country, world, and universe. Remember, we are held spiritually responsible for how we spend our lives, talents, energies and mind power.

People Changes

There is much talk about our coming transformation, ascension, and enlightenment. If you are wondering about this, consider Joni King's channeled message from Ptaah, "Every time you choose love, you change your frequency, lifting that rate of spin faster. Every time you choose love, you change the reality. Every time you choose love, you are changing your physical reality. It is a gentle unfolding ... This transition is about love."[4]

Spend your days sending love and blessings to the world at large. As you make their day better, you also improve yours.

> God grant me the Serenity to accept the things I cannot change ... Courage to change the things I can and the Wisdom to know the difference.
> —St. Francis of Assisi

The Universe

Extend your god/goddess awareness out into the universe. Behold the whole universe as a projection of your God-self, which at this level of observation, is at one with all beings. True love comes from your God-self. As you stand in your god/goddess power, your every thought is a blessing to the entire universe.

"You are a Child of the Universe, no less than the trees and the stars, you have a right to be here. And whether or not it is clear to you, no doubt the Universe is unfolding as it should. Therefore, be at peace with God, whatever you conceive him to be, and whatever your labors and aspirations, in the noisy confusion of life, keep peace within your soul... Strive to be happy."[5]

> I send my heartfelt blessings to be with you always.
> May you live in love, peace, and joy forever.

Bibliography

Every attempt has been made to properly credit material quoted or cited in this book. Any errors made in the research and editing process will be corrected in future printings.

The Truth About You
1. Krippner, Stanley and Daniel Rubin. *The Kirlian Aura*. Garden City, NY: Anchor Press/Doubleday, 1974.
2. Leadbeater, C.W. *Man, Visible and Invisible*. Wheaton, IL: Theosophical Publishing House, 1971.
3. Powell, A.E. *The Mental Body*. Wheaton, IL: Theosophical Publishing, 1927.

The Process of Creation
1. Besant, Annie and C.W. Leadbeater. *Thought Forms*. Wheaton, IL: Theosophical Publishing House, 1925. Wilda B. Tanner's reinterpretation of sketches from *Thought Forms*, used by permission. All other sketches in this chapter are the author's personal interpretation of what she has seen.
2. Newhouse, Rev. Flower A. *The Kingdom of the Shining Ones*. Escondido, CA: Christward Publications, 1955: 72–76.
3. Leadbeater, C.W. *The Hidden Side of Things*. India: Vasanta Press, The Theosophical Society, 1913.

Understanding Your Belief System
1. Tanner, Wilda B. *The Mystical Magical Marvelous World of Dreams*. Tahlequah, OK: Sparrow Hawk Press, 1988.
2. Lipton, Bruce H., Ph.D. *The Biology Consciousness*. C.E.L.L., 1995. Videocassette.

Changing Your Beliefs
1. Hay, Louise L. *You Can Heal Your Life*. Santa Monica, CA: Hay House, Inc., 1984.
2. Ray, Sondra. *I Deserve Love*. Berkeley, CA: Celestial Arts, 1976.
3. Tanner, Wilda B. *The Mystical Magical Marvelous World of Dreams*. Tahlequah, OK: Sparrow Hawk Press, 1988.
4. Ponder, Catherine. *Prosperity Secret of the Ages*. Englewood Cliffs, NJ: Prentice-Hall, Inc., 1964.

Decisions, Decisions
1. Wegscheider-Cruse, Sharon. *Choice-Making*. Pompano Beach, FL: Health Communications, Inc., 1987.

Goal Setting
1. Parker, Arthur Caswell. *The Constitution of the Five Nations or the Iroquois Book of the Great Law*. Syracuse, NY: Syracuse University Press, 1968.
2. *Rosicrucian Digest, The*. January 1987, p. 25.

Nurturing Your Creations
1. Gawain, Shakti. "Meditation: Getting in Touch with Your God-Self," *Creative Visualization*. Novato, CA: New World Library, 1995.
2. Sechrist, Elsie. *Meditation, Gateway to Light*. Virginia Beach, VA: A.R.E. Press, 1969.
3. Ornish, Dean, M.D. *Dr. Dean Ornish's Program for Reversing Heart Disease*. New York: Random House, 1990: 234.
4. Ingraham, E.V., *Meditation in the Silence*. Unity Village, MO: Unity School of Christianity, 1969.
5. Sechrist, Elsie. *Meditation, Gateway to Light*. Virginia Beach, VA: A.R.E. Press, 1969.

Body Talk
1. Tanner, Wilda B. *The Mystical Magical Marvelous World of Dreams*. Tahlequah, OK: Sparrow Hawk Press, 1988.
2. Steadman, Alice. *Who's the Matter with Me?* Marina del Rey, CA: DeVorrs & Co., 1966.
3. Northrup, Christiane, M.D. *Women's Bodies, Women's Wisdom*. New York: Bantam Books, 2002.
4. Allen, James. *As a Man Thinketh*. Kansas City, MO: Hallmark Editions, 1968.
5. Bailey, Alice A. *Esoteric Healing, Volume 4*. New York: Lucas Publishing Company, 1953: 133.
6. Steadman, Alice. *Who's the Matter with Me?* Marina del Rey, CA: DeVorrs & Co., 1966.
7. Wordsworth, William. *Ode on Intimations of Immortality*. In *Complete Poetical Works by William Wordsworth*. London: Macmillan & Co., 1888.

Mirror, Mirror on the Wall
1. Burns, Robert. *To a Louse*. Slightly Americanized from the original Gaelic, quoted here: "Wad some Power the giftee gie us to see oursels as ithers see us." In *Poems and Songs of Robert Burns*. New York: P.F. Collier & Sons, 1909.
2. Shakespeare, William. *Hamlet*. Act One, Scene 3: "This above all; To thine own self be true."

Surroundings as Symbols
1. Fox, Emmet. *The Mental Equivalent*. Kansas City, MO: Unity Village, 1943.
2. Ibid.
3. Tanner, Wilda B. *The Mystical Magical Marvelous World of Dreams*. Tahlequah, OK: Sparrow Hawk Press, 1988.
4. Findhorn Community. *The Findhorn Garden*. New York: Harper & Row, Publishers, 1975.
5. Fox, Emmet. *The Mental Equivalent*. Kansas City, MO: Unity Village, 1943.

Circumstances as Symbols
1. Murphy, Joseph. *The Power of Your Subconscious Mind*. Englewood Cliffs, NJ: Prentice-Hall, Inc., 1963.

Your Life, Your World, Your Universe
1. Laubach, Frank. *Prayer: The Mightiest Force in the World*. New York: Fleming H. Ravell Co., 1946.
2. Swami Beyondandonda. www.beyondandonda.com.
3. Newhouse, Rev. Flower A. *The Kingdom of the Shining Ones*. Escondido, CA: Christward Publications, 1955: 72–75.
4. King, Joni. *Sedona, Journal of Emergence* (magazine). January, 1999.
5. Ehrmann, Max. "Desiderata." © 1927, renewed 1954 by Robert Bell.

General Bibliography
Baker, Penny. *Meditation: A Step Beyond with Edgar Cayce*. New York: Pinnacle Books, 1973.

Besant, Annie and C.W. Leadbeater. *Thought Forms*. Wheaton, IL: Theosophical Publishing House, 1925.

Bradshaw, John. *Homecoming*. New York: Bantam Books, 1990.

Capacchione, Lucia, M.A. *The Power of Your Other Hand*. Hollywood, CA: Newcastle Publishing Co. Inc., 1988.

Cooke, Grace. *Meditation*. Hampshire, England: White Eagle Publishing Trust, 1955.

Erbe, Peter O. *God I Am, From Tragic to Magic*. Australia: TRIAD Publishers Pty Ltd., 1991.

Faraday, Ann, Ph.D. *The Dream Game*. New York: Perennial Library, 1974.

Fromm, Erich. *The Forgotten Language*. New York: Holt, Rinehart, and Winston, 1951.

Garfield, Patricia, Ph.D. *Creative Dreaming*. New York: Ballantine Books, 1974.

Goldsmith, Joel S. *The Art of Meditation*. New York: Harper & Row, 1956.

Green, Celia. *Lucid Dreams, Volume 1*. Oxford: Institute of Psycho-physical Research, 1968.

Kunz, Dora V.G. *The Personal Aura*. Wheaton, IL: Theosophical Publishing House, 1991.

Johnson, Robert. *Inner Work*. San Francisco, CA: Harper, 1986.

Jung, Carl G. *Man and His Symbols*. Garden City, NY: Doubleday, 1964.

Keyes, Ken, Jr. *A Conscious Person's Guide to Relationships*. Coos Bay, OR: Living Love Publications, 1979.

Leadbeater, C.W. *Man Visible and Invisible*. Wheaton, IL: Theosophical Publishing House, 1971.

Levine, Barbara Hoberman. *Your Body Believes Every Word You Say*. Santa Rosa, CA: Aslan Publishing, 1991.

MacDougall, Mary Katherine. *What Treasure Mapping Can Do for You*. Unity Village, MO: Unity School of Christianity, 1968.

Hill, Napoleon. *Think and Grow Rich*. New York: Fawcett Crest Books, 1960.

Pearce, Joseph Chilton. *Magical Child Matures*. New York: Bantam Books, 1985.

———. *The Magical Child*. New York: Bantam Books, 1977.

Ponder, Catherine. *The Dynamic Laws of Prosperity*. Englewood Cliffs, NJ: Prentice Hall, 1962.

———. *The Healing Secret of the Ages*. West Nyack, NY: Parker Publishing Company, Inc., 1967.

———. *The Prospering Power of Love*. Unity Village, MO: Unity Books, 1966.

Powell, A.E. *The Etheric Double*. Wheaton, IL: Quest Books, 1979.

Ray, Sondra. *Loving Relationships*. Berkeley, CA: Celestial Arts, 1980.

——— . *The Only Diet There Is*. Berkeley, CA: Celestial Arts, 1981.

Reed, Henry. *Getting Help from Your Dreams*. Virginia Beach, VA: Inner Vision Publishing Co., 1985.

Savary, Louis M., Patricia H. Berne, and S.K. Williams. *Dreams and Spiritual Growth*. New York: Paulist Press, 1984.

Truman, Karol K. *Feelings Buried Alive Never Die*. Las Vegas: Olympus Distributing, 1991.

Wegscheider-Cruse. *Learning to Love Yourself*. Pompano Beach, FL: Health Communications, Inc., 1987.

West, Georgiana T. *Prosperity's Ten Commandments*. Unity Village, MO: Unity Books, 1959.

Appendix I

Recommended Reading by Subject
From Wilda B. Tanner

Angels, Devas & Nature Spirits:
  The Findhorn Garden, The Findhorn Community
  Behaving As If the God In All Life Mattered, Machaelle Small Wright
  The Brotherhood of Angels and Men, Geoffrey Hodson
  Rediscovering the Angels, Flower A. Newhouse
  Insights Into Reality, Flower A. Newhouse
  The Kingdom of the Shining Ones, Flower A. Newhouse
  A Book of Angels, Sophy Burnham
  Perelandra Garden Workbook, Machelle Small Wright

Astral Travel
  Journeys Out of the Body, Robert A. Monroe
  Astral Projection, Oliver Fox

Astrology
  Astrology: A Cosmic Science, Isabel M. Hickey

Auras
  The Human Aura, Walter J. Kilner
  The Kirlian Aura, Stanley Kripner & Rubin Daniel
  The Personal Aura, Dora Van Gelder Kunz
  Hands of Light & Light Emerging, Barbara Ann Brennan

Bodies
  The Etheric Double, A.E. Powell
  The Astral Body, the Mental Body, the Causal Body, A.E. Powell
  Man and His Bodies, Annie Besant
  Man Visible and Invisible, C.W. Leadbeater

Dreams
  Dreams In the Life of Prayer, Harmon H. Bro

Symbolism the Universal Language, J.C. Cooper
Mass Dreams of the Future, Chet B. Snow, Ph.D.
Dreams, the Language of the Unconscious, Hugh Lynn Cayce *
Lucid Dreaming the Dawning of the Clear Light, Gregory Scott Sparrow *
The Sun and the Shadow, Kenneth Kelzer
Sexual Dreams: Why We Have Them, What They Mean, Dr. Gayle Delaney
Getting Help From Your Dreams, Henry Reed *
In Search of the Dream People (Nightmares), Robert Noone with D. Holman
Cinderella's Gold Slipper, Samuel Denis Fohr
Dream Power, Dr. Ann Faraday
Creative Dreaming, Patricia Garfield, Ph.D.
Edgar Cayce: The Sleeping Prophet (Edgar Cayce), Jess Stearn *
There Is a River, Thomas Sugrue *

Healing
Hands of Light, Barbara Ann Brennan
Light Emerging, the Journey of Personal Healing, Barbara Ann Brennan
Who's the Matter With Me?, Alice Steadman

History of Human Origin
Man: Whence, How and Whither, Annie Besant & C.W. Leadbeater
The Twelfth Planet, Zechariah Sitchin
The Explorer Race, Robert Schapiro

Meditation
Meditation, Gateway to Light, Elsie Sechrist *
The Art of Meditation, Joel S. Goldsmith
Meditation, Grace Cooke

Reincarnation
Return From Tomorrow, Dr. George G. Ritchie
You Have Been Here Before, Dr. Edith Fiore
Beyond the Ashes, Cases of Reincarnation From the Holocaust, Rabbi Yonassan Gershom
Death to Rebirth, Manly P. Hall

Many Lives, Many Masters, Dr. Brian L. Weiss
Winged Pharaoh, Joan Grant

Self-Help

Loving Relationships, Sondra Ray
The Prospering Power of Love, Catherine Ponder
The Family: A Revolutionary Way of Self-Discovery, John Bradshaw
Knowledge of the Higher Worlds, Rudolf Steiner
The Power of Your Subconscious Mind, Dr. Joseph Murphy
Thought Forms, Annie Besant & C.W. Leadbeater
As a Man Thinketh, James Lane Allen

Souls

Journey of Souls, Dr. Michael Newton
The Soul of the Indian, Charles A. Eastman
Soul Return, Aminah Raheem, Ph.D.

Spiritual Laws — Growth

The Path of the Soul, White Eagle
The Way of the Sun, White Eagle
Spiritual Breakthrough, John Van Auken*
Spiritual Unfoldment, # 1,2,3,4, White Eagle
Ye Are Gods, Annalee Skarin
Star Gates, Corinne Heline
The Mystery of the Christos, Corinne Heline
Initiation, Elisabeth Haich
The Prospering Power of Love, Catherine Ponder
Gateway of Liberation and Spiritual Laws, Mary Gray
Jesus and the Essenes, Dolores Cannon
UFO, ET's
Keepers of the Garden, Dolores Cannon
Light Years, Gary Kinder
The Gulf Breeze Sightings, Ed Walters

* *Books available from A.R.E. Press (Toll free #(800) 723-1112*

Appendix II

Reincarnation Facts And Quotes

> The body
> Of
> Benjamin Franklin, printer,
> (Like the cover of an old book,
> Its contents torn out,
> And stript of its lettering and gilding),
> Lies here, food for worms;
> But the work itself shall not be lost,
> For it will (as he believed) appear once more
> In a new
> And more elegant beautiful edition.
>
> —Modified by the Author
> From *Gale's Quotations*

Reincarnation Quotes in the Bible

In our search for proof of reincarnation as a fact, let us begin on common ground we can all agree upon, the Bible.

"Then the word of the Lord came unto me, saying, 'Before I formed thee in the belly I knew thee; and before thou camest forth out of the womb I sanctified thee, and I ordained thee a prophet unto the nations' " (Jeremiah 1:4–5).

"Naked came I forth from my mother's womb, and naked I shall return" [to be born again and again] (Job 1:21).

"Rabbi, who sinned, this man or his parents so that he was born blind?" (John 9:2). The questioner obviously understood the concept of reincarnation since he asked who sinned. If the man was born blind to pay for his "sin," he must have had a previous life, yet Jesus accepted the comment, without question or rebuke, implying agreement.

"They [the Pharisees] asked [John the Baptist], 'Who are you? Elijah?'" (John 1:21). Elijah had been dead for 500 years.

"Herod was told by some that John [the Baptist] had risen from the dead, others that Elijah had appeared and by others that one of the prophets had come back to life" (Luke 9:7–8).

"Jesus asked [his disciples], 'Who do people say the Son of Man is?' The disciples answered, 'Some say John the Baptist, others Elijah, and others, Jeremiah or one of the prophets'" (Matthew 16:13–14).

"Behold, I will send you Elijah the prophet before the coming of the Lord" (Malachi 4:5).

"For until John [the Baptist], all the prophets and the Law foretold it. If you care to accept it, he himself is Elijah who was to come" (Matthew 11:13–15). Again, Elijah had been dead for 500 years.

"'Why do they say Elijah must come first?' Jesus replied, 'Elijah comes but I tell you Elijah has already come and they did not recognize him, but have done to him as they pleased.' Then the disciples realized that he was speaking of John the Baptist [beheaded by Herod with a sword]" (Matthew 17:10–13).

"Whoever kills with the sword must be killed by the sword" (Revelations 13:10, Matthew 26:52). Elijah had seized the priests of Baal and slaughtered them with swords (1 Kings 18:40).

Another reincarnation quote is the story of the Prodigal Son, which is a description of mankind going out from the Father's house, squandering his talents [money], then returning home to be welcomed and forgiven by a loving Father (Luke 15:11–31).

"To him that overcometh, I will make him a pillar in the temple of my God and he shall go no more out" (Revelations 3:12).

Why Aren't There More Reincarnation Quotes?
Good question! The reason, not well known, is that the early church "fathers" actually decreed that all references to reincarnation be removed from the Bible! Check your church history.

Missing Books of the Bible

Second and Third Centuries:
In the second century, Irenaeus insisted there be only four gospels included in the Bible. This eliminated the Gospel of Mary, the Gospel of Thomas, the Gospel of James, the Gospel of Peter, the Gospel of the Hebrews, the Gospel of the Egyptians, and the the Gospel of Mattheus.

In the third century A.D., more books were excluded from the official Bible. Some references for further information are listed below.

Books Removed From the Bible
Baigent, Michael, and Richard Leigh. *The Dead Sea Scrolls Deception*. New York: A Touchstone Book, Simon & Schuster, 1991.

Baigent, Michael, Richard Leigh, and Henry Lincoln. *Holy Blood, Holy Grail*. New York: Delacorte Press, 1982.

Forgotten Books of Eden, The. New York: Bell Publishing Company, 1980.

Goodspeed, Edgar J., trans. *The Apocrypha*. Random House, 1959.

Gospel According to Thomas, The. Concord Grove Press, 1983.

Laurence, Richard, trans. *The Book of Enoch*. Wizards Bookshelf, 1983.

Lost Books of the Bible, The. New York: Bell Publishing Company, 1979.

Mack, Burton L. *The Lost Gospel*. Harper & Collins, 1994.

Nag Hammadi Library, The. San Francisco: Harper & Row Publishers, 1977.

Other Bible, The. San Francisco: Harper & Row Publishers, 1984.

Pagels, Elaine. *The Gnostic Gospels*. Vintage Books, 1981.

Secret Books of the Egyptian Gnostics, The. Rochester, VT: Jean Doresse Traditions International, Ltd., 1958.

Smith, Morton. *The Secret Gospel*. Clearlake, CA: The Dawn Horse Press, 1982.

Smith, Susy. *The Book of James*. New York: G.P. Putnam's Sons, 1974.

Fourth Century:
The First Ecumenical Council of bishops was called by Emperor Constantine in 325 A.D. The Creed of Nicea was formulated, setting up official church doctrine. About this time, scholars were commissioned to translate the New Testament from the Old Latin into "modern" Latin and to purge all references to reincarnation in the process. Sometime later, the Catholic Church ordered all the "old" Bibles to be publicly burned.

The recently-unearthed Dead Sea Scrolls, along with the Nag Hammadi Library, have revealed many changes, additions, and omissions in the older, non-altered versions of the New Testament. Could this be the reason the church delayed forty years in allowing the public to see the scrolls?

Fifth Century:
During the fifth century, a scholar named Augustine proposed a new doctrine; "All men are born in sin!" For this un-Christ-like remark, he was given the honorary title of "Saint." Thus encouraged, he soon made another statement declaring, "There is no salvation outside of the church." This is clearly out of line with the teachings of Christ. Yet this, too, was added to the growing "doctrine" of the church.

Augustine's twisted concepts later led to the practice of selling "indulgences" (forgiveness of sins) to the parishioners or their deceased relatives for large amounts of money.

Sixth Century:
The Fifth Ecumenical Council, 553 A.D., led by Emperor Justinian, condemned Origen (a highly respected historian) for writing about the preexistence of the soul. Once more, reincarnation was attacked and discredited, giving the church more control over the people.

Sixteenth Century:
Somewhere between 1512 and 1517 Martin Luther, a doctor of theology at Wittenberg, Germany, denounced the selling of "indulgences" with his famous *95 Theses* nailed to the door of All Saints Church in Wittenberg. Luther proclaimed what Jesus had taught, that salvation was given by faith alone. Yet the church leaders upheld Augustine's misconceptions and declared Luther a heretic, threatening him with excommunication unless he recanted.

Search for the Truth

As we peer more deeply for the truth about reincarnation, let us begin with some common-ground theories such as, "All men are created equal." Add to this, "God is Love." If these are true, and I believe they are, then are many situations that do not make sense if we only live once—such as the fact that some children are born healthy, wealthy, and happy, while others are born in situations of poor health, poverty, and hunger. Or that some people have parents who are drug addicts or alcoholics and still others are abused by their families. If we only live once, then obviously life is not fair.

Yet we know God is love and wants the best for all of us. "It is the Father's good pleasure to give you the kingdom" (Luke 12:32). Knowing this, how can we explain the differences in circumstances? The Bible explains it this way; "Whatever a man sows he shall also reap" (Galatians 6:7). To say it another way, "He who leads (others) into captivity shall go into captivity; he who kills by the sword must die by the sword!" (Revelations 13:10).

To this Jesus adds, "While heaven and earth endure, not one jot or tittle [~, a curl of the pen] shall be dropped from the law, until it is finished [paid up, brought into balance, complete]" (Matthew 5:18, Berkeley Version). All of which is saying that whatever we do to others will be done unto us, "Visiting the sins of the fathers upon the children unto the third and fourth generation" (Numbers 14:18). The Berkeley Translation says "He is One who on no occasion will leave the guilty unpunished; One who requires of the children to pay for the iniquity of their parents down to the third and fourth generation."

Cruel punishment? Not when you consider that those abusive parents must come back into the same family (third or fourth generation) to reap the results of what they have done unto others. This is the final balancing of the Law. It is also why we are advised to "Love one another," and to "Do unto others as you would have them do unto you"—because one's deeds, both good and evil, will return to their maker.

You have heard it said, "The wheels of God's justice grind slowly." There are no accidents, failures, or oversights, only justice. Hence, reincarnation.

Documentary Research on Reincarnation

Stevenson, Ian, M.D. *Evidence For Survival From Claimed Memories Of Former Incarnations.* (Dr. Stevenson traveled widely to verify the claims of those who claimed to remember their past lives and was one of the first credible researchers to publish his findings.)

True Stories of Reincarnation and Near Death

Brinkley, Dannion and Paul Perry. *Saved by the Light*. Harper Paperbacks, 1994. (5 months on *New York Times* Bestseller List.)

Church, W.H. *Many Happy Returns*. New York: Harper And Row, 1984.

Fiore, Dr. Edith. *You Have Been Here Before*. Ballantine Books, New York, 1978

Gershom, Rabbi Yonassan. *Beyond the Ashes*. Virginia Beach, VA: A.R.E. Press, 1992. (Surprising tales of non-Jewish people seeking the Rabbi with dreams and memories of WWII in Germany concentration camps and the horrors they lived there.)

Moody, Raymond A. Jr., M.D. *Life After Life*. New York: Bantam Books, 1979.

Ritchie, George, M.D. with Elizabeth Sherrill. *Return From Tomorrow*. (A true-life experience of death, the afterlife, and a surprising return to the morgue to reclaim his dead body.)

Stearn, Jess. *The Search for a Soul*. Garden City, NY: Doubleday, 1973.

Recommended Reading On Reincarnation

Hall, Manly P. *Death to Rebirth*. Los Angeles: The Philosophical Research Society, Inc., 1979.

Moody, Raymond A. Jr., M.D. *Life After Life*. New York: Bantam Books, 1979.

Richelieu, Peter. *A Soul's Journey*. Wellingborough, England: Turnstone Press Limited, 1972.

Richelieu, Peter. *Through Time Into Healing*. New York: A Fireside Book, 1993.

Sugrue, Thomas. *There Is a River*. Virginia Beach, VA: A.R.E. Press, 1994.

Whitton, Joel L., M.D., Ph.D. *Life Between Life*.

Recommended Reading on Hypnosis

An unexpected tool for uncovering former lives.

Bernstein, Morey. *The Search for Bridey Murphy*. Garden City, NY: Doubleday, 1989.

Woolger, Roger J., Ph.D. *Other Lives, Other Selves*. New York: Bantam, 1988.

Newton, Michael, Ph.D. *Journey of Souls.* St. Paul, MN: Llewellyn Publications, 1997. (Study of Soul Life between Incarnations.)

Weiss, Brian L., M.D. *Many Lives, Many Masters.* New York: A Fireside Book, 1988.

Other Recommended Reading

Cerminara, Gina. *Many Mansions.* New York: William Sloanes Associates, 1965.

Cerminara, Gina. *The World Within.* New York: William Sloanes Associates, 1965.

Goldberg, Bruce. *The Search for Grace.* St. Paul, MN: Llewellyn Publications, 1997.

MacLaine, Shirley. *Dancing In the Light.* New York: Bantam Books, 1985.

Montgomery, Ruth. *Ruth Montgomery: Herald of the New Age.* New York: Doubleday & Co., 1986.

Stearn, Jess. *Edgar Cayce: The Sleeping Prophet.* Bantam Books, 1967.

Sugrue, Thomas. *There Is a River.* Virginia Beach, VA: A.R.E. Press, 1994.

Weisman, Alan. *We, Immortals.* Malibu, CA: Valley of the Sun Publishing, 1977.

Proving Reincarnation for Yourself

The first time I heard about reincarnation, I wondered if this could be true. Since I was already working with my dreams, I simply asked, "If I have lived before, please show me."

It worked. I woke up remembering an extremely vivid dream and absolutely knowing that I was this Indian male in long, black braids, paddling a canoe somewhere in a wooded area. I was excited, as there was no doubt in my mind that we were one and the same!

You, too, can ask for a dream giving proof you have lived before. Be sure to write out your question, then have pen and paper handy. Record what you remember of the dream immediately after waking, before speaking or even thinking about other things.

Do this for several days in a row, preferably a week. Faithfully write your dreams upon waking. This should result in numerous insights on your past.

Watch for dreams featuring a different country, culture, style of architecture, or old-fashioned things. Any of these could be showing you yet another past life to consider.

Appendix III

Ceremonies and Rituals

Your power to clear and cleanse does not come from outside of you, but from deep within you.

Always have a clear purpose in mind before starting any ritual. It is important that each ritual or ceremony has a definite beginning and ending, with a firm feeling of completion. Otherwise, there are no hard-set rules. Use the outlines given and concoct your own variations. Prayers, chants, and oms are wonderful extras. Prayers do not have to be long. Simple is better. If you are doing this in a group, have each person say one sentence.

Beginning Your Ritual

1. Have your purpose clearly in mind.
2. Reverently set the scene (candles or incense lit and ready).
3. Open with a prayer.
4. Connect with your God-self.
5. State your purpose.

Burning Bowl Ceremony

Fire has long been a symbol of cleansing and transformation in many cultures. This particular ceremony is both simple and effective, often being used as a New Year's ritual. Happily, this can be done in just about any location, inside or out, and is suitable for one person or a group. (For a group, you could have a carefully contained outdoor campfire or use a charcoal grill.

1. Set the stage. Light a candle, dim the lights, and maybe burn some incense for atmosphere. You could even add some appropriate music. Prayer, singing, and chanting are always helpful to harmonize the group. If you do this alone, you could play some Gregorian chants or do some quiet oms on your own.

Set a fireproof bowl near the candle. (Place a wooden cutting board or other heat-resistant device under the bowl.)

If this is a group ceremony with much paper burning, you may wish to have a lid for the bowl, in case the blaze should get out of hand. It may also be wise to set the bowl on your kitchen stove under the hood with the vent turned on so all smoke will be safely removed. Observe all rules of fire safety.
2. Connect to your God-self.
3. Open with prayer and call in angels.
4. State your purpose.
5. Begin your ritual by having each person write on a small piece of paper something that is to be released. It can be some hard feelings, a long-held guilt, an unwanted emotion, or whatever is needed. This also works for old habits to surrender, an old love you want to relinquish, a message to someone whose whereabouts are unknown, or anything you feel is appropriate.
6. To release, take your note and walk slowly to the candle. Pause for some deliberate thought and/or a little prayer about what you want to release, then ceremoniously ignite the message in the candle flame and drop the paper into the bowl.

If you have a fireplace, you could follow the same procedure as above, then toss each note individually into the fireplace. If outdoors, you could drop each into a small charcoal grill or bonfire.
7. Replace that which has been released. In general, it is always wise to replace what has been released with something positive. In this case, you (or each person) can write out a new goal, a new direction, resolution, and/or a positive intent for the future. This can be kept in a hidden place, or you may wish to have it out in the open where you can see your new goal every day.
8. Close your ritual. For a group, you may want to end with some special music, then end with a prayer of thanksgiving.

Incense Cleansing Ritual

This ritual is good for a whole house cleansing. Again, you can do this alone or with a group.

1. Start with clear intent.
2. Set the stage with appropriate lighting and music. Have a holder or container designed for carrying your incense. (If you don't have one, you can set one end of your incense stick into a small, dirt-filled

flowerpot.) Start with a good, natural kind of incense such as sage, cedar, sweet grass, sandalwood, frankincense, or myrrh. These are some of the same materials churches use to clean out unwanted, negative vibrations.
3. Connect with your God-self.
4. Open with prayer and state your purpose. Call in angels, if desired.
5. Cleanse. With clear intent as to what you wish to cleanse, light your incense and slowly move all around each room allowing the smoke to enter into all nooks and closets. Go through the whole house, attic to basement. Pray, chant, or sing as you go, or play suitable music.

    If the home in question has had months or even years of old anger and other negative emotions, you may need to use additional efforts to clean these accumulations.
6. Replace. When finished, deliberately create or call in a beam of pure white light to finish purifying your chosen area. Let it pour in and through the room until it feels thoroughly clean, light, and refreshed. Next, send a pink cloud of love and forgiveness into the room and to all the people who may have been involved. When finished, return to your starting point.
7. Close with a prayer of blessings and thanks.

Having done this, especially if it is your home, try to be more aware of the kind of thought forms you or your friends and family are creating at any given moment. Keep your home cleansed regularly. Intend to think, live, and act with greater peace and harmony. Spend time radiating love and good will to all that enter your home, office, or auto. Always hold the thought of love and highest good for all concerned.

Personal Cleansing Ceremony

Especially good for cleansing and releasing your own, personal "garbage." This is also helpful for personal cleansing when you are feeling hurt, dirty, or guilty from being around negative people and situations.

1. Start with a clear intent as to exactly what you want to cleanse. Have your release statement written and ready. If feasible, have a symbolic picture, clay model, or item to represent the person, incident or memory you want to release from your mind.

    Decide on what ideas, goals, or qualities you will want to replace the old energies with. Have your replacement statement written and ready.

Decide what method to use to let go of the old, unwanted attitudes, emotions, or habits. If you choose to burn your list, picture, or symbol in a candle flame, be sure to place the candle within easy reach in a flame-proof tray to catch stray ashes. You can hold metal symbols in the flame with tongs. Soluble things can be dropped in the water. You can bury other things outside later. Choose your method of disposal and gather the necessary tools to complete your task ahead of time.

2. Set the stage. Once your tools are gathered, light a candle, dim the lights, put on some soothing music, or do whatever else you would like to set the scene. Fill the tub with hot water and add pleasant-smelling bath salts, herbs, or flower petals such as lavender or rose — any scent or oil that feels and smells uplifting to you.
3. Connect with your God-self.
4. Open with a prayer stating your intent. Call in your patron saint, Guardian Angel, or anyone else you would like to work with before you step into the tub. Climb in, get comfortable, and relax. Take at least three long, deep breaths to relax even more. Once you are deeply relaxed, begin the next step.
5. Cleanse. Say a brief prayer to release the wound. With reverence and clear, purposeful intent let go of your symbol by your chosen method of forgiveness and release. This ends your cleansing ritual. Relax and know it is done.
6. Replace. Read aloud your replacement statement at least three times. Say a prayer of renewal and fill your heart and mind with love and happiness. Feel love and light actually fill you where there once was pain and darkness.
7. Bask and luxuriate in a sense of cleanliness, abundance, and beauty. Be thankful. Be happy. Think of as many things as possible that you appreciate and are grateful for having. Give thanks for all that you have.
8. When finished, shower off all remnants of negative vibrations. Let the water carry away all sense of guilt, frustration, or resentment. Deliberately let go of all your cares.
9. Close with a prayer of thanksgiving for all the good that has come your way. Step out feeling cleansed, relaxed, and refreshed.
10. Afterward, indulge yourself with something special to make you feel good, especially when dealing with self-worth issues (flowers on your desk, a new CD, massage, jewelry, etc.).

Chakra Cleansing

For those who are familiar with chakras and their placements, this ritual helps cleanse, clear and balance blocked energies. For those to whom the chakras are unfamiliar, there are numerous books out on the subject so we will not go into this rather complex matter here.

1. Start with clear intent.
2. Set the stage with candles, appropriate lighting, and music.
3. Connect with your God-self.
4. Open with a prayer of intent.
5. Sit or lie with your spine straight.
6. Use any one or a combination of these (one at a time) depending upon your needs. Follow the process below using your chosen energy.
   - Pure white light and/or rainbow colors may also be employed
   - Earth energies strengthen, ground and balance.
   - Water may be used if a cleansing is needed.
   - Sun or fire energies can be used for transformation, clearing and lightening, especially when you feel heavy or depressed.
7. Picture your feet flat upon earth, water, or your chosen media. Bring the strong, grounding earth energies up through your feet and into your base chakra. Feel this chakra filled, strengthened, and grounded with powerful earth energy.
8. Cleanse. Release any anger or pain from your lessons. Let it now be transferred to the soul as wisdom.
9. As you feel balanced and empowered in the first chakra, send the energy up through the second chakra. Repeat this process through the third, fourth, and fifth chakras. Again, release any anger or pain from your lessons. Let it now be transferred to the soul as wisdom. For the sixth and seventh chakras, switch to a lighter energy such as pure white light or violet.
10. Replace. When finished, feel all of your chakras open, cleansed, balanced, and spinning. Open your whole aura at the top and allow yourself to be filled with God's pure white light, love, and any other quality you need. Intend to hold and treasure this heightened awareness of love and light as long as possible.
11. Close. Seal your aura with a layer of crystal light for protection. Pronounce it good. Give a prayer of thanks.

Instant Cleansing Ritual

This is a quick-fix cleansing you can use when you are "on the go."

1. Stop for a moment and say, "Father God, pass your violet consuming flames through my bodies." (Picture this happening all through your aura.)
2. Now say, "Sweep out and dissolve all that is less than perfect and fill me with your pure white light and guide me in the way I should go."

Quick Cleansing for Odd Places

This is a quick method to clean a room, bed, automobile, public seats or benches, funeral homes, and even a hotel room. This is especially great when traveling for you could work on any area, large or small, which you might wish to cleanse before using.

1. Start with a clear intent.
2. Connect with God-self.
3. Open with prayer of intent.
4. Cleanse. Begin by mentally creating a magic broom, vacuum cleaner, duster, or even a white tornado (whatever suits your fancy). Sweep down the walls, ceilings, and floors in each room or area. Pay special attention to closets and other nooks and crannies. Clean furniture, drapes, and rugs as well. Cleanse plane or car seats, toilet seats, hotel bed, and anything questionable.
5. Then, with firm intent, sweep or send all the thought form rubble outdoors, preferably into the sunshine, and let nature finish the purification job. (If this isn't applicable, use a fireplace to burn it, a magic wand to transform it, or any tool that comes to mind to finish the cleansing. If weather permits, open several doors and windows to air the area. Ask the universe to transform the negative energies into positive ones.
6. Replace. After removing the negativity, always replace the old stuff with something new and positive such as a blessing. No fancy words needed, just say what comes naturally and sincerely.

Get playful and create your own rituals based on the information, outlines, and suggestions above.

Index

abuse
    mental/emotional 47–48
    physical 56–58
Adelade, the Unpaid Maid 46–47, 156–157
Allen, James 73, 93, 183, 189, 217, 256
angel(s) 33, 104, 123, 163
    Archangel Michael 108
    Guardian 55, 90, 163–164, 171–172, 174, 176
anger 60–64, 238–239
    and health
        acid stomach 190
        arthritis 189
        blisters, burns 189
        cancer 189
        depression 190
        rash 190
    directed 22
    exploding 18
    hate and 26
    irritation 17
    jealousy 23
    resentment 18
    slow burn 17
    undelivered 22
Astral body. *See* body(ies), nonphysical: Emotional body
aura 5–7
    affecting others 9–11
    learning to recognize 8–9
    love thoughts in 18–20
    thought forms in 15–18, 25–26, 27–28
    unfinished business in 101–102
Aurelius, Marcus 155
auric field. *See* aura
awareness
    of God 164
    of our faults 211
    of the God-self 175
    practice 169–170

Bacon, Francis 135
Bailey, Alice 191
belief system
    check your 248
    understanding your 43–72
belief(s). *See also* belief system
    changing 73–91
    inherited 202–204
    power of 45–46
Beyondandonda, Swami 265
Bible. *See also* Elijah; Golden Rule; Herod; John the Baptist; Lord's Prayer; Mary; Pharisees; Prodigal Son; St. Paul; Ten Commandments; Ten Talents
    1 Kings 284
    1 Timothy 55
    Acts 6
    Deuteronomy 67
    Exodus 65
    Galatians 1, 10, 35, 287
    Genesis 13, 31, 32, 33, 34, 183, 258
    Jeremiah 283, 284
    Job 28, 35, 113, 142, 150, 270, 283
    John 5, 203, 268, 270, 283, 284
    Luke 48, 142, 151, 239, 284, 287
    Malachi 284
    Matthew 2, 13, 34, 43, 66, 87, 107, 142, 156, 200, 254, 258, 261, 284, 287
    missing books 285–286
    Numbers 287–289
    Proverbs 34, 67
    Psalms 2, 142, 155, 163
    Revelations 284, 287
    Romans 34, 113, 202

bioplasmic field. *See* electromagnetic field
blame 66–67
bliss
    find your 126
    follow your 264
    ignorance is not always 193–194
    upliftment, personal 265
body signals 170–171, 188, 248
body talk 183–198
    dis-ease
        and repeating patterns 242
        as a signal 185, 188
        body/mind related 189–192
        healing 196
        mental/emotional/soul malfunction 195
    disenfranchisement 184
    healing 196–198
    how illness speaks 187–192
    how your body speaks 186–187
    personality development 184–185
    solar plexus 192
    souls born in physical bodies 183–184, 185–186
    tension 192
    when illness strikes 194–196
body(ies), invisible. *See* body(ies): nonphysical
body(ies), nonphysical 1, 5–7, 88
    Astral body. *See* Emotional body (below)
    Buddhic body 6
    Causal body. *See* Intuitional body (below)
    Emotional body 6, 13, 48
    Etheric body 6
    Intuitional body 6
    Lightbody. *See* aura
    Mental body 6, 10, 17, 60, 157
    Spiritual body. *See* aura
body, earthly. *See* body, physical
body, physical
    as a tool 1
    as a vehicle 5, 6–7, 252

    as bearer of messages 185
    associated with Low-self 164
Buddha 6, 31
Buddhic body. *See* body(ies), nonphysical: Buddhic body
Burke, Michael 167
Burns, Robert 199–200
Burr, Dr. Harold 6

Causal body. *See* body(ies), nonphysical: Intuitional body
ceremonies. *See* rituals
chakra. *See* rituals: Chakra Cleansing
change(s). *See also* symbol(s): circumstances; thought(s): changing
    Earth 270
    foundation for 140–141
    helping one another 265–266
    making 132
    people 271–272
    your thinking 240
choice(s) 114, 118–119, 229. *See also* decision(s)
Christ 6, 164. *See also* Jesus
    consciousness 123, 164. *See also* God-self
circumstance(s). *See also* symbol(s): circumstances as
    choosing 47–48, 74, 78
    creating 2, 4, 10, 13–14, 29, 31, 140, 199
    victim(s) of 2, 4, 7, 69–70
clear intent 157–159
co-creator(s) 1, 2, 3, 29, 32–34, 107, 109, 139, 149, 257–258
Cocoon 5
colors
    black 18, 22, 25, 26
    blue 18, 19, 181
        dark 9
        light 181
    brown 16, 17, 18, 22
    gold 19, 20, 181
    gray 17, 22, 25, 26

green 16, 19, 23, 181
   in auras 6, 9
   in meditation 181
   in thought forms 16–20, 22–23
   lavender 18, 19, 181
   orange 18, 181
   pastels 19
   pink 16, 18, 19, 20, 22, 25, 131, 181, 293
   purple 9, 181
   rainbow 175, 181, 295
   red 14, 17, 18, 22, 61, 181
   rose 19
   violet 295, 296
   white 9, 181, 293, 295, 296
   yellow 16, 18, 23, 181
community, improving 267
confrontation 221
conscious mind. *See* intellect
consciousness 3, 137
   altered state of 15
   building a new 141–144
   Christ. *See* Christ: consciousness; God-self
   Gaia 103–104
   planetary 269–270
   race 23–24, 270
   self- 109
   soul 165
   Super. *See* God-self
Constantine, Emperor 286
Cosmic Clock 3–4
Cosmic Law 13, 62
creating
   a better life 116
   and fears 37
   balancing point 97
   Basic Stance 137–138
   building a new consciousness 141–143
   changing your thoughts 138–139
   choosing goals 139–140
   Feeling Thermometer 148
   guidelines for 228–229
   joyful 264

Laws of Creation. *See* creation(s): Laws of
   laying the foundation 140–141
   our own reality 3
   process of 144–153
   putting it together 160
   Quick Check Summary 147
   simple outline 153–154
   timing 136
   your future 269
   your heart's desires 135–154
creation(s)
   Laws of 31–38, 139, 261
   manifestation(s)
      accuracy of 34
      and prayer 174
      delayed 28–29
      equation for 32
      God as power source for 123
      practice goals 143–144
      timing 136
      with joy 264–265
   nurturing 155–162
   process of 13–29

Dead Sea Scrolls 286
decision(s) 99–119, 244
   conform to your belief system 45
   failure to make 115–116, 225
   fuzzy, unclear 100
   hasty 100
   make clear 116
   no 99
   people-pleasing 99
   poor 99
   take responsibility for 201–203
   vacillating 99
Delgado, Jose 6
depression 25–26, 102–103, 190
discipline 157
Dr. Dean Ornish's Program for Reducing Heart Disease 173
dream(s)
   as guidance 96–97

299

daydream(ing) 7, 161, 186
    nightmares 53, 186
    precognitive 186
    symbolic 186

Earth School 1, 60, 106
Eckhart, Meister 1
Ecumenical Council
    Fifth 286
    First 286
ego 164, 165, 185. *See also* personality
electromagnetic field 5–6. *See also* aura
elephant. *See* thought(s): limited
Elijah 284
Emerson, Ralph Waldo 159, 163
Emotional body. *See* body(ies), nonphysical: Emotional body
Etheric body. *See* body(ies), nonphysical: Etheric body

failure 113
faith 113
fear(s) 37–38, 52–55, 239
flea. *See* thought(s): limited
forgiveness 80–81, 87, 106–107. *See also* self-forgiveness
    act of 107–109
Fox, Emmet 217, 227
Franklin, Benjamin 283
Funk & Wagnall 184

Gaia 103–105, 270–271. *See also* Mother Earth
Ghandi 271
Ghost Wolf, Robert 184
goal(s). *See also* thought(s)
    check 244–245
    choosing 139
    negative 113
    no 242–243
    rewards for reaching 95
    setting 121–134
        daily 127–128
        get it on one page 130–131

goal book 131–132
goal cards 129, 161, 249
guidelines 123–124, 126
hints 133–134
planning 122–123
preparing the way 129–130
purpose 125–126
true and false 124–126
yearly 127
your direction 123
ultimate 1, 3
God
    image and likeness of 1, 2, 7, 124
    is love. *See* love: God is
    seed 1
God spark 147, 164. *See also* God-self
god(s)/goddess(es) in the making
    and power 269
    and creating 118, 135
    and the search for truth 75, 78
    recognizing the God-self 164, 171–172
    we are 2, 3, 7, 11, 29, 33, 109
God-self
    answers from 167–168
    getting in touch with. *See* meditation
    guidance from 168–172
    recognizing 164
    rediscovering 163–172
    working with 167
Goethe 132
Golden Rule 48
Great Laws of the Iroquois Confederacy 269
growing up 68–70
Guest, Edgar A. 266

halo 6. *See also* aura; electromagnetic field
Hay, Louise 142
Herod 284
High-self 164. *See* God-self
Holmes, Oliver Wendell 121
Holy of Holies 174
Holy Spirit 164, 173. *See also* God-self

home. *See* symbol(s): surroundings as
impulses 171–172
intellect 43
    vs. intuition 117, 170
intention 117–118
intuition 43, 116–117, 146, 169–170, 185
    vs. intellect 117, 170
Intuitional body. *See* body(ies), nonphysical: Intuitional body
Irenaeus 285–287
Iroquois Nation 125

Jesus 2, 22, 37–38, 65, 107, 151, 164, 173, 174, 239, 254, 261, 267, 268, 284, 287. *See also* Christ
John the Baptist 284
journal 93–97, 152, 159
    recording meditations in 180
joy team 160
joyful stance 127, 159–160
Justinian, Emperor 286

karma. *See also* Law of Cause and Effect
    and Blame Game 66–67
    and Law of Love 64–65
    and Universal Laws of Attraction 64
    balancing, karmic 66
    clouts, karmic 100
    lessons (karmic) and family 201–202
    payback, karmic 37, 64
    seasons and cycles 200
King, Joni 271
Kirlian photography 6

Laubach, Frank 261
Law of Attraction 24, 35, 36, 137, 208, 211. *See also* like attracts like; Universal Rules of Attraction
Law of Cause and Effect 35, 47, 65, 203
Law of Chosen Lesson 65–66
Law of Love. *See* love: Law of
Laws of the Universe. *See* universe: Laws of
life field. *See* electromagnetic field

Lightbody. *See* aura
like attracts like 13, 18, 37, 140, 149, 210, 214, 229. *See also* Law of Attraction; Universal Rules of Attraction
Lord's Prayer 108
love
    God is 2, 37–38, 87, 107, 123, 149, 164, 262
    Healing Power of 86–88
    Law of 2, 3, 28, 59, 64–65, 69, 70, 97, 109, 117, 149, 157, 164, 203, 255, 263
Low-self 164, 165, 174. *See also* personality
Luther, Martin 286

Man with the Hose, The.
marital agreements. *See* promises
Mary 6
meditation
    additional ideas for 181
    and nurturing goals 153
    and visualization 161
    comments on 176
    contacting God-self 167, 173–180
    for clarity of purpose 192
    for peace of mind 197
    mini 181
    prayer as prelude to 173–174
    prayer without words 174–175
    preparation for 176–177
    recording 180
    seed thoughts 180–181
Meditation—Gateway to Light 173
Mental body. *See* body(ies), nonphysical: Mental body
Message of My "House from Hell" 221–222
mind field. *See* electromagnetic field
mirror(s)
    authority figures as 207–208
    coworkers as 209
    Earth as 158
    family as 200–206
        parents 200–201, 204–205

siblings 206
friends as 206–207
how they work 210–212
life as 199–215, 254, 263
mates and partnerships as 208–209
of the soul 27
relationships as 199–200, 246
reprogramming and 214–215
surroundings as. *See* symbol(s):
   surroundings as
morphogenic field. *See* electromagnetic field
Mother Earth. *See also* Gaia
   aura of 24
   mistreatment of 33
Murphy, Dr. Joseph 231

Nag Hammadi Library 286
neighborhood 266–267. *See also*
   symbol(s): surroundings as
New Age 29, 165
non-decision 109. *See also* unfinished
   business; procrastination
Northrup, Christiane, M.D. 187

Ornish, Dean 173

people pleasing 83–85
personality. *See also* ego; low-self
   and "dis-ease" 191–192, 195
   development of 184–185
   is easily sidetracked 165
   soul vs. 192
Peterson, Wilferd A. 99
Pharisees 284
Polka-Dot Car 226–227
poverty
   a learned condition 41–42
   and your belief system 55–56, 67
   teachings 40–41
Powell, John 125
Power of Your Subconscious Mind, The
   231
prayer
   and meditation 173–175, 176

and nurturing goals 161
and the Holy Grail 117
healing forms 19
power 149
protective 19
problem(s)
   broken promises 212–214
   dealing with constructively 234–235
   disappointments 255
   lessons in disguise 253
   messages 90–91
   minimizing 215
   people 210–212
   perpetuators 36
   prevention 255–256
   repeating 242
   stimulate our growth 253–254
   typical 238–239
   when things go wrong 241–259
procrastination 114–116, 224–225. *See*
   also non-decision; unfinished business
Prodigal Son 37–38, 284
promise(s)
   broken 212–214
   choosing and keeping 110–112
   marital agreements 105–106
   others 110–111
   self 110
   things-to-do list 111–112
   what is a 100–101
Ptaah 271

Ramposhki, Llama 270
reincarnation
   and karma 47, 59, 66, 201–202, 203
   Biblical references to 1–2, 37–38
   books 280–281
   facts and quotes 283–289
ripple effect
   and change 266
   and connection with your God-self 269
rituals
   beginning 291
   Burning Bowl Ceremony 291–292

Chakra Cleansing 295
Incense Cleansing Ritual 292–293
Instant Cleansing Ritual 296
Personal Cleansing Ceremony
    293–294
Quick Cleansing for Odd Places 296

Saga of Broken Promises 212–214
School of Life 70
Schweitzer, Albert 196
Sechrist, Elsie 173
self-esteem
    good 76–77
    poor/low 46, 48–52, 68
self-forgiveness 79–81
self-talk 88–89, 249–250
Shakespeare, William 214
Sheldrake, Rupert 6
soul(s). *See also* spiritual being(s); spiritual
    self
    -connection 66, 69
    and joy 245
    and free will 70
    and healing 196
    and journal writing 94
    feeding 167
    knows 171
    lessons. *See* karma
    purpose 3, 124, 165, 166, 167, 183,
        185, 192, 204
    you are a 1, 5, 7–8
spiritual being(s). *See also* angel(s); soul(s)
    and self-talk 88
    you are a 3, 5–8, 109, 171,
        183–184, 252
Spiritual body. *See* aura
spiritual law 10, 31, 34, 37, 64, 252
spiritual self 164. *See also* soul
St. Augustine 8, 286
St. Francis of Assisi 272
St. Paul 34
Steadman, Alice 195
Story of Two Brothers 73
stress
    addressing 248
    and illness 189–192
    and solar plexus 192–193
    in the workplace 188
    Stress-O-Meter 247
subconscious mind
    and self-talk 88
    can sabotage intentions 110
    power of 43–45, 231
success
    groundwork for 248–249
    is a state of mind 112
    planning for 122–123
Super Being. *See* God-self
super conscious mind. *See* intuition
Super Consciousness. *See* God-self
symbol(s)
    circumstances as 231–240
        attitude 240
        boundaries 235–238
        cycles 233
        dealing with problems 234–235
        patterns of change 232–233
        signal(s) for change 232,
            233–234
        typical problems 238–239
    surroundings as 217–229
        automobile 226–227
        disorder 225
        home 217–221, 221–224
        neighborhood 227–228
        workplace 224
synchronicity 186

Ten Commandments 65, 87
Ten Talents 258
thought form(s)
    boomerangs 28
    collect in your aura 27–28
    common 15–20
    construction of 13–15
    directed 21–25
    effect of 25–27
    floating 20–21

thought(s). *See also* thought form(s)
    and health 189–192, 196, 197
    are things 32–35, 128, 135
    as attractors 58, 64, 228
    aura and 9–10
    changing 76, 79, 138, 228
    creation and 31, 32–33, 34, 72, 104–105, 121, 155, 231, 241, 251, 261, 269
    goals are 123
    limited 39–42, 154
        flea and the elephant 39, 41
        learning limits 39–40
        perceived limitations 41
        poverty teachings. *See* poverty: teachings
    Man With the Hose, The 138–139
    of revenge 67
    power of 249
    recording 88, 93–97
    reflections of 158, 217, 227
    return to the sender 35, 87, 107, 135–136, 200
    seed 129, 180
    stored 45

unconditional love 125
unfinished business 101–103. *See also* non-decision; procrastination
unforgivingness 102, 204
Unity Church 142, 252
Universal Rules of Attraction 64. *See also* Law of Attraction; like attracts like
universe
    abundant 41
    as reflector 212, 235
    as source 104, 118, 122, 137, 146, 150, 239
    as teacher 10, 211, 231, 232, 233, 242
    free will 44
    in tune with 263–264
    Laws of 2, 64–65, 123, 157, 191, 257–258

    safe and loving place 10, 70, 117, 151, 158, 240
    spiritual 241, 252
    thought-created 32, 72, 139, 157
    your 261–272

vibration(s)
    affect your surroundings 227
    and anger 61
    and attraction 64, 135, 137–138, 141, 250
    and creation 32, 261–263
    and thought forms 13–14, 21
    and your aura 10, 11
    cycles of 107
    gentle-loving kindness 255, 257
    positive vs. negative 87–88, 97
victimhood 57–59, 59–60. *See also* abuse: physical
victimization 68, 113, 252. *See also* victimhood
visualization
    and creating 160–161
    and dreams 186
    and goals 131, 132
    and reprogramming 145
    and self-talk 88–89

walk your talk 153, 156, 250
weather 267–269
Weisenbaum, Joseph 114
well-being 89–90
will power 43
Wordsworth, William 198
worry
    and attraction 31, 35, 36
    and vibrations 262
    is negative goal setting 113